HOLY WAR

HOLY WAR

THE LURE OF VICTORY AND
THE PASSING OF AMERICA AS A WORLD POWER

James A. Thomas

0886476

ARLINGTON HOUSE·PUBLISHERS
NEW ROCHELLE, N. Y.

63092

For Sylvia

Library of Congress Catalog Card Number 73–10835

MANUFACTURED IN THE UNITED STATES OF AMERICA

Library of Congress Cataloging in Publication Data

Thomas, James A   1933–
  Holy war.

  Includes bibliographical references.
   1. United States—Foreign relations—1945–
2. United States—Military policy.   I. Title.
E744.T48   327.73   73–10835
ISBN 0–87000–215–5

Contents

INTRODUCTION
WARS AND WORDS,
LEARNING AND WISHING

The country got burned dabbling at the liberals' wars, far worse, very likely, than anyone is at present able to gauge. A messianism which developed largely as a faith cult during the Depression years was made lethal by a world war, fatal by the miniwars that followed. The lure of final victory and the pursuit of the millennium has now gone full circle, from New Deal to Nuremberg, Korea to Vietnam.

The impulses are not dead, but instead are being redirected—from foreign to domestic affairs—from which they first sprang. They are expressing themselves in a chant. Never Again! say the righteous and the self-righteous. Vietnam was one of a kind, Korea never happened, World War II was bliss. As they speak there is the fresh scent of ashes.

A more honest view of current affairs means the recall of decades protected by time. For it is only in terms of the past that the present makes any sense. It means recalling the periods following World War II and Korea, when there was a faithfully unconcerned public, rifles without bullets, soldiers who were convinced of their own irrelevance.

There is a difference between then and now, but the difference is not to be found by making ethical distinctions, nor by chanting Never Again! The difference rests in the fact that we have gone a long way toward demonstrating our inability, as a nation, to wage limited, Vietnam-type wars.

The purpose of this book is to raise some issues which we Americans, ahistorical people that we are, would as soon leave undisturbed. That is just what we did before, to our discredit and disservice.

What is required is a survey of the recent odyssey of the American spirit as it struggled through both indecisive Asian wars. To speak of "both wars" will strike some as irksome. Already that other winless, loseless conflict on an Asian peninsula is slipping, or being pushed, into the land of myth.* But it must be brought forward and looked at again. Despite the apparent differences between Korea and Vietnam these wars share at least one powerful characteristic: we lost, but without suffering defeat. One thesis of this book is that Korea revealed, or should have revealed, some fundamental forces operating within the American character which preclude our successful participation in limited, ideologized war.

An obvious reason for our disenchantment with limited wars is this: Whereas most people like winners, Americans demand them; limited wars, just because they are limited, cannot be won. In this context, however, the hidden is of greater value than the obvious. Americans do not have the crush of defeat on their minds. Instead we suffer from an undefined, bitter melancholia which superimposes itself upon the sure knowledge that we didn't win in Vietnam. On a scale running from total defeat through all-out victory we would perhaps rank ourselves somewhere within the lower quarter of the scale. Thus, we are denied the sense of completeness, finality, closure which rest at either end of the scale would offer us.

These feelings and the convictions which undergird them are peculiar to the post-1945 period. This fact provides a clue as to how we got to where we are. Therefore, it is important we examine the reasons the nation confidently tells itself World War II was won (which is, in fact, the last conflict to which we apply that term). For the words "win" and "lose," "victory" and "defeat" have meanings today which are specific not simply to Americans, but to Americans living during the last third of the twentieth century. We shall focus upon the process by which such common terms took on such uncommon meaning.

The years just before and immediately following the Korean War,

*An example is D.J.R. Bruckner's column in the *Los Angeles Times,* February 2, 1972. He says that "Gen. Eisenhower demonstrated the only reasonable method in Korea. He stopped the fighting and then negotiated the exchanges."

Apparently the Chinese Communists didn't share Bruckner's faith in President Eisenhower's reasonableness. On June 10, 1953, they launched their greatest offensive since Spring 1951. It came to a halt when a sufficient number had been killed, on July 20, 1953. Seven days later the armistice was signed.

and the terrible years of the war itself, form a watershed in the spiritual life of our country. For our inquiry this time-frame is important. Events prior to World War II are of minor interest only, the flavor of that era being more important than specifics. Coming at the end of an age, and our study, the Vietnam War is to be seen as the unfolding of latent contradictions. As this period of limited war is traversed an evolution in the meanings we give to "war," et cetera, will unfold.

To show that this evolution is genuine rather than invented, it is necessary now to meet the argument that Korea and Vietnam were unique, each specifically its own. This is a favorite theme of sometime office seekers.[1] In some uninteresting ways the two wars are of course different, but these differences are trivial when attention is centered on the similar ways each conflict attacked the American soul. The manner is more important than the degree of damage inflicted.

Even at the level of observation the wars are not so different. Note the following.

—Both wars were limited. This fact continues to be indigestible for us as a people. Each war thus had undefined, indefinite and shifting goals to which we never were able to adjust; goals, indeed, to which we were forever dumb.

—In both cases our response was both incremental, and from the point of view of our people, something of a surprise. *Our* response rather than enemy action provided the opening drama.

—In each instance the long-standing counsel of the military concerning intervention was disregarded, the results being that we had to engage in ground combat with enemies who could do little else. As a result of the first such war, Korea, there developed among top military leaders what Roger Hilsman calls the "Never again" club, with the most profound of implications for the conduct of the second war, in Vietnam.[2]

—Both wars showed us that an alliance is more the nature of a negotiable contract than an unalterable commitment.

—Each was, according to that theory's author, a misapplication of the doctrine of containment.*

—In Korea and again in Vietnam there was an initial and substantial upsurge in public and Congressional support for the actions undertaken, and those promised, by the respective administrations. In each case our people interpreted the use of American forces as an implicit promise for explicit American victory. In both wars

*The development of containment is discussed in Chapter 2.

support remained relatively strong for about a year, the plug being pulled in each war only when it was understood there would be no unconditional surrender by the other side.

—Presidential candidates twice won and lost on the issue of war, and in both cases the winner tended publicly to disregard facts concerning the required unraveling of the war; and he implicitly promised the people either (a) victory in the case of Korea, or (b) something better than defeat in the case of Vietnam. These successor presidents were in fact locked-in by enemy battlefield strength and by the actions of their predecessors, with few genuine options available to them upon taking office. In fact, the policies of the GOP were, in both wars, basically continuations of processes set in motion by their Democratic predecessors.

—Following the end of the dream of final victory, and the subsequent retreating, public and private disavowals could be heard alongside the development within us of an overwhelming need to let the events be engulfed by history. To insure the latter the early reinstatements of domestic priorities were twice urged by the leaders, and as a result of this need to flee into the future, and into ourselves, a thorough understanding of what the nation had endured was twice made impossible. As a result of our guided introversion—and especially is this true of events following the Korean War—the psychological and moral preparation required for the successful waging of limited war, by this nation and in this century, was precluded, the increasing likelihood of such wars notwithstanding. Therefore, it was absolutely required that we relive some of the anguish of Korea, but with a far greater intensity, when we were plunged into Vietnam.

—We have twice been deeply involved in places ruled by despots, though time has been kind to President Rhee.* On both occasions we displayed a conpulsion to disregard the traditions and institutions of those we were aiding in order to satisfy a selected view of history and domestic political needs.

—In the final half of each war military tactics were dictated by the demand from home that casualties be held to a minimum, as the enemy displayed his talent for fighting while negotiating.

—On both cases we demonstrated our incompetence, as a nation, to wage limited war.

—Only three matters of importance distinguish the two wars: Korea was linear whereas Vietnam was a fluid "war in the crowd";[3] in the former America held absolute command of all friendly forces,

*The Korean Conflict is discussed in Chapter 3. President Rhee was denounced as a tyrant by his people and ousted April 27, 1960.

and in the latter was officially an adviser; the Cartwheel Factor* was barely visible during Korea but was in full swing even before the Vietnam War. The first two matters were worrisome in Vietnam, the latter decisive.

Something turned sour in both wars. Let us reformulate the problem, staying within the grasp of recent memory.

In the summer of 1965 it was the will of the American people that Ho Chi Minh's head be set atop a pike, there to be displayed in public. Developments in the war showed this was unlikely, and later impossible. Then it became the will of our people first that we get out, later that we stay out, of Vietnam. Finally, the will asserted that we never again become involved in such unsatisfying wars.

For those who demand a permanent end to involvement in Vietnam and in other limited wars, there are two pieces of evidence held to be convincing. First, the Vietnam War is immoral. Second, the Vietnam War has torn asunder the fabric of our society. The last statement is as unprovable as the first is self-serving and irrelevant, for concerning society's discontent it is clear there were forces at work much in advance of the build-up of 1965, forces which have for some time been nudging us off history's stage. As for the ethical status of the war, beneath the will of the people, within their heart of hearts, there is a pulsating message: "we lost."

What is being proposed in this work is an analysis of ideologized America at limited war.** This requires that we look beneath the sheath of indictment and praise which has served to protect this subject from the embarrassment of examination, and then see what we shall see. We will take a critical look at the descriptive and normative fibers which make up the American banner of war, as it has been unfurled during a quarter of a century of limited conflicts. In so doing we will have sketched both cause and effect of our incompetence to fight such wars.

Our approach will be analogous to the work of a therapist, who coaxes forth the origins of the patient's belief, or wish, or affliction.

*The Cartwheel Factor is discussed within the context of the Vietnam War in Chapter 7.
**The twofold classification of war into general and limited is inadequate but useful. In a general war the survival of the nation is directly at issue, whereas in restricted conflict the aim is to secure or defend political goals which are highly desirable but which are not required for the nation's continued existence. There is some question as to the utility of this dichotomy during an era when war can take such varied form. Such terms as "sublimited" and "subterranean" have been used to describe insurgencies and the like, but are unsatisfactory. What is required is a rethinking of war as such, which would permit a more fruitful taxonomy. Most of all, war has to be dedivinized.

The process will resemble the construction of a developmental chart, showing circumstances and factors which influenced our beliefs. It is hoped that by laying out the causes of our shortcomings something of a prescriptive nature will emerge, for verily it is written: Never Again!

Moral indictments have made up the air we breathe for so long, some statement about war's morality is expected. The ethics of war is not the point of this study. Consequently, let us look briefly at the three traditional conceptions of war,* get them out of the way, and return to the first order of business.

The settled notions about the nature of war are clear, reasonably concise, and internally consistent; they are the products of ideologies long in development. They are also incompatible with each other, and cannot be combined. These ideas are of interest here principally because of the ways in which they have been appropriated by some of our leaders, and because of the consequences flowing from such importing from abroad. Since they may not be familiar to the reader, a series of brief scenarios will make these notions clear.

Assume that Bruce is a tenured professor, who lives in Superbia along with his son, Goliath. Assume further that one afternoon Goliath is struck by another child. Chances are good that Goliath will defend himself. Provided the odds are not overwhelmingly against him he will, if he survives the first onslaught, go on the offensive with sufficient vigor to insure the act is not immediately repeated.

The reaction seems perfectly natural to most of us, even desirable to some. Abstract from and magnify Goliath 200 million times and one has approximated the defensive conception of war. For the child to defend himself is, we say, a natural thing; for the nation, an inalienable right.

According to this view of war, though the defense was natural the initial assault was not. Supporters of the defensive conception see international strife as an unnatural, cataclysmic upheaval, an erupting and destructive force. War is a radical departure from the normal course of things, and the quicker the cracks are papered over the better. It is as if history has been lifted off its tracks by alien powers, realizes it, and strives to resume a normal course.

*Variations and elaborations on the basic arguments can become extreme, with such matters as proportionality, intentions, etc. receiving careful attention. We will consider only the basic forms, since these most nearly accord with statements on war made by our public officials—our concern.

If war is unnatural, then it is also unnecessary. Arguing from analogy, using a benign model of man as the basis, our defensive view has it that a state never is forced into war, that legal or other nonviolent redress is or at least ought to be made available. War is no more a requirement of life between nations than are social abberations within our nation.* It is this thrust of faith—that war never is a necessity, and that moral freedom is a fact for man and nation alike—that forms a bridge between the descriptive and normative aspects of the defensive idea of war.

Supporters of Goliath's position (which include most Americans) seldom feel it necessary to give any ethical justification further than to say that they, or their country, is engaging in self-defense. The right to defend oneself is inalienable, indubitable.

It is also either confused or morally perverse.

Returning to the example of Goliath, son of Bruce, we recall that he had been struck by another, and then defended himself. A morally unimpeachable reaction. Perhaps.

Let us flesh out the picture by giving the little fellow who defends himself, thus hurting others, a loathsome character. Let Goliath now have a character that complements his name, so that he becomes a swinish and tyrannical bully. For amusement he clubs the neighborhood children into submission. If we accept the defensive view of war, then at a minimum our impulses must give us a headache. On the one hand, we would argue that Bruce's son had every right to defend himself, thus inflicting pain on the aggressor. On the other hand, given the disposition and track record of Goliath most Americans would feel that the tyrannical little bully had the thrashing coming to him.

Multiply by 200 million.

Rotating matters on their axis we discover an equally displeasing sight. A necessary consequence of the defensive notion is that one never is justified in striking the first blow, or a nation in launching the first armed attack on another land. This means that regardless of the perversity or the heinous goings-on within the boundaries of another country, despite the institutionalization of evil across the border, and regardless of Goliath's nature, we never have the moral right to correct the situation by use of force.**

Multiplying by 200 million one learns that, contrary to its appeal, the defensive conception of war is of the coarsest moral material. A

*This is the basis for the mistaken belief that interpersonal ethics ought to or can apply to state relations.

**The ethical basis for America's disavowal of preventive war. (Preventive war is called "active defense" by nations which practice preventive war.)

nation which follows this doctrine must ignore the justness of the respective causes, the righteousness or evil of existing regimes—including that which one is defending (or else elect a pre-Tonkin Gulf liberal).

A possible way out is to say that what one is defending is of transcendent worth. But in that case "defense" takes on a new meaning.

Going again to the case of the child who actually threw the first punch, imagine that his assaults on others result from his conviction that it is right and just that the pummeling occur, that eternal peace and justice can reign along the block only if its social transformation is complete.

Let us further imagine that those against whom the pummeling has been directed are convinced that the other kid is not just bad but evil, and that suppression of his acts is required not for reasons of self-defense but for overarching moral reasons. (One might visualize an alliance of like-minded preschoolers being formed, each member of which is pledged to oppose, for example, Son of Bruce.)

If the members of the alliance (or, as is more likely, a portion thereof) jointly resist assault, perhaps inflict pain on Goliath, it is important that they be clear as to whether they are resisting aggression or Aggression, whether they are stopping a breach of the peace along the sidewalk or punishing a crime against humanity. Otherwise, some of the members will be confused as to their aims.

Multiply both sides of the above illustration by a billion or two and one is again at the level of principle.

This second view of war goes by a host of titles, the most appropriate being "eschatological." Here war is seen as cosmic heroism, with the forces of light battling the forces of darkness (the light and shadows depending, as the example of Goliath versus the alliance suggests, on one's perspective). Such an appraisal of war tells us that history and reality are in the making, to be grasped and reordered according to an eternal template by the righteous victor. War is the opportunity for the arrangement of nature according to man's interpretation of immanent moral truth. Forces hurl themselves into the fight on a universal scale, the goal of the participants more certain than the outcome of battle. The unpatriotic are idolators.

The eschatological doctrine is one of severity and retribution. It is not sufficient to strike back when attacked, nor to hold the other at bay. It is not sufficient either to retrieve what one has lost. Least of all is it permissible to reach an accord: doing so would be making a pact with the devil. Thus, the destruction of the enemy—his physical annihilation—is required. The punishment must fit the crime, and the end does not justify but instead specifies the means. The latter are properly harsh.

Every war of this century has been justified by our leaders by appealing to the defensive, the eschatological, or an argument combining both elements. The consequences have been ruinous. Before considering those, however, there is one other justification for making war.

William James won for himself ample if undeserved criticism from European intellectuals around the turn of the century with his use of such terms as "cash value" to describe the philosophy of pragmatism. Even before then Americans had prided themselves on being shrewd businessmen, on getting a good deal, and in bad circumstances on knowing when to cut one's losses. Such a doctrine makes sense when elevated to the level of the state in time of war only if one's goals are variations on the primal urge for national survival.

The idea has a respectable lineage. It never has gained much public favor in America because of its lack of moral grandeur. Here end and means must always be in tandem, though not as a moral goal, with permissible method. The emphasis is upon identifying, gaining and holding the political ends which are necessary, possible and desirable. This ordering is all-important, as important as disavowing the position in public.

The political view of war involves another analogy of human to national conduct. But the model of man considered here is different from the defensive conception. The current model is one of the rational guiding the irrational, intellect over emotion, idea astride need. If war is awful it is also natural, as are fights between different species. There are indeed laws of nature and of history, and the point is for us to understand and take advantage of them.

In terms of values this way of looking at war maintains there is but one sure end, which was implanted by nature. Keep what you have, and get more if needs, conditions, and capabilities are in harmony. Realize that "peace" and "war" are words only, marks created by man to indicate, respectively, acceptable and excessive levels of violence. Realize, too, that other justifications for war can be the ploys of charlatans and knaves who, to escape the guilt of the very bad acts one commits during war, a guilt the bearing of which might make for better humans were it ever within one's conscience, hide behind the shield of the eternal, pretending they can divine the intent of our Creator. Harshness is preferable to hubris.

A political view of war was of supreme importance to the United States in the conduct of both the Korean and Vietnam wars, if only because of our inept grasp of that conception.

Experience must be categorized, and to do so we employ words. One such word is "war."

Returning again to the child with the swinish and bullying ways, one would have to suppose that his opinions would not receive universal acceptance along the block unless the fear of a thumping stands behind them. It is conceivable that he one day decides to try bringing his friends into line through the force of argument rather than through force of his arms. Were this to occur most of us would hail it as evidence of progress on the part of the son of the tenured professor. Goliath, it would appear, is moving along the road to rationality.

Let us assume that the favorite subject for discussion by Goliath and his preschool friends is the use of force for the gaining of ends. Let it further be assumed that there is a grubby little war in one of earth's more distressed pockets, a war holding a special if painful delight for our hero. Both he and his colleagues hold very powerful convictions concerning the justness of that conflict. In line with his change to a gentler life style, let us imagine that Goliath unequivocally opposes the involvement and aims of one side in the war.

A boy from up the block who wears thick glasses (let us call him David) was last seen taking a drubbing from his bullying friend. He has again been approached, this time to be engaged in an argument about "the war." An early impasse is reached. Since the dispute is about words David offers to settle the issue by going to the source and standard of all words, the dictionary.

His labor goes unrewarded. His father's dictionary gives not only a series of different and confusing definitions, but it shows how a word ought to be used, depending upon the needs of the time and of those involved. There is the War of the Roses and economic warfare, warring factions, and the warrior ethic. Following the War to End Wars there are warmongers. Having succeeded too well, the dictionary and its complexity are left behind.

In an effort to save the discussion from collapse the disputants might agree on ground rules so that the conversation can continue. The lad with weak eyes begins by laying it down that "war" will mean certain things for purposes of the argument; the converted bully, still not entirely at ease in his new environment, gives cautious assent. Words fly, the arguments develop, progress is made as the meaning is whittled and honed to fit the desires of the more verbally sure David.

In fact there is zero progress, and the dispute ends with the pummeling of David by Goliath.

Our purpose in recalling the little bully to duty should be clear, since his conduct has been repeated on innumerable occasions in our nation's recent past. Nearly everyone is a student of language and logic, either as participant or as observer. Nearly everyone either has been involved in or has stood on the periphery of arguments of this sort, on "the war." Nearly everyone has left these festivities muttering obscenities, convictions intact.

Under these circumstances definitions and dictionaries are worthless—the former being irrelevant, the latter potential missiles for Goliath. Even on the unlikely assumption that agreement on words is reached, feelings and acid levels remain unchanged. Pascal wrote that the heart has its reasons: to which it might be added, so do the adrenals.

The principal reason for the other fellow's continued refusal to yield is not hard to find: the dispute is not over words and their content but over attitudes and the actions they ought to produce. There is something infuriating about presenting indisputable facts and impeccable logic, and still failing to convince one's opponent of the justness or venality of the point of the argument. This atom of irrationality will likely remain at conviction's core, unresponsive and unmoved. Both sides refuse to budge, yet this is precisely what they each insist upon: giving intellectual ground is not enough, and a change in conscience must issue in action. Especially in questions of social ethics it is clear that resolution of debate be only preliminary to resolution in practice.

But resolution at the level of argument must come first, which means one side must convince the other, must generate a corresponding ethical experience within his opponent. When the issue is war, and the debate is within the United States, the larger experience which resolution and unity presuppose has to approach the classical sense of *pathos*. Short of that, one side must persuade, or browbeat, the other.

In no other area is the role of persuasive definitions—definitions involving fundamental convictions—so pronounced as when war is being discussed. If the war in Southeast Asia has had one effect which no one can deny, it is that the term "war" in contemporary discussions evokes immediate evaluative, largely pejorative, overtones even as that term inserts itself into the discussion. A result is that the very devices through whose use one must investigate the subject of international violence have been corrupted virtually beyond use. Simply stated, "war" is for most, today, invisibly and inextricably tied to moral considerations, for example, "immoral war," "just war." These are in practice irreducible terms. A further result of this implicit coupling is that the objective study of one war in particular, or of war as such, is today looked upon as a form of neocromancy,* principally because we didn't win.

Presumably Americans have learned, or have been taught, what "war" means.**

In order to insure their continued survival as a group, or at least to make sure that survival comes to an end only at man's pleasure, fish often are bred and fattened in an environment of man's choosing. After an appropriate period of time the fish may be returned to his homeland, perhaps to a pleasant mountain brook, where he can start life anew. The fish is still in possession of his warm memories of the keeper, and of the regular feedings he received, and of the shadow signaling the coming of supper as the keeper approached the water. Recalling repeated incidents of this sort, it is not surprising that the fish, now in the stream high in the hills, will move over to the bank as he sees the shadow approach. Not surprising, either, that the bear whose shadow falls upon the water, and whose paw breaks beneath the surface, is pleased that the new fish is so accommodating.

One might conclude, then, that the fish picked up a thing or two while in captivity; and possibly he had a vague notion of at least one form of war.

*It has recently been proposed[4] that an approach different from that of categorizing wars solely in terms of purpose (defensive, just cause, etc.) be used. This method consists of identifying morally relevant characteristics a given war possesses; not surprisingly, this method invariably shows World War II and Vietnam to be poles apart in terms of moral acceptability.

One of the difficulties with this technique is suggested by the following. Assume (as the article cited seems to) there are ten characteristics (aggression, etc.) which, if all present, define the perfect unjust war. (Assume that "unjust," "immoral," "utterly wicked," and "venal" are synonymous, as opponents of the Vietnam War tended to do.) In elementary logic one says that a complicated statement (made up of simple statements) is true just in case all the simple component statements are true. For example, the statement "Bruce is a tenured professor and Bruce is a make-believe revolutionary" is true just in case Bruce is a tenured professor and Bruce is a make-believe revolutionary. There are four possibilities here: Both statements true, the first true and the second false, the first false and the second true, both false. The rule is 2^n, where n = number of simple statements. The possible combinations, and the one condition under which the statement "Bruce is a tenured professor and Bruce is a make-believe revolutionary" is true are shown by constructing a truth table. If one were to build something analogous in order to make statements about the truly unjust war, then with ten characteristics defining such a conflict, the rule 2^n would yield 1,024 possible combinations. Does it then follow that only once in 1,024 wars one is privileged to witness the totally unjust war (and, by implication, the totally just war —with zero characteristics present)? If so, we are truly privy to the diastole and systole of ethics in war, with the best (World War II) and the worst (Vietnam) placed before us within a span of just thirty years.

**Beginning with Chapter 1, it will be shown that this has been a crucial if unintended function of major American leaders over the last three decades.

Our interest is in Americans learning about American wars. It is not clear at what point on the learning scale this type of acquisition belongs. Perhaps it should reside alongside the fish in the hatchery; perhaps in the cage with the starved rat who will push bars, climb stairs, pull triggers for a crumb or two; perhaps it belongs in the category with the piegeon who, having been fed by someone without having first done anything other than bow and scrape, thinks hard and, convinced no pigeon gets something for nothing, repeats his bowing and scraping in hope of being fed again. Perhaps one's appreciation of war is fully as superstitious as the hungry, bowing bird.[5]

Almost every American has an opinion on war in general, and war 'X' in particular. Few of us can trace this opinion to a book, to a moment of conversion during a discussion. Nor have many taken a course entitled, "Introduction to War in General, and to War 'X' in Particular." At this time no one knows the factors which exerted themselves in teaching us what we were taught, any more than we know where to plot such learning along a scale. Neither do we understand why there was general approval (if meager comprehension) of World War II, and late in the game a general disapproval (if meager comprehension) of the Vietnam War.

The answers, if ever such are found, probably will come more from an understanding of the fish and pigeon than from the ritualistic denunciation of war "X."

It is the purpose of this book to suggest some factors which gave us our outlook on war in general, and on war "X" in particular. What is required to conclude this introduction, then, is a statement of the existential construction Americans place upon "war" today, a brief mention of war and democracy, and then the foundation for our historical survey will have been established.

As for the American conception of war, it is not a conception at all. Instead, it is a wish pleading to be fulfilled. This wish is the historical product of the overlapping and interpenetrating of the defensive and eschatological doctrines of war, even though these two sets of ideas logically exclude each other. Our wish says that war must have a beginning, identified by some violent dislocation of history; a middle, a time of reversals and resolve; and an end, an event which happens in time but which transcends time, something reaching into and through the temporal order to envelope, make sense of and give moral sanction to the intermediate acts. War is linear, thus permitting us to translate distance into time, obstacles into plans of action. Obstacles are not to be gone around but through. This linearity applies essentially to the temporal order rather than to the geography of occupied areas. It is essential that war have a beginning, a middle, and an end, rather like a good story. Rather like World War II.

By this wish, and by acts of recollection of wars which have gone well for us, a distorted picture of war, idealized beyond practical use, is kept alive. By the same acts other wars are distorted, too, then are rejected as being first incomprehensible, then as unwinnable, and finally as immoral.

Thus if a war lacks one or more of the three characteristics of time, especially an ending, then the possibility of psychological closure is removed. If no sense of ultimate completion is before us the war will not, cannot, fit into our ingrained categories of explanation. After passing a critical, discernible point in time and/or exposure,* we will take back our moral support.

It was on psychological, perhaps aesthetic, grounds that after learning no victory laurels were to be had a few of us called Korea immoral, though with voice muffled. We would later vent the genetically identical outrage when Vietnam's time had come, and passed. On this occasion there would be an unmistakable clarity.

We approach wars armed with a wish, or expectation. What is important in a study of the American at limited war is to look at the promises made, whether explicit or implied, which the people held as we prepared for and then plunged into war, or as we failed to prepare for and then stumbled into war. Such is the danger of ideology armed.

These expectations fuse with persuasive definitions of "war" and moral justifications for conflict. This fusion is the result of our democratic society, the nature of modern war, and the genius of a Corsican. It is due in large measure to Napoleon that we learned what we learned, due to our own prophets that we learned as we learned.

The French revolution gave rise to war and to war propaganda, creating what William Pitt called "armed opinions" and Jomini "wars of opinion."[6] With the rise of Napoleon came the rise of war as a democratic, evangelical, and ideological force, sweeping all older conceptions, and most armies, before it. For the first time there appeared in battle a fully self-conscious Frenchman.**

A rediscovery of this impatience could not long be restrained within the borders of France. Nor was it. This truth of war as salva-

---

*Advances in communication technology, plus the absence of restraints, make exposure more important than time. See Chapters 6 and 7 for a discussion.

**Napoleon should be taken as symbolic of an emerging mentality. See A. A. Palmer's work, note 6.

tion and salvation through war, hidden since the Crusades and Peter the Hermit, erupted and lay claim to all Europe.

As with the revolutionary messianism of that earlier day, war and those who rode its crest were carried onto the throne of Eternal Truth and Eternal Justice. French nationalism gave way to a chiliastic fever, as liberty, equality and fraternity ceased being aims of citizens of France and became instead rights of all mankind. War, like the rights of man, thereafter knew no limits. It crossed the Atlantic.

By conceptual trickery a defense of France became a defense of the transcendent. By the same deceit Napoleon layed down the rules of engagement for all future wars of opinion. World War II was a war of opinion, fitting well Jomini's description of a war enlisting "the worst passions, and become vindictive, cruel and terrible."[7]

Limited wars, like rights, are pre-Napoleonic. To conduct a limited war as if it were a war of opinion is to introduce into the life of a nation such as America, which is itself founded on opinion,* a fatal contradiction. Korea and Vietnam were limited wars.

When an American leader presents his justification for taking us into war, that justification will contain within it promises as to the course that war will chart, along with promises of the values we will, because of the war, see realized. His argument will also tell us what is expected of us, and what is expected by how many of us. Promises produce corresponding expectations. An ethical justification for war which promises the realization of universal values cannot set limits upon the expectations of the people. Attainment of values of such dimension in wars of opinion place an obligation on each of us, as members of a democracy, to participate in the quest. To that degree a nation at war is unified, even if artificially.

But to limit wars is to limit the values to be realized, as it means we will settle for political goals of a determinate size. It also means placing restrictions upon the number of those among us who will go forth to secure those goals, and those values. Most of all, to limit a war is to limit expectations of the people. This is done by making carefully limited promises. To that degree a nation at war is not unified.

The last thing one wants in limited war is universal participation, universal promises, universal expectations.** Ideology is inflexible.

*Which is to say, the will of the people.
**Thus the all-important qualification "as a nation" when discussing our incompetence to wage limited war. By no sensible military or political standard could we be said to have lost either in Korea or in Vietnam. Those are verdicts of the people, their final opinion, as it were.

To conclude: the fears and desires of the American people, and the promises of the American leaders, will emerge during our study as the most crucial factors which operate when our nation is at war. To focus upon the promises and expectations of American leaders and the public, respectively, and to observe just how and if the two mesh—promises made and kept, wishes asked and fulfilled—is to chart the course of war as that experience has registered itself in the American soul. Such a focusing is to show what the terms "war" and "peace," "victory" and "defeat" mean to us. Simultaneous with these displays it will be revealed why we are incompetent to wage limited war.

All analogical arguments are invalid, all comparisons dangerous. Buried within us there is the compulsion to compare wars, to view the worst in the light of the best. If the comparison is made, the analogy constructed, then the contrast should not be limited to moral characteristics alone. To do so, and to ignore those other aspects which are causally related to our attitudes about the moral nature of a given war, aspects which are the stuff of the analogy, is to beg the issue.

Preparatory to our journey alongside the American at winless war, let us return for a fleeting glance at a war of unlimited promises, total participation, and expectations gorged; a time when a misreading of Clausewitz was fueled by the unread Jomini, piloted by disciples of a new social order.

Let us return to World War II.

I OF VICTORY AND VICTORY GARDENS

> Thus was revealed to me by the living Paraclete all
> that has been and that shall be, and all that the eye
> sees and the ear hears and the thought thinks.
> Through him I learned to know every thing, I saw the
> All through him, and I became *one* body and *one*
> spirit.
>
> —Mani

WAR AND GNOSTICISM

We called it "reeducation." They called it "retraining," and it amounted to thrusting one's fingers through another's skin, grasping the insides, and fashioning something worthy of our moral approval. By whatever name it was called, this attempt by us to restructure the German character was to mortar what the judgment at Nuremberg was to a copestone. Both were consistent with and derivative of our insistence upon total satisfaction and, as a result of the latter, our conviction that we had gained a handle on total, ideological truth during those war years.

August 1946. The smell of ashes and of defeat were permanent parts of the air the Germans breathed. It was the stated purpose of our "Long-Range Policy Statement on German Reeducation" that ashes remain a part of that defeated people's atmosphere[1] and landscape, thus providing a scaffold onto which we would erect a civilized and moral state. In due time that state could be crowded with civilized and moral Germans.

Another American plan was operative at the same time, and in the same place. This was the agreement reached at Potsdam, by which the Yalta declaration for the total destruction of Nazi Germany was made operational. That agreement was still on the books in 1946, and at the level of day-to-day living took the form of Directive 1067. The latter was an articulation of American policy toward Germany as seen through the eyes of the creators of that directive, the U.S. Joint Chiefs of Staff. With an air of Hamurabi about them the American military planners remarked without emotion that suffering by Germans was inevitable, and that it should be brought home to those defeated that what was happening was proper retribution for the ruthless destruction waged by their destroyed, satanic leaders.[2]

The contradictory avenues of approach to the hearts and minds of postwar Germany is apparent only. At the subterranean level there was consistency, though it was a consistency of impulse rather than concept. At war's end we were dispensers of eternal justice, a role which provided that we scourge the body of the defeated even as we refashioned his character. Such are the advantages of a democracy waging, and winning, general war.

April 1, 1944. The beginning of the end for the body of the Nazi Reich, as well as for our President. Mr. Roosevelt was speaking to his people that day about the previous year: "The total harvest from victory gardens was tremendous. It made the difference between scarcity and abundance." Not only was virtual starvation averted; that little strip of land or the window box gave "every citizen an opportunity to do something toward backing up the boys at the front."[3] The results were identical though not equatable.

As the President campaigned in Chicago later that year with the sure knowledge he would be roared back into office for still another term, Mr. Roosevelt said he was confident that his people agreed with the objectives, "—that they demand them—that they are determined to get them—and that they are *going* to get them." What the people truly wanted, and what they would get was the unrelenting pursuit of the guilty. After this we would "deliver them up in order that Justice be done."[4] His use of the capital "J" was intentional, for only so could we be satisfied, totally and completely.

World War II had its beginning, so far as Americans are concerned, in the butter-soft breeze over Hawaii, as Captain Fushida led the attack against the music which rose softly from Radio

Honolulu. The middle occupied three years of promises—first of survival, then of punishment of the wicked. The end was the deck of the flagship *Missouri,* after which Toshikazu Kase, one of the members of the surrender party, told the Americans by way of his emperor that our side had won because of a nobler idea, and added "the real issue was moral—beyond all the powers of algebra to compute."[5] Our side deserved as much. Promises had been made and kept, expectations had soared only to be sated, and the vision of being attacked, regrouping, and launching the counterattack to claim complete victory, had been etched for decades to come into the tissue of the American character.

The American people's desire to be left alone in their isolation before World War II is well known, and needs no belaboring. "Let us turn our eyes inward." When the governor of Pennsylvania made that remark on Armistice Day, 1935, he was speaking for virtually every citizen of the nation.[6] One year later, when asked if we should join with an attacked nation to repel the invader, 71 percent of us screamed No! During the Spring of 1937 virtually the same number believed entry by the United States into World War I had been a mistake, and 95 out of 100 were utterly against going back into Europe in the event of another war. By the Fall of 1937, as war engulfed Spain, two-thirds of the American people rejected entry into the League of Nations. Six months before the invasion of Poland and the beginning of the war,* two-thirds of us were unwilling to help those nations which the attack on Poland had dragged into the fighting: England and France.[7]

Even after a term-and-a-half of social legislation the people were still as exhausted as their soil, introspective, bitterly cynical over the unfulfilled promises of President Wilson and his war, and categorically against lifting their vision, and expectations, much above ground level.

Entry into the World Court had been thrust aside resolutely both by the people and by the Congress, the President's request for discretionary powers to decide whether an embargo applied and, if so, to which nations, was likewise rejected. Congress' response in the latter case was to pass a neutrality act** designed to shackle the Chief Executive, to express their horror at categorizing nations as good and evil, then recess.[8]

In the years just before the war popular attitudes swayed and

*That is, the beginning for some other nations. So far as Americans were concerned we definitely were not at war in 1939.

**Neutrality Act of 1935, signed August 31 of that year. See note 8 for the convoluted course of U.S. neutrality 1935-40, and the various acts.

sagged, and occasionally convulsed. There appears to have been two rather distinct strata of opinion, one more basic and consistent than the other. This more fundamental stream of feeling responded less violently to the upheavals abroad, but measured and absorbed their impact, and grew progressively in accordance with the rise in international hostility. It forced FDR to step quickly away from his "quarantine" speech of October 1937, and to lie low for two years.

Surface opinion fluctuated with passing events, and gave pollsters fits as to just what the people were thinking.* In general, from the time of the invasion of Poland in 1939, there was a growing but largely unconscious realization among the people that war was probably inevitable. At the same time, though, there developed a corresponding desire to avoid war at almost any cost. One year before Pearl Harbor nearly two out of three opposed FDR's request that the Neutrality Act be amended to permit our ships to carry war supplies to England.[10] In the same breath 90 percent favored extending help to England if this was the only way to save her from defeat.[11]

The other side of the world presented an entirely different picture for Americans. Japan's push into Manchuria and China, even the sinking of our river boat *Panay,* had not been greeted with much more than the yawn of the irritated. In February 1941, a healthy majority could not identify with the Dutch East Indies and Singapore, and were unwilling to offend Japan to the point of risking war.[12]

These opinion polls were of abiding interest to the President. Through one of his assistants, Anna Rosenberg, Mr. Roosevelt had expressed his interest to one of America's pioneers in the field of measuring opinion, Hadley Cantril. The work the psychologist had been doing out of the Office of Public Opinion Research concerned the reaction of our people to the events unfolding in Europe; the President asked he continue and share the results with his government; and Dr. Cantril obliged. The question, "Should we help England?" became a "trend" question, asked again and again and again.[13]

Polls were used to gauge public opinion regarding what our government ought to do in certain situations, and asked how much the citizens agreed with what the U.S. Government was in fact doing. FDR maintained he never made a radical alteration in his policies as a result of these polls. If there were discrepancies between his

*For example, the defeat of the French in 1940 saw a spasm among our citizens for defense measures. Six months later 83 percent were opposed to our entering the war against Germany and Italy.[9]

views and those held by his followers, it was his avowed duty to convince the people of the rightness of his position. To such ends public opinion polls could make a unique contribution, that is, not to measure but to mold opinion.

The war that, in FDR's opinion, had to be fought* would be a classic example of a "war of opinion." That presupposed an evangelical unity, and the President did not countenance obstruction.

An example of the President's impatience with disunity occurred during his press conference of February 21, 1941, just as his nation had completed its slide back into the doldrums of isolation. A reporter raised the issue of the moral function of the fourth estate, and its corollary right to print what it had learned. The President made an interesting distinction by affirming the reporter's right to get the story, but the editor's obligation not to print it. After discussing morals and ethics and patriotism, Roosevelt was asked what the "final test" of sensitive information might be. The answer? "What the commander-in-chief of the Army and Navy thinks would be harmful to the defense of this country to give out."

There was, he added, "no question of censorship." The reporter asked, "You want the papers to figure on some method of their own?" Our President nodded his head, agreeing, and thus brought into being the best of all controls: self-censorship.[15]

Four months later Fuehrer Directive No. 21 was implemented, Operation Barbarossa got underway, and the German and Russian dictatorships began their battle unto death. As the Panzer units encircled and cut to pieces entire Soviet corps, Dr. Cantril began a new sampling of our opinion. The new differed from the old in that it was knowingly slanted,[16] its purpose being to solidify support for England. This would not be the final time polls became vectors of social attitudes.

Even before the invasion of Russia FDR had established the parameters for the waging of general war by this democracy, when he spoke "not with the voice of one man but with the voice of one hundred and thirty millions." The decision having been made, "It is binding on us all." That which was binding was opposition not to country X, but to "tyranny and the forces of oppression."[17]

At this point, however, it is pretty clear that the unity the President wanted, and needed, did not exist. On the very eve of Barbarossa well over half the people favored a war referendum before permitting Congress to send American soldiers overseas,[18] FDR's

*While still a President-elect FDR told Rexford Tugwell that war with Japan might as well come now as later. Shortly thereafter FDR allocated National Recovery funds for warship construction.[14]

denunciation of "defeatists and appeasers" and his declaration the previous May of an unlimited national emergency notwithstanding.

Throughout the summer of 1941 he railed against his countrymen's lethargy, and chided them about "an oasis of liberty surrounded by a cruel desert of dictatorship." A majority believed we were already at war "for all practical purposes," but clung to an inbred optimism.

During that summer he also met with Former Naval Person— Prime Minister Churchill—and shortly thereafter began waging an undeclared if thin war against the German Navy.[19]*

Two out of three of us applauded our Navy's shooting Germans on sight,[20] applauded FDR's likening them to coiled rattlesnakes. Every other person expected war with Japan in the near future.[21]

Pearl Harbor satisfied our expectations, and molded our need that war have a certain symmetry. Pearl Harbor likewise satisfied the requirement that the threat, and thus ultimate evil, be universal. This would permit a universal response, in the quest for universal moral entities.

"The American people in their righteous might will win through to absolute victory." The words, and the sentiments they expressed, were the President's as his voice radiated into our homes that first Monday following Pearl Harbor. The people's initial reaction to the attack was anger pure and simple, not the outrage of the righteous. But he did speak for Americans as they would be within a few months, as enemy atrocities embellished American defeat.

Already *jihad* was inevitable, as Roosevelt simultaneously promised and insisted upon, in the name of his people, not the destruction of Japanese treachery, "but the sources of international brutality, wherever they exist . . ." The force we would soon exert, and the killing we would undertake, would not be in the defense of the United States but in defense of the eternal: "When we resort to force, as now we must, we are determined that this force shall be directed toward ultimate good as well as against immediate evil."[22]

With the promise of victory and punishment came the additional promise of freedom from fear.

ARMS FOR THE DEFENSE OF THE ETERNAL

But a war of all against all which would remove evil and fear forevermore requires men and arms.

*FDR had met Mr. Churchill during World War I while serving as Assistant Secretary of the Navy. Mr. Churchill served as First Lord of the Admiralty. "Former Naval Person" was the title the Prime Minister used in his telegraphic communication with the President prior to U.S. entry into World War II.

Our modern military establishment was brought into being in 1920 through the National Defense Act. A standing army of about a quarter of a million was authorized even as the grip of cynicism and isolation was tightening. A year after Hitler became Germany's ruler, our army stood at less than half its authorized strength. Each year the core of career officers justified their work during the previous year, assessed threats and capabilities, and requested the funds to recruit up to the authorized limit. Each year of the depression they were turned down.

The combined report and request of 1934* was written in the apologetic, introspective language of the larger society, whose values were being reflected: The army would block hostile invasion, perhaps; but this was only a "possible necessity."[23] Overwhelmed with its own feelings of irrelevance and impotence—feelings which would return after every war—the army aided its detractors in the very act of asking for additional monies.

Congress' fist loosened only for a crack, and only for a moment, in 1939. Two months prior to the partitioning of Poland by Germany and the Soviet Union our representatives bought a few airplanes, and reinforced our garrison in Panama. The money also permitted the National Guard to meet 60 instead of 48 times each year.[24]

The "phony war" made the pleas of FDR and his generals appear at best ludicrous, at worst like warmongering. On the eve of the fall of France a request to put together a defense force in Alaska was denied. Suddenly, the nation was seized with the vision of tyranny victorious and, as General Marshall later recalled, "the pendulum of public opinion reversed itself, swinging violently to the other extreme, in an urgent demand for enormous and immediate increases in modern equipment and of the armed forces."[25]

Sensing that the wind was at his back, if only temporarily, the President struck. Within a two week period he asked for $2 billion, got it, and sat bewildered as our representatives gave him 120,000 more soldiers than he had asked for.[26] Trying to stay with a winning hand Mr. Roosevelt asked that the National Guard be federalized (thus side-stepping the issue of massive inductions). Four months and much parliamentary maneuvering later, the first guard units were brought into federal service. On the same day, September 16, 1940, the Selective Service Act was signed by the President.** The

*Included in the Baker Board, a report chaired by Newton D. Baker, Secretary of War during World War I. Its primary purpose was to investigate U.S. air power.

**On the hunch that money to house the hoped-for troops would come from somewhere, FDR diverted $30 million from his emergency fund for barracks construction on August 2, 1940.[28]

cutting edge of our armed opinion soon stood at a million and a half.[27]

One year later the edge was blunted, then it began to rust. Those men brought on through the National Guard and by the draft knew from the outset their contracts were for twelve months only. Jubilance among the soldiers mounted as Summer 1941 crawled toward them. With the arrival of hot weather the jubilance faltered and collapsed. It appears there was some very fine print to those contracts, something about extension in the event of a national emergency.

In August, four months before Pearl Harbor, Congress approved FDR's national emergency request of a month earlier.[29] For the next four years jubilance was a commodity restricted to presidents and generals only.

About the time the draftees were getting the bad news some American laborers were being dispatched to Northern Ireland, with instructions to build a naval base; some American soldiers were settling in for the occupation and defense of Iceland; and some specialists from the American Treasury were trying to figure out exactly what to do with the Japanese assets just frozen.

A couple of weeks before Christmas 1941, all bets were off, all questions suspended, for the duration.

VOX POPULI

"President Roosevelt has asked the public to think up a good name to call the present war. What would you suggest (other than 'Second World War' or 'World War II')?" April 29, 1942. As disaster compounded itself, an attractive lady with time on her hands, some polling experience, and a desire to help the war effort, put this question to her portion of carefully chosen American citizens, then recorded their spontaneous and unrehearsed responses. No title was a walkaway winner, though "War of World Freedom" was chosen by one out of four.[30]*

It was an ingenious use to which polls were being used, as it was discovered that opinions could, under the guise of measuring them, be generated, directed, controlled. The dilemma of the equality of opinion was on the road to solution.[31]

On issue which nagged us during the first two years of the war, one over which there was less than uniformity of attitude, concerned

*Runners up were the less resourceful "War of Freedom" (14 percent), "War of Liberty" (13 percent), "Anti-Dictator War" (11 percent). The lackluster and morally neutral "Survival War" skimped along near the bottom with 7 percent.

unconditional surrender. The President announced this as a required goal if we would take our designated place in history, following the Casablanca meeting in January 1943. The quiet furor the announcement generated among his less evangelical advisers was squelched immediately. Nor was public discussion of the likelihood of this demand stiffening enemy resistance, or of our premature display of intentions, overly encouraged. The buzz word was allowed to remain, suspended, above the American body politic.

Some of the wires suspending the notion showed signs of fraying, though, so a month after the initial announcement that our enemies must meet the precondition of placing their fates in our hands, the President received a memo suggesting he set "unconditional surrender" in its true perspective by outlining the history of the German Army, emphasizing the continuing menace to world peace its existence threatened.

A problem of no mean proportion developed, though. More than one in four distinguished between Hitler and his army. Thus, if Hitler were out of the way a goodly number of Americans would be willing to talk peace. As Dr. Cantril, who was involved in this measurement-control program, remarked, these people "still did not understand the full meaning of 'unconditional surrender' . . ."[32] That is to say, there were still some who had not yet been persuaded to accept the definition, incidentally, which was integrally related to other definitions: "war," "peace," "victory," "defeat."

In the end the true definition was accepted. Beginning with a spasmodic fear response (five months after Pearl Harbor almost 90 percent believed our government ought to take over and run those war-related industries whose owners refuse to produce) the people progressed to the point that by Summer of '42, half of us would force workers to move anywhere in the country in order to do war work, more than three-quarters were in favor of a tribunal to suspend any law that slowed the war effort. Though the meaning of "unconditional surrender" remained hazy, only 2 percent thought we should bother with courts-martial before putting the Nazi leaders to death.[33]

On it moved, and as the engines of war creaked with their burden and as we closed out the first full year of fighting a third of the people had no clear idea of why the war was being fought.[34] This fact about our comprehension remained constant throughout the war, though it came into contact with new facts. During the great German offensive through the Ardennes every third American wanted Germany totally destroyed as a political being, her territory to be chopped up into small, benign countries; fewer than half opposed the use of poison gas during the final month of the war;* finally, after so long a time, and after so much effort, almost 90 percent demanded of Japan what we had gotten with slightly less popular support from Germany—unconditional surrender.[36]

The road had been long and convoluted. It had, in fact, been a multitude of roads whose terminus was solidified opinion in this most perfect war of opinion.

"The Government is entitled to do anything it wants toward winning the war. Hollywood is concerned because it wants the Government really to get what it asks for."[37]

Walter Wanger was an important individual in the motion picture world, and when he spoke his audience usually was attentive. It was his hope that the professional image builders who had given their talents to the government for the duration of the war would pay as much heed to his written word.

What bothered Wanger was not propaganda but bad propaganda, and the latter was what the amateurs were turning out, the same individuals who, among other things, wanted all of Hollywood's motion picture scripts submitted before production.** They were showing "a growing desire to write *things into scripts.*"*** Left to their own devices Lowell Mellett and friends would succeed only in putting films together that would empty theatres. So wrote Wanger in 1943, his feelings hurt that after all the work without profit that Hollywood had done, even after 20th Century-Fox had budgeted 40 percent of its next year's outlay on war propaganda films, Washington could be so insensitive and stupid as to send amateur propagandists out to meddle in production. There was no question of government's right to have certain lines of thought it considers important stressed in films. The sole issue was how best to persuade the American public. Concerning the latter there could be no substitute for experience to buttress patriotism.****

Mellett was liaison officer from the government to the motion picture industry, and was only doing his job when he insinuated himself into the production of commercial films. He had been

*By this time a majority of Americans believed that "Japs" are a naturally cruel and brutal race of people, so it is not surprising that so-called laws of humane warfare were held inapplicable in their case.[35]

**Hollywood, and Mr. Wanger, drew the line at this suggestion, though not because they disagreed with the manipulative use to which movies were being put.

***Mr. Wanger's italics.

****Our Government produced movies on its own during those days. When Congress cut off the funds, the motion picture industry, which had already been producing half the items on the Government's program, undertook to do it all.[38]

chosen because of his dedication to the President, and because of ability demonstrated while part of something called the Office of Government Reports.

In early 1933, just a few months after taking office, President Roosevelt was approached with the idea of making available to the public information on what he and his advisers were doing for the welfare of the people. He liked the idea, enough that when his temporary executive Council was streamlined and condensed to form the National Emergency Council there was created, to supersede the Division of Press Intelligence for the U.S. Government, the U.S. Information Service. The function of the latter was to keep the people informed of federal recovery programs.

With more serpentine developments and Executive Orders, and with the creation of the Executive Office in 1939, all these informative functions were transferred to the President's Office.[39]

The purpose, here again, was to provide information for our democracy. That was, at any rate, one of the functions. Actually, there was some question, raised principally by President Roosevelt's detractors, as to the degree to which the information disseminated was to (a) educate the public, or (b) insure FDR's reelection. But then there are always Doubting Thomases.

His critics were on somewhat more solid ground with their other gripe about OGR. They suggested, as those out of office tend to do, that what we really had in OGR was a government-sponsored public opinion, or popularity, poll. Were their complaints not without grounds, Mr. Roosevelt would have had a disproportionate advantage. President Roosevelt's admirers' response was to repeat that the OGR simply kept him informed of citizen complaints. If, in the process, he learned something of their opinions and desires, well, no harm done.

Director Mellett (who would shortly move to Hollywood)became a bit testy in the final months before Pearl Harbor when the issue of propaganda and OGR was raised. "It may be," he snapped, "that we propagate the doctrine of democracy.... If that is what is meant by propaganda, let us hope we are guilty."[40]

With the outbreak of war many persons who had gained their experience with OGR moved to OWI. Some, like Mellett, moved both to OWI and to Hollywood.*

*The influence commercial films exert upon public opinion probably is too complicated to investigate. In any case an *ex post facto* experiment would be required which, in turn, would mean reversing the flow of time. It is of interest to compare the fims made during World War II, Korea and Vietnam, and the atmospheres into which they were discharged. Obviously, assigning cause and effect their proper positions is necessarily difficult.

In the jumbled, flaming months which followed Pearl Harbor there were eight government agencies more or less responsible for handling news of the war: the Division of Information of the Office for Emergency Management, the Office of Facts and Figures, the Foreign Information Service, the Coordinator of Inter-American Affairs, plus the Departments of War, Navy and State. There was also the Office of Government Reports. Clearly, such an arrangement would not do if the speedy and accurate dispatch of news was one's goal.

The news was hideous and could be expected to worsen. Thus, while our frayed and already-beaten soldiers were withdrawing to the Bataan peninsula for a final defense, back home in Washington the Bureau of the Budget drew up a plan creating a unified agency within the government for the timely dispatch of news, thus making scattered attempts superfluous. On June 13, 1942, FDR issued Executive Order 9182 by which the Office of War Information was given birth.* By the same device Roosevelt created the Office of Strategic Services.

Soon after this act the OSS began running operations against its selected targets. The OWI did the same, to insure, as its mandate read, "an intelligent understanding of war policies, activities and aims of the Government."**

When his office had been at work for about a year the director of the home-front propaganda battle, Elmer Davis, wrote that he was doing just what old Ben Franklin had been doing while working on his British audience so many years ago; recoiling from his bad analogy, he parried, telling us that if "propaganda" is a word in bad odor in this country, well, there is no public hostility to the idea of education as such, and "we regard this part of our job as education."[41]

"This part of our job" amounted to telling the American people not only how the war was doing, "but where it is going and where it came from—its nature and origins—what (besides national survival) our government hopes to get out of victory." Central to the efforts of OWI is the need "to help remove confusion from the public

*The OWI had a foreign and a domestic branch. In this chapter only the latter is of concern.

**Two months before Pearl Harbor, Colonel (later General) William J. Donovan was appointed Coordinator of Information by FDR. Colonel Donovan established a Foreign Information Service, and became deeply interested in psychological warfare and strategic propaganda. After much wrangling, the OSS, which Colonel Donovan headed, was given jurisdiction over "black propaganda," that is, strategic untruths. The legacies of the OSS would persist and come back to life with the birth of Special Forces. See below, Chapter 5.

mind." The best therapeutic device for this is to build up in the mind of the citizen "the full realization" that the United States would win.[42]

By the middle of 1943, then, the meaning of "victory" was being inflated to mean something far more than self-preservation, the latter having been rejected as pusillanimous by FDR a year before our entry into the war. By 1943 there were strong indications, gained from the soundings pollsters had been taking, that there was a receptivity among the people for a shift from the defensive to the eschatological interpretation of what our roles in World War II should be. This newer, final definition would be self-consciously held by our people, or a determining majority of our people, only after another year. In mid-1943 it was sufficient to promise victory, arouse the desired expectations, and relate both to "the true nature of the war."

As the nation's moral adventure accelerated, citizens were encouraged to look toward their government as a cooperative partner in the quest. The Association of Advertisers could receive assistance from the Bureau of Campaigns, as could teachers and librarians. This was a joint effort, in which all could, and ought, participate.

Teachers were especially important in the OWI's educative effort. Elmer Davis admitted that to tell intelligent teachers what they ought to think seems contradictory. Abhoring contradictions, he recommended only that they teach, as he said, "the obvious: that the earth is round, that this is a global war, and that premature peace means more Pearl Harbors." To those in his audience who might want him to retrace his most recent steps, he offered this counsel: "practical operation is more important than theoretical principles."[43]

These would be busy and trying times, with little left over for reading. For those who found the time, though, the OWI stood ready to give assistance. The librarian could, indeed was asked to, peruse the *Magazine War Guide*, "a monthly summary by the OWI Books and Magazine Bureau," a product designed as an aid not only to librarians but to editors and writers in planning their future publications. Our government would bend over backwards to aid all those who would see the war as it had to be seen if one were to perceive truth.* By 1943 the truth already meant the incineration of our enemies.

Facts and figures are always a bore; to make them less so, to con-

---

*Two OWI employees saw the truth from a different angle, disagreed on our making buddies of Admiral Darlan and Marshal Badaglio, and exposed these government machinations in public. They did not become heroes. They became unemployed.

nect the few shortages we suffered with the moral surety being sought, was the job of Archibald MacLeish. He was aided by a superb publication, the change in the title of which directly paralleled the shift in our argument to justify our war-making.

The publication in question was a magazine. It began publication on the final Friday of August 1941, just after the signing of the Atlantic Charter. The title was *Defense,* had been put together to make anticipated economic controls palatable, and could be had at the preposterously low price of 75¢ for 52 issues! It spoke of manpower and finance and production, and the initial issues were as exciting as stock averages are for the unemployed. This magazine, like this people, required that history explode before it was energized.

Indicative of our goals if not our mood in the months of defeat which trailed after Pearl Harbor, the name and magazine soared. The title now became *Victory,* the contents now were not so painful to read. Services, like the title and the magazine, outstripped previous efforts. A publisher could get free posters for the asking, along with the ever-popular cartoon mats of the hideous Tojo. Feature articles changed alongside war aims, and in mid-1942 one could read of the just treatment of Japanese "evacuees" who were reclaiming 8,000 acres of the Mississippi Delta.

As our armies stormed the hedgerows of France the reader of *Victory* was offered a slick-paper, multicolored affair, but had to shell out $5 for what 75¢ would have bought at the time of Pearl Harbor. Teaching techniques improved over the years, as the relationship between money and war was demonstrated, as reports of domestic economic controls formed captions for a picture of a soldier pumping liquid fire into a cave full of Japs.

MORALITY, WAR, AND THE FOURTH ESTATE

The censorship code for publishers was voluntary.* Undergirding every viable social rule is an ethic which, at a minimum, condones the law. The most efficient laws are unwritten, self-imposed laws. Which was the idea behind voluntary censorship.**

With information from the government centralized in the OWI the job of the newsman was made not more difficult but easier, and the reports by the civilian press were reinforced only when we, the people, thought the ordinary media would not give "adequate cover-

*There was an office of Censorship during World War II, but its concern was not the control of domestic news.

**Those newsmen who disagreed with FDR's war policies were solemnly condemned as examples of "the copperhead press" by Mr. Davis.

age."[44] In any case, as Davis stressed in his final report to the President, his job was not to serve the press itself but to help the press better serve the people.[45] The circularity went unnoticed at the time.

The war's symmetry required a symmetry of controls, only one of which concerned civilian attitudes. Our common effort required a division of labor appropriate to the task. There were soldiers, and reporters, and there was no need of stirring up trouble by letting the two get together and air their gripes.

A month after Pearl Harbor a hastily written document was thrust into the hands of field commanders the better to control undesirable gripes. By today's standards the document[46] is remarkable. It must be judged by what it demanded rather than by what was permitted, more by the society which urged its enactment than by the few who escaped its force.* By this set of military rules the following statements would be grounds for censorship: those false in fact or by implication; those injurious to the morale of our forces, the citizens back home, or to our allies; remarks which proved embarrassing to the United States, to our allies, even to neutral nations; even exaggeration of activities only contemplated was flatly prohibited. Finally, newsmen would not quote officers, not even anonymously, without specific authorization of the theatre commander.**

There is in this field manual a keen appreciation for war's universal nature in the modern age, and for the handicaps a democracy operates under when it goes off to war. The solution, as offered by this document and by the controls at work inside the continental United States, was to jettison parts of democracy "for the duration."

In the spring of 1971 about 20 Vietnamese maneuver battalions crossed into Laos. United States artillery and tactical air power were in support. A quarter of the Vietnamese troops took a mauling at the hands of an alerted North Vietnamese force.

In an effort to put this phase of countering a Communist revolutionary war into its proper setting for the viewing audience at home, TV reporters solicited the opinions of some of the American GIs who operated the fire support bases. In the main, the soldiers reckoned that with the mosquitoes and all, the Laos push was bad strategy. And probably immoral.

*One of the most famous of those who did not escape was AP's Ed Kennedy, who defied a rule and filed a story prematurely of Germany's surrender after hearing it on German radio. He was suspended as a correspondent and discredited. (After the war full rights were restored to him).[47]
**The document makes no mention of interviewing enlisted men, for reasons never made clear.

Nineteen forty-three was a marvelous year, and radio stations were asked not to play "Deep in the Heart of Texas" lest they unintentionally let fly a secret code word. Our "Man in the Street" program was taken off the air for good. Through the misuse of nitrogen we corrupted our soil while going in search of the perfect victory carrot, as the aged painfully, carefully dragged scrap metal to the collection station never knowing it was destined to be thrown into the sea as economically irretrievable. Those of us in grade school were permitted time out from study to hoist the School-at-War flag, then plaster Victory stamps over the face of the hideous Tojo. Kate Smith got $30 million pledged for war bonds in one night.

We left World War II convinced that war has a beginning, a middle, and end; that we have been splendidly endowed by the Creator with a moral sense which calculates the moral qualities of a war as easily as a child counts the spots on a cow. The algebraic sum of the good and the bad in World War II was in the plus column ; therefore, the war demanded—and got—our total support.

Our propaganda efforts directed against ourselves during those years can be understood as variations on three principles: involve everyone as completely as possible; deprive each until he is uneasy but not irritated; win the war.

Most of all, win the war.

II

ANTIMATTER

We must be content, then, in speaking of such subjects and with such premises to indicate the truth roughly and in outline, and in speaking about things which are only for the most part true and with premisses of the same kind to reach conclusions that are no better.
—Aristotle 1094[b]

EPILOGUE

It resembled a globe of the earth fashioned from delicate ceramic, perched atop a tripod. The three supporting legs were interdependent, and a sharp movement in one was immediately recorded in the other two. On such occasions the globe trembled.

The policy of containment can be likened to the ceramic piece. It was viable only so long as its supporting structure was intact, only so long as the three legs of the tripod remained in balance.

The supports amounted to: an idea, reasonably consistent and found acceptable by our leaders; a defense establishment to implement the idea forcefully should that become necessary; and an at least passive, at best applauding, Congress and public.

There was one other supporting, unifying, feature, as basic as the concept, popular acceptance, and an armed force: the ability of the United States to wage limited war.

Containment lasted for a quarter of a century.

THE DOCTRINE OF FLUX

Containment was neither doctrine nor policy. Less still was it an ideology.* It was an attitude inconsistently shared by specific individuals who, for specific reasons, had been entrusted with the fate of the nation. Its ending can be dated with more precision than can its origin.

The attitude was in being, to one degree or another, at least as early as September 1945. President Truman suggests that a chilling and hardening of our relations with the Soviet Union dates from that time, when the Council of Foreign Ministers was meeting in London. Molotov was enthusiastic in his demands that French and Chinese participation be minimal. We were just as adamant.[1]

A year and a half later the President received the first draft of the address he wished to deliver to the Congress, an address in which his doctrine for the defense of at least Greece and Turkey, at most all who deserved freedom, would be set forth. The draft sounded like "an investment prospectus," and the papers were returned to Acheson asking "for more emphasis on a declaration of general policy."[2] Still another rewriting, the term "must" replacing "should," and America was on her way to points uncharted, pushed by forces unknown.**

The official date of the opening of pre-threshold hostilities of March 4, 1946, is clearly arbitrary. Winston Churchill's Iron Curtain speech given that day at tiny Westminster College in Missouri can hardly represent Day One. The question of whether the attitude the speech represented was action or reaction would one day split the nation's intellectuals into bitter foes.[4]

Such an attitude gave damaging comfort to a people habituated during the World War to viewing the world as the battleground of cosmic forces.

President Truman wanted his policies fashioned by intellect not feelings. It was with this in mind that within a few days of Churchill's speech he approved the establishment of a Policy Planning Staff in the State Department. Two months prior our knowing Charge d'Affairs in Moscow had sent to his superiors a gargantuan 8,000-word telegram—a political tract in reality—which predicted a Soviet program of unremitting subversion and political warfare. A second theme of the telegram, one whose importance was ap-

*For a discussion of ideology, see Chapter 7.
**Mr. Truman tells us that coordination of the planning which undergirded the Truman Doctrine was done by then-Under Secretary of State, Dean Acheson.[3]

preciated fully only by its author, was the potentially fatal effects of misplaced moralisms and threats of annihilation.[5]

George F. Kennan, author of the long telegram, accepted the position as head of the new Policy Planning Staff.

His superior would be the most accomplished staff officer our Army ever produced, George C. Marshall. His mission would be to look "beyond the vision of the operating officers caught in the smoke and crisis of current battle," and to see into the next valley, into the next conflict.

At the end of his tenure Kennan would reflect over the past few years and, in assessing gains and losses, pinpoint a flaw in our national character which no amount of policy planning could overcome: "something that I might call the legalistic-moralistic approach to international problems."[6] Thus, even as he and his colleagues limited their ethics to prudence and national self-interest, the country as a whole retained the rhetoric and habit patterns of eschatology.*

So did some of our national leaders.

Official history has it that containment was a slowly evolving but relatively seamless notion, understood and accepted by those at the helm and by those working below deck.[7] If one takes as containment's center of mass President Truman's Doctrine concerning Greece and Turkey and examines the statements of the principals involved, then the first requirement for making containment a viable policy—common acceptance of fundamental principles—is not met.

The story is roundabout, and begins with a meeting between Stalin and Churchill late in 1944. An imperial decision on the control of the Aegean was made that day between the two rulers, according to which the British were ceded 90 percent, the Soviets 10.

Stalin reneged precisely while the last German soldiers were withdrawing from Greece. Rather than using tanks and troops to extend his slice of the pie,** the Georgian dictator supported nationalistic and Communist-led partisans. The initial result was civil or revolutionary war.

Great Britain was all but bankrupt at war's end, the Greek government was, in Acheson's words, "a pretty weak reed,"[8] and American

---

*Kennan's fame rests, ironically, upon an article he must wish he had never written. In response to Secretary of the Navy Forrestal's request, Kennan wrote what was shortly thereafter published as "The Sources of Soviet Conduct." His mention of "containment" was not new. The term soon became popular and, as a result, thoroughly misunderstood.

**Currently referred to as "securing her flanks" by left-revisionists.

leaders were not in the retrenching mood of the American public. Isolated centers of thought began whirring.

One such mind, as already mentioned, was that of George F. Kennan. His view of what our posture should be as we moved from the shadows of World War II into the thicket of an era of neither war nor peace was expressed with characteristic precision. Our rule should be the "vigilant application of counterforce at a series or constantly shifting geographical and political points."[9] The emphasis would be upon finesse, diplomacy, economic warfare. Physical violence is jointly recognized as largely unsuitable as a policy measure.

That was one view, the view expressed by the reputed author of containment. There were other minds operating, however.

A very important mind, perhaps the most important of all, belonged to the President. It had engaged itself with the massive question of Soviet-American relations while the ceremonies on the deck of the U.S.S. *Missouri* informed our people officially that war had ended, peace had begun.

Peace and war intertwined, and a Soviet force dispatched during the great anti-fascist coalition days to protect Iran and the Middle East stayed beyond its deadline, and beyond the next, and beyond the next.

Finally the Russian soldiers left Azerbaijan, but only, the President was convinced, because of our display of strength and resolve. Friendly reminders of promises made were worthless. Pressure would have to be applied to counter Soviet pressure, of a type the Soviet leaders understood.[10]

When the Communists reached out to strangle Greece and Turkey, President Truman tells us he "moved to make this policy clear and firm."[11]

In the President's mind, then, there was indeed a policy in being, waiting to be instantiated, before his decision of March 1947. But already there were signs of divergence from the austere and surgical approach recommended by the head of his Policy Planning Staff.*

The question of a mutually understood, mutually accepted concept which critics of the time labeled "containment"** is worth

*It is not even clear that Truman's great confidant, Dean Acheson, always distinguished the desirable from the possible. Yugoslavia was used as a "safe area" by Greek Communists, and the border had to be closed if the insurgency was to come to an end. Only Tito could close it. He was slow deciding. Titoists shot at out planes throughout 1946–47, Acheson was all for an immediate and aggressive use of U.S. air power over Yugoslavia. General Lauris Norstad had to point out the military facts to the future Secretary of State.[12]

**Called by left-revisionists, "the *fatal* theory of containment."

pursuing, for if such cohesion were not present—as appears to be the case—then a partial explanation for some of the nation's difficulties will have been discovered.

During the last days of February 1947, President Truman told his Congress as well as his people of the course he had decided to pursue in the Mediterranean crisis. As he described the situation he waivered, spoke in two tongues, invoked reasons for our acting which are often as not mutually exclusive.

First, using the sleek and colorless words of his advisers from the State Department he told of the vested interest we had in the survival of a friendly Greece and Turkey, of the Dardanelles and their relation to our overall foreign policy.[13] Simply stated, the President advised us that we should aid Greece and Turkey for reasons of self-interest. The response from his listeners was so-so.

As he spoke on the tenor of his words changed, as did his expression, and his sincerity. Reaching back to the rhetoric of his predecessor and of World War II, the President tried his hand at gnosticism: "This was the time," he later recalled, "to align the United States of America clearly on the side, and at the head, of the free world."[14] Americans must go forth boldly, "stamp out the smoldering beginnings of any conflict that may threaten to spread over the world." To fuel the crusade we would employ the greatest resource of this nation: "the spirit and the character of the American people."[15]

Perhaps the use of such language was unavoidable. The ashes of World War II still smoldered, the moral glow on our faces still remained. In any case a fundamental contradiction was implanted, a cautious egoism feeding upon part of our spirit and character, pulling us in a specific direction, while at the same time a different part of our being poured out its energy in the service of an ideology which promised us understanding and realization of eternal moral truths.

The implications of the Truman Doctrine were not lost on the two most powerful Republican Senators of the day. Senator Arthur Vandenberg devoted himself to the measure's passage, seeing it as the most signal development in U.S. foreign relations since the Monroe Doctrine. Unlike the openly selfish doctrine for the protection of the Western Hemisphere (and, therefore, the United States), Mr. Truman's proposal was, as we have seen, patently ambiguous regarding moral goals.

The Michigan Senator seized upon the ambiguity, made only passing reference to US self-interest, then stated his price for support of the bill: the subordination of American to United Nations control.[16] It was the problem of freedom vs. Freedom, defense vs. Defense, war vs. War, the problem generated by revolutionizing war, of making war democratic and messianic.

By open agreement Senator Vandenberg, who had insured bipartisanship during the world conflict just passed, would be the GOP voice in foreign affairs. Senator Robert A. Taft of Ohio would concentrate on domestic issues.

But if time and two wars proved anything about containment, it was the impossibility of forcing an absolute distinction between foreign and domestic affairs.

During the first of the wars fought under the banner of containing communism, Senator Taft surveyed the carnage in Korea, noted our natural desire to make freedom universal, and then observed that the brute force of war will, by its very nature, contradict precisely those democratic principles we are striving to advance.[17]

Two decades and still another war would find these right-wing words appropriated by the parlor revolutionaries of the left.

There are two things about Americans George Kennan dislikes. The first of these, the moralistic-legalistic compulsion, already has been mentioned. The second characteristic which he doesn't think much of proved to be as indelible as the first, though even more damaging.

When the discussions over aiding Greece began, Kennan agreed we should, but only with the understanding that Greece be considered a unique problem requiring a unique solution.[18] He was soon to learn that we Americans respond not nearly so well if the cause is aiding one faction in a civil war as we do if a nation is being threatened by Aggression.

During the hearings which preceded passage of the Truman Doctrine Acheson felt his patience strained as he answered time and again the same question: Would we advocate doing the same thing everywhere under all conceivable circumstances? With the icy impatience for which he was loved, he answered in the negative. Senator Vandenberg seemed satisfied.[19]

Shortly after his meeting with Congress Acheson had to make the same promise against a blank check policy to Kennan.[20]

The head of the Policy Planning Staff gave the highest marks to sophistication, consistency, and clarity of concept. No high grades were to be forthcoming from Kennan.

President Truman had gone over the head of Congress and into the living rooms of America as he mounted the crusade. At the same time he had confused Greece with Turkey (or Turkey with Greece

—the President used first one, then the other, as justification for his program). Worse, he had permitted some of those in the defense establishment to take advantage of the situation, twist it to meet their own schemes, and "to infiltrate a military aid program for Turkey into what was supposed to be primarily a political and economic program for Greece."[21]

The source of the disarray was what the President described as "the greatest resource of this nation . . . the spirit and character of the American people." In Kennan's restrained malice, "the congenital American aversion to regional approaches, and the yearning for universal ones. . . ."[22]

In retrospect, considering the language and imagery employed by our public leaders to stoke the furnaces of the crusade, the yearning for universal answers seems unavoidable.*

There was a final difficulty with the concept. It was minor, didn't cost much and, in any event, was irresolvable. President Truman reminds us: "Thus, even as we undertook to bolster the economy of Greece to help her combat communist agitation, we were faced with her desire to use our aid to further partisan political, rather than national, aims."[23]

PROVIDED AN UNCOMMON DEFENSE

Military doctrine—ideas as how best to maneuver armies in the field and how to make palatable to an ally our advice—has to be based upon available money and men. Especially men. The latter has been the nagging preoccupation of the Army throughout modern times. It leaps to the surface as soon as the shooting stops,[24] subsides only with the onset of the next war. Then, with the shooting going on, men and money cease to be problems. And following the time-honored formula of working the soldiers around the clock, no one in the Army has either the time or strength to give much thought to doctrine.

In what is considered his first public "get tough" speech against the Soviets, President Truman partially gave in to the demobilization hysteria which engulfed our people. Six weeks after the indelible experience of the U.S.S. *Missouri* HST announced he would

*Reference is to the words and images experienced by the population. The Top Secret policy planning paper, NCS-68, completed April 25, 1950, never has been made public. When it is declassified it will be interesting to see the relative weight given to national self-interest, on the one hand, and service to the transcendent, on the other.

flush out the barracks as quickly as possible, but still make us remain the greatest naval power on earth. Some power still had to be retained.

Arms were required, he told us, for two reasons. First of all, there were the defeated Japanese and Germans who had to be forced to live up to the terms of peace.

A distant second reason was cited, one which was lost upon all save the Soviet Union. We must, he said, "fulfill the military obligations which we are undertaking as a member of the United Nations . . ." The latter is required to secure the millennium: "to support a lasting peace, by force if necessary."

As he was speaking 15,200 men were daily shedding away uniform, memory, and expectation. The result was, to use his expression, "disintegration."[25] He reread Kennan's 8,000-word telegram.

It was the President's desire to retain the largest peacetime army in our history. The figure and date selected by him were, respectively, just under two million men and June 1946. That figure was to be cut in half,[26] the date thus rendered meaningless.

The question of numbers was complicated by the problems of reorganization and unification.

In August 1944 the Department of War issued Circular 347, in which Army manpower recommendations for the remainder of the decade were set forth. Disavowing all inclination to emulate the system of elites and caste of Germany and Japan, the option selected would determine American domestic and, therefore, foreign policy for three decades. The recommendations of the 71-year-old adviser to General George Marshall for "organized units drawn from a citizen army reserve" became the basis for future law.[27] The other recommendation, and a cornerstone for the thinking of the day, was accepted neither then nor later. As soon as the guns had silenced, any thought of universal military training was futile.*

Discussions about reorganizing and unifying the services preceded World War II, and continued throughout that conflict. Sensing what he believed to be irreconcilable differences between the Army and the Navy, knowing the two sides had to be reconciled,

*Two months after World War II ended Truman praised UMT, but would himself undermine the proposal later on. Initially arguing for UMT in order to get the draft extended (September 26, 1945), he cooled to the idea when the apparent implications of air power and nuclear weapons were seen. Selective service was extended to March 31, 1947, UMT having been set aside. Truman argued that the military aspects of UMT were minimal, that what he wanted was the improvement of youth. In 1951, after announcing that UMT had again been shelved, the President's cranky Congress passed just such a law—when there was no chance of its being implemented.[28]

Secretary of the Navy Forrestal engaged a successful investment banker and former member of the War Production Board. The result was the Eberstadt Report.[29]

The report's conclusions were equivocal. On the one hand the report very shrewdly emphasized the notion that the central problem of unification was not coordination of the various services but coordination, integration, of military ideas with national policy. To effect the latter Mr. Eberstadt recommended what would two years after war's end come to be known as the National Security Council.

At the same time, the report's author both gave the wartime JCS more praise than it deserved, and also revived Elihu Root's fears concerning the "Prussianizing" effects of overunification.

The result was a sulking, fearful Navy, a loose and plodding JCS.[30]*

The Navy sulked and feared simply because it was responsive to the law of self-preservation. Unification threatened the Navy's existence—as the latter had come to be enjoyed at war's end. The principal source of this fear had less to do with the world's oceans than with the atmosphere above.

By the middle of World War II the air-minded soldiers who had survived the purges of the 1920s and '30s were convinced that strategic air power demanded a separate air arm. Creation of nuclear bombs at war's end had elevated this perception to the level of revealed truth. The way to a separate existence was unification, though it was admitted that with the dwindling defense slice of the budgetary pie such a move had to be at someone's expense, namely, either the Army, or Navy, or both.

Both the latter services were convinced not only of the way strategic thinking would be colored given a separate air arm; they also were sure those civilians who encouraged reexamination of strategy with an eye toward integration could care less about strategy. What really prompted all the encouragement from without, they were convinced, were the twin desires of justifying an already runaway demobilization and the omnipresent need to reduce the budget.[31]

Top soldiers and sailors responded in kind, concentrating more on sheer survival than strategic doctrine.

A different language was being spoken by each contestant: the U.S. Army, whose members saw reorganization and unification, plus the birth of an air force, as largely inevitable; the Navy, whose

*The principal difficulty of the JCS at this time was inability to reach emergency decisions, this in turn flowing from the requirement that their decisions be unanimous. It was not until August 1949 that our military chiefs of staff had a chairman authorized, not until six weeks into the Korean War that the change became effective.

people had let the President know even before the end of the war what they thought of being pushed out of the emerging nuclear strategy by an air force and unified defense structure;[32] those civilians who generated reports calling for streamlining, without having to consider traditions, loyalties, or habits; a President who was fumbling toward a new foreign policy the nature and content of which even he was unaware; and a Congress and public equally anxious to reorder priorities, divert war monies to the building of schools and hospitals, and snipe at the Chief Executive every two years.

"There are no easy black and white solutions for the problems which face this country."[33] The words are those of James V. Forrestal, Secretary of the Navy, later first Secretary of Defense, later still a discouraged and despondent man seeking release from life. As he wrote this line to the industrialist Robert Wood, in October 1948, Forrestal was aware he was leaving the government his goal of a defense organization a healthy balance of integrated arms and ideas nearly as distant as it had been so long ago when he first suggested to his new President that postwar consolidation of services was a necessity.[34]

Consolidation or unification was an issue which probably could have stood or fallen by itself. But after the Secretary had asked Eberstadt to study that issue, an entirely new one was produced, namely, the question of the uses to which this integrated armed force would be put. Eberstadt's principal recommendation, as we have seen, was for the creation of a policy-forming and advisory body of top Government officials.

Congressional hearings were held on an irregular basis for two years, roughly from the end of World War II to Summer 1947. There was considerable cutting and bleeding, as idea merged with idea, desire cancelled out desire. The Army agreed to an independent Air Force, so long as there was genuine coordination. The Air Force, for its part, wanted a monopoly on the world's monopoly of nuclear bombs. The Navy wanted an understanding, preferably in writing, as to its strategic share of the nuclear stockpile. Secretary of State James F. Byrnes wanted a centralized intelligence agency, whereas his Undersecretary, Dean Acheson, wanted intelligence brought back to his department, and thought the idea of transferring intelligence functions out of State gross stupidity.[35]*

---

*At the end of August, 1945, President Truman transferred to the State Department the foreign functions, facilities, and personnel of the Office of War Information. Soon two branches of the Office of Strategic Services were given to State. On January 22, 1946, Mr. Truman issued a directive moving primacy for intelligence to the Executive

And Eberstadt wanted the National Security Council.

Our national search for something like the NSC goes back to World War I. The effort acquired tangible form in 1938 with the Standing Liaison Committee, headed by Secretary of State Cordell Hull. This grew into a more stable but still temporary Coordinating Committee joining representatives from the Departments of State, War, and Navy. Even the latter temporary arrangement took more than two years of war before it could come into shape.[36]

It took two years of peace and four months of the Truman Doctrine for legislation to emerge. The National Security Act of 1947 was signed on July 26 of that year. Two months later the national military establishment was created with James Forrestal as its Secretary. There was something for everyone, not nearly enough for anyone.

The most prominent feature of the act was the production of an Air Force, which immediately went to war with the Navy, and a permanent body of top civilian and military people, who quickly showed they were incapable of producing coherent strategy and, therefore, guidance.[37]

This group, the National Security Council, was made up of Truman, his three service chiefs, Forrestal, Marshall (his Secretary of State), plus an expert on national resources.

So far as the development of containment went, the important consequences of NSA were these. First, of the 56 meetings held between September 26, 1947 (the initial meeting) and June 25, 1950 (the start of the Korean War), President Truman attended only 11. It is clear, and consistent with the man, that the President wanted there to be no doubt as to who ran the country, and of the purely advisory not decision-making functions the council's members would be permitted.[38] Some of those Congressmen who had voted for the defense act did so in the hope the testy Truman could be forced at least to seek out advice from certain people before reaching a decision. The President left no question as to where he stood on this issue,[39] and sought advice where and when he saw fit.**

If Mr. Truman had an excess of power, the same could not be said for Secretary of Defense Forrestal. The services had been federated not unified, lines of authority tangled and fragmented.[40] The Secretary was squeezed from above and below.

The Joint Chiefs of Staff were excluded from the National

Office of the President; hence, the loss to the Department of State.
**His favorite sources of counsel were Marshall, Forrestal, and Acheson.

Security Council, and in their isolation and austerity developed independent notions as how best to defend the country. By independent means all three services arrived at the same conclusion: nuclear airpower was relatively cheap and absolutely decisive, the foot soldier irrelevant. The latter became the principal motivating force for the Army.

Fourth, and finally, the Bureau of the Budget not the National Security Council established the nation's military parameters: military plans neither were presented as the basis for money requests, nor seriously considered when the reductions in force were demanded.[41]

In describing the first months following the mid-1947 attempt to develop simultaneously a coordinated defense establishment and to put together a group of individuals who would articulate strategy at its highest levels, Truman was lavish in his praise. His overworked, overconcerned, already-sick Secretary of Defense was singled out. Forrestal was unceasing in his efforts to suppress grievances of such long standing, the President said. The Secretary's chief problem, we are told, was in specifying missions and roles for each of the services.[42]

The President's rendering of the events of those times does not do complete justice, for it does not specify other personalities who stood between the nation and a viable defense apparatus. In a word, Truman ignored the role he, himself, played in smothering most attempts to fashion a military adequate to the demands of the late 1940s. Nor did he stress his decisive role in forcing Secretary Forrestal's resignation.

The President decided not only to cut the defense budget in the election year of 1948, but not to spend all he had requested. This marked the beginning of the end for Forrestal, and for any idea of a credible force.[43] He made these decisions during a time when military crises were becoming a way of life. At this time, Spring 1948, his Secretary of Defense expressed hope that our military defenses were bottoming out,[44] then recanted.

The "bottoming out" amounted to an Army of 2 1/3 divisions, only one of which was deployable within the foreseeable future, not even one of which, the departing Chief of Staff* despaired, had been given weapons developed late in the last war. General Marshall, for the past year our Secretary of State, noted during a February 1948 meeting of the NSC the basic irrationality of making military

*General of the Army Dwight Eisenhower. The remark was made February 7, 1948. The General went on that day to argue for UMT.

threats in Greece when we had nothing available with which to quash the flames we were fanning.[45] The Czechoslovakia coup two weeks later went uncontested.

The limits of our vacuous threats occurred during the summer and the Berlin crisis of 1948. With our surface access routes denied us there was some talk of shooting our way in. General Lucius Clay, our military governor of Berlin, said "20 good divisions" would stop the Reds. It was pointed out to him, in the manner one points things out to generals, that if we gave it all we had we'd still be short 19 divisions.[46]

The degree to which unification had unified was shown during a goodwill meeting in March of that election year at Key West between Secretary Forrestal and the Joint Chiefs of Staff. After amenities, and after discussing the need for better civil-military coordination, and how a "function paper" which set forth specific missions was to be interpreted, the four-day meeting broke up with the usual smiles for the photographers.

Within a week the Navy and Air Force were back to haggling over their respective share of the nuclear button, the minimum strength for each of the services levitated, and the President accepted his Defense Secretary's function paper as an improvement over the past.[47]

A month after the Iron Curtain had descended on Czechoslovakia, President Truman was pleading with his Congress to once again extend the draft.* Volunteers were hard to come by, reenlistments in a do-nothing, impoverished Army scarcer still. Public passions having been temporarily aroused by the then-current Czech crisis, (the official alarm still was not based upon a broad strategic plan) the 2 1/3 divisions would over the next two years skyrocket into an Army of ten divisions whose regiments had two rather than three battalions, buttressed by a 45-day supply of obsolete ammunition.[48]

After the election, Secretary Forrestal asked that the defense structure be gone over. His request was granted.** He asked that his views concerning the weight of the defense budget carry over those of the President's budget chief. His request refused, Forrestal left his post to his successor Louis Johnson.

*On March 31, 1947, the Selective Service Act of 1940 expired. It was reinstated for a one-year period three months later.
**Forrestal's recommendations became law August 10, 1949 (Reorganization Plan No. 4) after he had left the government. The Department of Defense thus came into being, the Army, Navy and Air Force became military departments, and a chairman of the Joint Chiefs of Staff was authorized.

NATO was approved by the Senate the fourth week of September 1949. Johnson enforced his President's economic directives with a special vengeance, directives flowing, when the last fiscal budget before Korea went up in flames was being massaged, from a unified concept.[49] It was the first such guiding concept, and was straightforward: If the Red bastards cross that line, Nuke 'em.

REPRESENTATIVES. . . .

"The fundamental issue is whether the President shall decide when the United States shall go to war or whether the people of the United States themselves shall make that decision." [50] The words were not spoken by a Democratic presidential hopeful while our Army, tail between its legs, crept from the Indochinese peninsula. They were instead voiced by a Republican whose party would never give him the Presidential nod, while the U.S. Eighth Army was fighting for its very life, on the Korean peninsula.

Senator Taft's bitterest rival, describing, as was the Senator, not a specific war but states and governments and survival, responded by admitting the niceties of checks and balances. Coming directly to the point the patrician Acheson made it plain that the real issue is survival, which means continuity of policy, which in turn means "over a period of years the maintenance of distasteful measures."[51]

The third and final leg of containment—congressional and popular support—waved and buckled from the outset. Like revolutionary war, the attitude of containment had minimum and maximum domestic objectives. At best, there is enthusiastic, directed support by Congress and by the people for what the Executive branch is doing. At a minimum, the fish and sea analogy demands noninterference and compliance on demand.

It was the first leg to collapse, after two wars, four Presidents, and twenty-five years.

Between the fall of Germany and the incineration of Japan, Truman sent his Congress a message requesting a de facto extension of FDR's first War Powers Act. Knowing the end of the war was at hand the legislators balked. During the first week in September of the final year of war he again approached the Congress, though this time his argument rested on his desire to insure a smooth war-to-peace transition. The mention of domestic controls revived congressional memories of some of the excesses of Roosevelt, excesses winked at by those who shared his vision, pointed to by opponents as evidence that the lure of a new social order was more precious than freedom.

The balking continued, despite Truman's straightfaced assurance he was not seeking more government controls.[52]

Inflation did for HST what his pleading could not, and one week before Christmas 1945 the second War Powers Act was passed. The accretion of discretionary power to the Executive accelerated into the third decade, though no longer fueled by the passions either of a democracy at war, nor of a democracy threatened with starvation.

Bipartisanship in foreign affairs can be viewed either as means or ends by those outside of government who theorize about such matters. To those who are enmeshed in the workings of the machinery, such as Dean Acheson, a less abstract, more accurate description of a truce between factions of government during time of war is possible. Nonpartisanship, with its tacit assumption that those who supported FDR would be protected by the umbrella of executive immunity, was "the holy water sprinkled on a political necessity."[54] So far as most conservative legislators were concerned, whatever necessity there had been came to a halt with the close of the war. And so far as Acheson, Kennan, and Truman were concerned, the kaleidoscopic world into which we passed following World War II demanded more presidential latitude than ever before. This was so precisely because there was no overall plan, no strategy, no doctrine. Nor would there ever be.

What would emerge between 1945 and 1950 was a series of uncoordinated acts motivated by men of divergent interests.

Divergence of an even more basic nature began with the GOP sweep of the 1946 elections, the first such cause for rejoicing in 16 years. With the flow of congressional power came, it was believed by many Republicans, the moral obligation to present opposition to Truman and his attaché case diplomacy. Senator Vandenberg was chairman of the Senate Foreign Relations Committee, GOP spokesman in Congress in the realm of foreign affairs, and Senate president. He was also the source of Acheson's "holy water," and with war's end and the Republican victory a year later he came under increasing pressure from his party members to follow the people's mandate and oppose Truman.[55]

The Senator agonized and concluded there was no solution. In today's world, he reasoned, bipartisanship is indispensable (a point for Acheson). At the same time, if the two-party system is to survive such an understanding is never possible on a permanent basis (a point for Taft). He never resolved the dilemma. Instead he tried to muddle through as his conscience dictated, the result being that his own party charged him with practicing an obsequious "me too-ism."[56]

As he saw it, the Senator and others in positions of authority confronted not a theory but a condition to which we had to respond. The most famous case in point was, again, the President's decision to aid Greece and Turkey.

On January 6, 1947, Truman called a bipartisan congressional group together. Even as sympathetic a man as Senator Vandenberg was rankled that the President allowed so little opportunity to look the matter over.[57] That was not likely to cement bipartisan bonds. The President's decision to go over Congress' head, and his total failure to consult "Mr. Republican," Robert Taft, prior to the Truman Doctrine speech was in time sure to tear such bonds to shreds.

On the day following the speech announcing the President's intentions regarding Greece and Turkey, Senator Vandenberg pleaded for a total policy, one which will both "primarily consult American welfare," but also one which will "keep faith with the pledges to the charter of the United Nations. . . ."[58]

That contradictory remark, combining egoism and altruism, ran headlong into the Kennan-Acheson school of thought. More important, it collided with the inclinations of Harry Truman.

As for the duo here referred to, it is clear they considered congressional intrusion into foreign relations at best benign and amateurish attempts to be helpful. At worst, that is, when partisans chose to be partisans, the Congress represented thickheaded interference with professionals.*

For example, Senator Vandenberg had indeed supported aid to Greece and Turkey, but only after amending the bill to circuituously bring the Truman Doctrine under the UN. The President's speech had intentionally been made before consulting the world union, for which Acheson took full credit. The Soviets would have vetoed the proposal. Besides, appeal to the UN was to dabbling in the futile. And Senator Vandenberg's muddle-headed amendment was justly labeled as silly or cynical, not only in Moscow but in Paris and London as well.[59] This was Congress at its best and at its worst, simultaneously.

The workable ideal for those days during which policy was being pieced together was stated succinctly by Kennan. It is better, he later mused, to increase congressional restrictions on the Executive branch if need be, so long as such a program "left somebody free to use his head when it needed to be used."[60] This would be Congress at its best.

At its worst, Congress is uneducated opinion bowing to public

---

*Acheson likened American foreign policy to a sick patient, the Congress to ignorant relatives, himself to the physician.

pressures. Whereas Acheson and the rest of the executive people bring initiative, proposals for action, and other good things, legislators can do no better than criticize, limit, veto. As a result, this model of diplomacy by finesse "learned to bear the irrelevant with more than patience as it ate up precious time,"[61] as he laboriously educated the Senate in fundamentals.*

In the end, that is, after the eruption in Korea, the Vandenberg thesis went unsupported, the spheres-of-influence agreement with Senator Taft tossed aside, partisanship and strict construction again the order of the day.[62] The other cells were in revolt.**

... AND THE REPRESENTED

One of the major differences between then and now is that then —during and immediately after World War II—any analysis of the strategic interests of the great powers was totally lacking in the public statements of our statesmen. Public discussions by the people in 1945 centered more on a new product—frozen orange juice—than on wartime coalitions and their history. We faced the new day less with historical reference than with hope.

The President recognized this as a problem, that Americans are brought up believing peace and harmony are theirs by inalienable right, requiring no effort. Conflict of interests was believed to end with the last shot.[64] There is either peace or war, never both.

While he was speaking of the vast undertaking and eternal vigilance peacekeeping required, the President himself unintentionally forced his people to look inward when, on September 6, 1945, his 21-point Fair Deal package was sent up to Congress. Its 16,000 words had the effect of drawing the opaque curtain of self-concern between the voter and the world beyond.

One day after the President's social legislation request went to the Congress an aide to then-Secretary of the Navy Forrestal reported to his boss on the results of a trip just concluded. The traveler said his

*Acheson enjoyed analogies, besides the physician-patient-relatives comparison, he also likened himself and his kind to "thinking cells," the other branches of government simply "the other cells." His humility endeared him to the conservative opposition.

**Another basic issue which insured a rupture in executive-legislative relations was secrecy. Possession of atomic energy and Truman's creation of a Civil Service loyalty board were major sources of Congressional distrust. Senator Homer Ferguson, who made opposition to Truman a living faith, claimed classifying of documents was inspired principally to mask incompetence and dishonesty. The feeling that President Truman and his career foreign officers and appointees were an exclusive clique was widespread throughout this era.[63]

investigation showed the country would be violently opposed to the continuation of conscription, unalterably opposed to Universal Military Training.

Forrestal and Secretary of War Henry L. Stimson simply refused to believe such was possible.[65]

Nineteen forty-six was the year of attempts at social advance and retention of a Democratic Congress. Inspired by both goals the Employment Act (originally called the Full Employment Act, being more in line with Truman's promises) was passed, with conservative condemnation and laissez-faire amendments, on February 20. The Democrats' bid for a continuing majority in the two houses now raced with the inevitable pull of voter's personal needs.

During the year a meandering inflation and a chronic shortages of meat were of far greater concern to the citizen then diplomatic notes to the Russians about some tardy troops in the north of Iran.* The effects of the meat shortages would soon disappear. Those of the letter Secretary of State Brynes drafted to the Soviets would persist through three decades.

Truman's honeymoon with the New Deal** and labor ended, despite his explicit promise to carry forth and enlarge upon FDR's social programs, despite the advance assurance he gave that he would veto anti-labor legislation.*** Despite all his efforts the President lost steady ground in opinion polls as the fall election approached, as did his party at the polling booths in November. As much a result of domestic politics as an insistence from the people that we not simply turn but rivet our eyes inward, therefore, an explanation of Azerbaijan to the people (assuming, which is doubtful, that there was agreement at the top of just what it meant) would have been forced to compete with real, not abstract, near-at-hand, not distant, issues. Consequently, the attempt never was made to inform the electorate of the first urgings of containment.

Even more out of the question was an explanation of China, and the rise of a second hostile power.[67] In later years Truman and those

---

*Soviet troops occupied the Iranian province of Azerbaijan in 1942. The American fear was that an autonomous entity subject to Soviet control would be created. On March 24, 1946, apparently in response to a note the President described as "blunt," Stalin announced the immediate withdrawal of all Russian troops.[66]

**Following a speech in Madison Square Garden in September 1946 by Henry A. Wallace, President Truman reassessed the Secretary's mental soundness, disliked what he found, and ten days later fired the last New Dealer.

***The President vetoed anti-labor legislation in 1946, while he still had a Democratic Congress that could resist a veto. He vetoed the Taft-Hartley bill the next June. Senator Taft went on the radio, then back to the Senate floor where he engineered an immediate and successful veto.

surrounding him, people who made a career of anti-communism, would be chided about their soft ways. Frozen orange juice and Taft-Hartley were more important at the time and, in any case, the times when it is said we should have been hard were precisely those times during which one could poke a hole through our defenses. As for our offense, Truman reminds us of the total impossibility of imposing our will on China and/or Russia. For one thing, we didn't have the soldiers do anything more provocative than engage in rifle drills. And for another, during the only feasible time when force might have played a useful role in China—1945–46—the people were unalterably opposed to any military venture,[70] and certainly opposed to any campaign whose necessity had not been explained to them.*

Containment never was explained to the American public for two reasons. First, there was no rational system, no plan, no strategy to be explained. Still less was there agreement between the principals of the time. What one finds are unabashed nationalists: Truman, Acheson, Kennan, Marshall, Forrestal; men who shared, at best, a subconscious hunch about the world, and about the friends and enemies who inhabited it.

Secondly, assuming one man had been elected sole spokesman for this group, the bloodless, detached, amoral language he would have used (had he not been playing to the gallery and simply stating his case—as a corporate attorney might present his argument in favor of an unknown client), then the people would have thrown him aside. The principal reason for this was that the people constituted the gallery, and the people were in the habit of being played to.

The play is the thing, and war is a moral drama. Of this much we were certain. This fact was the bane of our policymakers. And it still is.

About their fellow citizens Kennan and Acheson are without equivocation. It is obvious, the first tells us, that we dislike to discriminate, that we like to attribute universal significance to decisions made for limited and selfish reasons: World War II, Pearl Harbor, the Atlantic Charter. Worse, as we sat in the gallery and heard ourselves pictured as both arbiter and dispenser of eternal justice, the words filtered down and became permanent features of

*Explanation can be counterproductive. During the Greek crisis of Spring 1947 the new Secretary of State called for national calm during one of his press conferences. General Marshall explained soberly how the State Department was handling matters. The result was a general war scare.

our national character. The result is emotionalism and long-obsolete habits of thought. And to our discredit a thoroughly professional foreign officer corps, insulated from the irrationality of public opinion, is probably a chimera.[69]

Dean Acheson was just as explicit. He spoke repeatedly of the "pragmatic rewards of probity" and a "cool and detached appraisal of national interest." As to pressure from public attitudes, the regal Secretary responded with the conditional, "if the public knew and cared enough to have an attitude. . . ."[70]

After a quarter century of laboring for his government, Kennan returned to civilian life. In that summer of 1950, as skeletonized battalions were being thrown onto the Korean chopping block, he paused to write of the unprecedented confusion in the public mind concerning our foreign policy. Truman didn't understand it, neither the Congress, nor the people, nor the press. Instead, they had all joined hands and entered into a "labyrinth of ignorance and error and conjecture . . . in which there is no recognized and authoritative theory to hold on to."[71] Nevertheless, we went ahead and fought the war.

THE ARMS OF KENNAN

For lurking beneath the crisp diplomatic exchanges and witticisms and disdain for the unknowing, uncaring public, there was both the threat and the promise of war. It was the substructure upon which the tottering legs of containment were mounted that gave strength and credibility to containment. It was an alien, unnatural kind of war, carefully hidden from public view. In retrospect it was, to paraphrase Dean Acheson, a pretty weak reed.

In April 1946, George Kennan was assigned as first deputy for foreign affairs at the War College. His mission was to teach senior government and military people the inseparability of statecraft and war. His fundamental premise was the implacable hostility of the Soviet Union, this flowing from an automoton psychology peculiar to ideologized Russians. The second premise broke into a pair of reciprocal facts: our atomic monopoly and technological superiority, and the insanity of unleashing our power. His preface to the course of instruction was straightforward: "If our policies are wise and nonprovocative," then we and our allies ought to be able "to contain them both militarily and politically for a long time to come."[72]

Coupling premise and preface, the problem was defined: How can a tyrannical, evangelistic opponent be checked without inviting the annihilation of the United States?*

Before the problem could be refined, and an answer formulated, more hard thinking on the interrelatedness of war and politics was needed, more information, more concepts. As he cast about for something viable in the way of ideas, he discovered there was nothing in print less than a hundred years of age which even addressed itself to Clausewitz's dictum. One major reason for this void was nothing other than the unending string of American military successes. This experience had produced in military and civilian minds an unspoken assumption, namely, "that the normal objective of warfare was the total destruction of the enemy's ability to resist and his unconditional capitulation."[73] In its turn this state of mind obliterated any distinction between force and objective, permitting us to seek open-ended political goals. In a word, history had treated us kindly and, in so doing, had punished us, damaging our ability to compete in a world of mottled gray.

In order to find a workable idea Kennan and his students split their forces, diverting one to Greece with its current civil war, sending the other back through time and onto the continent of Europe. Gaining the results they wanted, they regrouped to compare notes and ideas.

Those who had studied the agony of Greece, as it was slowly being devoured by communists, loyalists and, in no small measure, by major powers, concluded this war had the shape of things to come. An American response probably was required, though nuclear bombs raining on the heads of a political underground as the latter moved among the populace didn't seem appropriate. Indeed, if money, advice or political pushing and shoving would secure our limited goals there, the use of force was to be avoided.

The fact that our goals and, conversely, our interests in the post-war world are largely limited, dovetailed with the findings of the other expeditionary force, that which leaped backward in time, to the eighteenth century.

What they found in pre-Napoleonic Europe was warfare practiced on a carefully modulated scale. America had rediscovered limited war, the importance of which was not hidden by Kennan: "If weapons were to be used at all, they would have to be employed to temper the ambitions of an adversary, or to make good limited objectives against his will—." Then came the punch line: "not to destroy his power, or his government, or to disarm him entirely."[74]

The memoirs covering his career between the years 1925 and 1950

*By this time (mid-1946) it was not a question of if but when the Soviets would possess atomic weapons.

were published in 1967. In the same year General Ridgway's recollections of the Korean War were likewise set into type. With his nation again neck-deep in an Asian war the general wondered aloud whether Americans even at this late date really understood what limited war is.[75]

As phrased by the general, the question is misleading. By 1967 many millions of Americans still could recall Korea, and the 36,000 Americans killed, wounded or captured during the two years of mindless, futile truce talks. The understanding was present, even if at a subliminal level. What was and probably will remain absent was a spiritual acceptance of the austere, aristocratic, and necessarily amoral nature of limited war.

What Americans of 1947 and 1967 understand *and* accept is the portrayal of war as moral drama, the preface to which was read aloud by Douglas MacArthur as he appeared before Congress, even as General Ridgway cautiously worked his way to the next phase line in Korea: "But once war is forced upon us, there is no other alternative than to apply every available means to bring it to a swift end. War's very object is victory—not prolonged indecision."

Those most deeply involved with crafting state policy sensed the likely response from the American public were the issue of limited ends and limited force ever aired in public. For in order to translate this language of the engineer into that which people can grasp would have meant the explicit admission that we would, under certain conditions—conditions which could not be announced in advance, since they were not known in advance even at the highest levels of government—send an unspecifiable number of American soldiers into combat for an unknown length of time, in pursuit of political goals we might possibly be able to survive without.

"To many this seems an unfamiliar and wrong idea," Acheson ventured. Amen! comes the response of the American electorate.

"It did not seem so to the Europeans of the latter half of the seventeenth and the eighteenth century"[76] is his imperious answer. Right on.

The second grave defect in containment's presupposing limited war centers not so much on our addiction to waging wars of opinion as on the Congress' intransigence when it comes to relinquishing all control over the waging of war.* Just before and immediately fol-

---

*A third problem was the creation of a small, mobile force of soldiers to enforce Kennan's open-ended policy. It never came into being. Instead, money and opinion resulted in "a counteroffensive force built around a fleet of bombers, accompanying planes, and long-range missiles."[77]

lowing the Korean affair the resistance to "executive privilege" was led by those Republicans with rib of rock. NATO and UN membership, they feared, might automatically commit us to war.

In the grief and bitterness of the Vietnam War it is precisely those who roost on the opposite end of the political spectrum who insist upon severing alliances, pulling in our heads, eschewing power and its correlative arrogance.

Many of these leaders were around during those pivotal years, basking in the heat from the great war drama of '41–'45, insisting the President be given an ever-freer hand for his social schemes and international visions, reminding their constituents each election year of our mandate to resist Aggression, and all the time pushing our soldiers ever deeper into the sloth of garrison life.

It therefore became necessary for us to fight the one war we were totally unprepared to fight, armed for the most part with contradictions.

PROMISES, PROMISES

We obviously dislike to discriminate.

—George F. Kennan

Why, my soldiers asked of me, surrender military advantage to an enemy in the field? I could not answer . . .

—General Douglas A. MacArthur

MORE ON MYTHS

June 25, 1950 marked the two-month anniversary of NSC Policy Planning Paper Sixty-Eight. President Truman celebrated the event with a quiet dinner in Missouri, Secretary of State Acheson with a sense of well-being as he listened to voices again demanding his resignation, and the Koreans by butchering each other.

Even before the killing was halted there began circulating half-truths, and worse. These would in time become the official literature. Later still this history by consensus would attain the status of secular mythology, at about the time the nation crept into its next Asian war.

These mistaken myths are important, for they bear directly upon our self-conception as a nation. For following the Korean affair we felt considerably less virtuous as a people, and were gaining the conviction that rule by the deliberative sense belonged to an era long past.*

PURSUIT OF PEOPLE'S JUSTICE

The Thirty-eighth Parallel exploded at four o'clock in the morning that June day,** sending south bearers of liberation and of immanent truth. Wearing mustard-colored clothes, men of the People's Army of North Korea swirled across the border, 110,000 strong. A thousand and a half pieces of artillery flung steel shards ahead of the advancing troops, into the flesh of the waiting South Koreans. One hundred and twenty-six tanks added their dimension of terror, as they roared across hill and road and human being.

This attack followed traditional invasion routes,[2] avenues over which suzerain and plunderer had traveled throughout remembered time. Its center was down the Uijongbu-Tongduch'on corridor, with secondary fronts on the Ongjin peninsula and in the Kaesong-Korang-po area. An hour or two later patiently concealed guerrillas sprang from their hiding places, declared the south independent, and killed villagers and farmers who fled in panic. Then the guerrillas linked up with regular NKPA units from the north, attacking down the east coast with a vengeance of the righteous. Primitive assault boats put some additional northern soldiers onto the coast. They, too, would begin the race south, liberating and killing.

Facing the torrent from the north was a South Korean force numbering, on the books, 100,000. Fully a third were on leave when the storm broke. Those remaining made up little more than a constabulary force, without effective artillery, air, or even a weapon that would penetrate the steel of the terrifying Russian tanks. This was at best an underequipped police force: no match for the trained and politicized opponent they now faced.*** And so the retreating began. And continued.

---

*The Korean War is a depressing example of confused justifications for war-making. That the grounds were not defensive can be seen from General Ridgway's statement to his Eighth Army, January 21, 1951: "What are we fighting for? The real issues are whether the power of Western Civilization, as God has permitted it to flower in our own beloved land, shall defy and defeat Communism ... the issue is ... whether Communism or individual freedom shall prevail."[1]

**The attack was launched at three o'clock Saturday afternoon, Washington time. Whether Korean or Washington time is being used will be clear by the context.

***South Korea's pathetic state of readiness is in part understandable. The North Korean government had a clandestine guerrilla net in operation south of the Thirty-eighth Parallel, and the Rhee administration was having little success in destroying it. Acheson thought Pyongyang would rely on this tactic of "spontaneous insurgency"

Most of our five hundred advisers who were serving out their time in Korea were spending their usual weekend in Seoul when the attack began. The thankless job of trying to train a nation of farmers and peasants for mechanized warfare, without funds or equipment or personnel, had taken its toll. Only the ready availability of inexpensive liquor and leisure made the stay bearable. They were an irrelevant force in an irrelevant country.

Then the flood hit. Frantic shouts for trousers and boots, a hasty clearing of cobwebs and a wish the weapon had been zeroed. Out to the vehicles, or at least to the road where a ride could be thumbed, then back to the unit that was being "advised."

Had the pilots of the Russian-built Yak aircraft been able to see the faces of those they were trying to kill, men sitting behind the guns at Suwon airfield, they probably would have been surprised to find that the anti-aircraft gunners were Americans, doing their level best to kill the attacking pilots first. In so doing they were following neither UN mandate nor Presidential proclamation, but only the most basic law of all. This spontaneous, improvised and directionless behavior would be the leitmotif for the next few weeks.

INTERJECTION

Nothing interprets itself, but the Korean War aids the interpreter by dividing itself into distinct, orderly segments. These divisions are five in number, each of which possesses two aspects, i.e., a decision-making and a battlefield side.

The five segments consist of the following. (1) Late June to mid-September 1950 typified by the NKPA attack and advance, and the ROK-U.S. forces fighting delaying actions while withdrawing into the Pusan perimeter. (2) Mid-September to late October 1950, MacArthur's brilliant counterstroke at Inchon, breakout from the Pusan perimenter by the allied forces, and the crossing of the Thirty-eighth Parallel. (3) Late October 1950 to mid-January 1951, intervention of Chinese Communists and the forced retreat of allied soldiers to a position considerably south of the Thirty-eighth Parallel. (4) Mid-January 1951 to late June 1951, the second allied coun-

rather than make a frontal assault. Consequently, our lackadaisical attitude toward arming and training the South Koreans.

When writing of his own insurgency experiences on Cyprus years later, General Grivas correctly noted the mistake the North Koreans made in using conventional force, for the United States would have had great difficulty in going to war to save such a repressive regime as that of Syngman Rhee in what clearly was a civil insurrection. Witness Vietnam.

teroffensive and second recapture of Seoul. (5) Late June 1951 to July 27, 1953, a period of negotiations and limited combat action.*

It is with respect to these natural lines of demarcation that the war in Korea should be examined. To that we now turn, looking first at the war front, then at the decisions.

BELOW THE PARALLEL

The front had been blazing and altering its course by pressing south and overwhelming everything and everybody in its path for the hour and a half which separated the initial assault, and President Rhee's awareness of the attack. By 6:30 A.M. Sunday hundreds of his soldiers lay broken and dying as the Korean president received the word.[3] Many times that number had either fled in horror upon confronting the Russian tanks, or had simply failed to go near the front. In isolated spots South Koreans had charged the tanks, arms bulging with smoking sticks of dynamite. Usually they were shot down before they got close enough to jump under the tracks. Sometimes they were successful.

At 8 A.M. Muccio, U.S. Ambassador to Korea, heard the news. Conferences and a demand for accurate information followed. The former could be arranged, and were, but the latter was nearly impossible because of the absence of communication. By half-past nine Ambassador Muccio was satisfied that this was not a repeat of guerrilla harassment or sporadic shellings, and he issued a cable to his government.

Twenty minutes later a correspondent for United Press sent a cable of his own, to his superiors in New York. The press dispatch moved faster than the official communique, and was received a half hour before the ambassador's cable.[4]

By noon of the first day the untrained and virtually defenseless ROK soldiers were quickly decomposing as a fighting force. Leaderless, they fled.

Some members of the US military mission found themselves in ground combat, contrary to all expectations, contrary to promises made by recruiting sergeants.

Almost immediately after getting the news in Tokyo, John Foster Dulles held a quick meeting with General MacArthur, then cabled Washington. Dulles maintained from the outset that United States forces ought to be committed. After that the United Nations would

*It could be argued that the fifth and final phase began with President Truman's press conference of April 11, 1951. But that was simply a signal to the other side that we would be content with pursuing strictly limited goals. In June our opponents made a proposal, which amounted to an acceptance of the President's April offer.

be asked to join in if that body was so inclined.[5] The message was received by the American government 10:30 Sunday morning, U.S. time, thirteen hours after the initial cable from Ambassador Muccio.

As the front disintegrated, an AP dispatch from Seoul on June 25 told us, "Drive seen curbed." It wasn't, and wouldn't be.

Faced with collapse of the ROK army, our senior military personnel turned over in their minds the sort of aid that might be required —or possible. Naval and Air Force leaders thought their aid might be enough, were it so ordered. It was, and early on June 28 Air Force sorties began. Their primary targets: the Soviet tanks. Air warfare looked good, and just might be sufficient.

But the man on the ground had a different perspective, and General MacArthur's personal surveyor, Major General Church, told MacArthur that nothing short of U.S. ground troops could be expected to stop the North Korean blitz.[6] This was on the third day of the war, noon of June 28, 1950, Korean time.

An hour later elements of the Royal Navy were sent to Korean waters by the British government, just about the time NKPA troops entered the shattered city of Seoul, proclaimed Communist liberation, and began the ritualistic slaughter of those selected as "enemies of the people."

On the fourth day General MacArthur decided on ground reconnaissance in person. He left Japan and his office in favor of a hilltop south of Seoul, from which he could view, analyze, and speculate.

By three o'clock that afternoon, after looking at the lines of straggling ROK soldiers a last time, he concluded without fanfare that if Korea were to be saved, American infantrymen would indeed have to put their lives on the line. He asked his government for immediate commitment of one regimental combat team. This would, hopefully, buy time enough to go on the offensive. For the latter he would need two divisions, so he asked that they be outfitted and trained in Japan right away.[7] Events were to prove him optimistic.

It was a full week before US forces were officially engaged in ground combat. This American presence was a battalion "task force," an imposing title for so tiny a unit. But Lieutenant Colonel Charles Smith, after whom the task force was named, plunged into battle north of Osan on July 5 with the sure knowledge that the United States was now in it for real, and that in the end the enemy would be punished and victory proclaimed.[8]

With this in mind he deployed his 500 men against an army of 50,000.

The men under Colonel Smith fought better than they were capable, as thirty tanks ground our infantry to pieces. Cursing the worthless rocket launchers, the men of Task Force Smith withdrew under pressure dragging their wounded, and rejoined the rest of their Twenty-fourth Infantry Division which had just arrived from Japan. Near the city of Taejon the first war stories were swapped, as the eighteen-year olds in outposts just south of the River Kum praised themselves.

Three days after initial contact between American and North Korean forces, July 8, 1950, MacArthur made his first call for reinforcements. As he did so, the dream of an early counterthrust receded, like the steadily shrinking American battle lines. And with the promise of more troops on the way, the sky became the limit for U.S. involvement.*

General Walton Walker was given command of the ragtag assortment unfairly dubbed "Eighth United States Army." He established a headquarters in the squalor of Taegu and, at the request of President Rhee, agreed to command all ROK forces in addition to U.S. soldiers.

A major battle, and the first real test of our army of occupation, was shaping up—to the northwest.

The battle was joined in truth at the first big foothold our forces gained. It was essential Taejon be retained. The battle lasted just twelve days, during which time the Seventh Division, destined to be the sole combat division left in Japan, was cannibalized for men and equipment to fill out other units. During those days stockade doors in Japan were flung open, the inmates removed and rebaptized, then sent quickly along the pipeline which opened onto the loading dock at Pusan.

In the end, after twelve days, Taejon fell. The Twenty-fourth Division had been given the task of stopping five enemy divisions, and the rules of arithmetic were unyielding. The division commander, William Dean, attacked an enemy tank with a pistol, and shortly thereafter became the only U.S. general to be captured in battle in Korea.

Pusan is sheltered and watered by the Nam and Naktong rivers,

*The Selective Service Act empowered the President to order reserve components to active duty for not more than twenty-one months. Failure of Air, Navy and limited Army efforts required this act be invoked. The open-ended nature of the commitment forced just that decision. On September 1 two National Guard divisions (the Fortieth from California and the Forty-fifth from Oklahoma) were federalized. Within six months a total of eight divisions, three regimental combat teams, and 714 company-size units were mobilized. Their state of readiness was ghastly, and the two divisions which saw combat—the Fortieth and the Forty-fifth—were held in Japan for a full year before being committed.[9]

whose confluence resembles two outstretched but drooping limbs of a tree. The last natural barriers to Masan and the ultimate goal of the invaders, Pusan, these rivers provided the landscape for a drama that was beginning to resemble the early days of Bataan. Inside this semblance of cover moved the Twenty-fourth Division, where toward the end of July it met the clean faces and uniforms of men freshly arrived from Japan. By drawing the life's blood from the Seventh Division, it had been possible to put together Twenty-fifth and First Cavalry divisions, and hustle them into what soon became the most violent little pocket on earth. Before the final act still more Americans, soldiers from the Second Division who had come all the way from the green splendor of Washington State, and still more from the Fifth Regimental Combat Team, fresh from the lavender breeze of Hawaii, had arrived. Finally, U.S. Marines wearing helmets with green and brown spots arrived. They came with more than camouflage. They came with a pride the Army couldn't match, and their own close ground support air power. Esprit de corps and tactical air combined to provide the needed edge to stave off, then crush the tiring enemy tanks.[10]

On July 29, 1950 the city of Chinju, astride the Nam River, fell to the enemy. Any serious exploitation of this breach in the western defense of Pusan meaning complete destruction of his forced, the commander, General Walton Walker, ordered his men to stand and fight and, if need be, die in place. They all stood, many died, but the enemy's assaults were smashed every time.

By the first day of August all friendly forces were inside the Pusan perimeter which, cramped though it was, now gave our side the advantage of simplified and shortened supply and communication lines. The reverse was the case for the North Koreans, who were showing clear signs of faltering just as the final goal came into their view.

The next six weeks are recorded as "the days along the Naktong." They were days of the fiercest fighting of the war, when hand-to-hand combat often was the rule rather than the exception. Thirteen divisions of howling riflemen and a division of tanks grown senile moved in for the kill.

NKPA troops hurled themselves time and again, but each time there were fewer to regroup for the next assault. Worse, the inflexible Communist tactic of hitting everywhere at once, of continuing to cut away until the unprotected rear was reached, was predictable. The goal was always just beyond reach, their punch always too light.

American lines thinned, too, but they were destined to hold.

Rocket launchers that could penetrate the armor of the Soviet tanks were now readily available. The newer units had brought M–26 tanks along, whose guns also meant death for enemy armor. Finally, the Marine tactical air proved itself not simply as tank killers but as a very sound matter of doctrine. Largely as a result of the success of integrated air-ground operations the Army would, years later, reintroduce its own air arm with the coming of the helicopter.[11]

By the end of August the British Twenty-seventh Brigade was in the pocket, the first such contribution by a UN member state. Deep penetration by the NKPA was now out of the question, as the latter soon became one of beating the overextended communists to death.

As the two forces inside and outside perimeter sought and found equilibrium, General MacArthur conferred in Tokyo with high-ranking civilian and military officials. The general spoke of smiting the enemy at his flank and, in a single move, destroying him. Averell Harriman, and Generals Norstad, Almond, and Ridgway listened, but were not convinced. Rather than pleading, MacArthur treated his audience as students, and instructed on what he considered to be elementary points of grand strategy. He continued the instruction during his nightly telemetric conversation with the Joint Chiefs of Staff. While the world was coming down upon those in the Pusan perimeter, and while serious plans for pulling all our forces entirely off the peninsula were being put into final form, MacArthur, showing total confidence in his own judgment, held firm. He convinced first one, then another, and in the end cast his spell upon all who would listen.[12]

With September rapidly approaching, the general agreed to write out a statement to be read before a meeting of the Veterans of Foreign Wars. In that paper MacArthur argued for a more thorough understanding of oriental psychology, for decisiveness, for aggressiveness. Even at that early time it was suspected in some quarters that there was a connection between his call for expertise and forcefulness on the one hand, and his classically beautiful scheme for destroying the enemy through seaborne invasion on the other.[13]

Halfway through September the soldiers inside the perimeter of Pusan were confident they could not be pushed off the point of land and into the Japan Sea. On the other hand, any attempt to break out of the pocket met with a sheet of steel from a well-dug-in enemy.

Stalemate.

Then rumors began circulating, rumors of ROK guerrillas operating behind enemy lines seventy or eighty miles north of the perimeter on the east coast, and of something similar happening on the other side of the peninsula, where the Kum empties into the Yellow

Sea. There were lots of rumors, most of which were true. These were diversions for MacArthur's day of brilliance. And as the U.S.S. *Missouri* shelled the hills from its spot in the Sea of Japan, around the tip and half way up the other coast at the port city of Inchon, the spectacle was getting underway.

The decision to land troops in a spot that suffers from twenty-seven-foot tides and mud flats, and all the decisions which preceded the judgment to put troops ashore, form a hinge in American history.

BELOW THE POTOMAC

After deliberating the problem and possible courses of action for about an hour and a half, Secretary Acheson placed the first of three telephone calls to Independence, Missouri. It was 11:20 P.M., June 24, 1950. Saturday night.

The problem was that Acheson thought the man who ran the defense establishment, Secretary of Defense Louis Johnson, was still on tour in the Far East. Johnson had returned from his trip, and had this fact been known the course of recent American history might have been a bit different. But because the Secretary of State believed his brother Secretary to be gone, he described the situation as he understood it to the President, then recommended that State assume control of the Korean problem. He added that the President need not return at this time. Mr. Truman agreed, then went to bed.

Ten minutes after the first Acheson-Truman phone conversation, the Secretary-General of the United Nations got the word of the invasion. Considering the acts of the North Koreans almost a personal affront, Trygve Lie wanted a meeting of the Security Council immediately. But a UN fact-finding commission on Korea was still in the field, so the Secretary-General concluded, angrily, that he must await its report.

Two hours into Sunday morning the phone in Independence rang for the second time, as Secretary Acheson updated the President on the flow of events across the Korean peninsula. Communication with the Far East continued to be poor, there was no precise estimate of the situation, and the Secretary of State for the second time argued, successfully, for the President to remain in Missouri.

On the afternoon of Sunday, June 25, 1950, the Security Council met at the express request of the United States, where the American position paper was read. It was a little after 2:00 P.M. The language of the State Department paper was clear and firm, and a bit too harsh for some of the ears present. Our use of such terms as "armed invasion," and "cease aggression" had to give way to "armed attack" and "cease hostilities."* The U.S.-drafted UN resolution was sharply softened, with "order" and "resolution" being thrown out. In their place it was decided in the interest of unanimity the words should say everyone "calls upon" the NKPA to desist. The resolution requested an end to the killing.[14]

Just as the first Security Council meeting was getting underway, Acheson phoned President Truman for the third time. With the gravity of the bloodletting in Korea genuine, with the wholesale collapse of the South Korean forces only a matter of time, Truman decided it was up to him to act, and to return to his base of operations in Washington. Before hanging up he instructed Acheson to assemble the Joint Chiefs of Staff, and to order that body to have its composite recommendations concerning Korea ready for the President's eyes not later than dinner that day. The President then collected his working papers and headed back to Washington.[15]

After landing at Washington's National Airport about a quarter-past seven, Sunday evening, some of his first words were to his Secretary of Defense: we would "Hit them hard." Several hours later that evening he added that we could not let the UN down.

An hour after touchdown the President met with his political and military advisers at Blair House, where the Joint Chiefs of Staff presented their recommendations. One of the initial questions asked by Truman concerned usable troop strength in Japan, and the time required to get them onto the battlefield. The JCS's chairman, General J. Lawton Collins, said we had 23,000 men strung out unevenly between four infantry divisions. General Collins interjected, with General Bradley's concurrence, that some American soldiers definitely would have to be committed.[16]

Other matters brought up concerned the longer and more unpleasant view of things. How about a mobilization of reserves? The U.S. Army at that time had 592,000 men under arms, and at this early hour of the contest they were thought, or at least hoped, to be sufficient. Then someone mentioned, if only briefly, the possible political costs to the President for what he was about to do. By all published accounts the President "snapped." It is possible he was more explicit. In any event, domestic political questions would not be discussed.

As the meeting was concluding, with our commitment already taking definite form, the President thought of how surprised the Russians would be at American action.

*As will be seen, much confusion and misery resulted because of the President's continual interchange of "attack" and "aggression" while addressing his American public.

And George F. Kennan, who would leave his government post in two months, said what was on everyone's minds: if the ROKs proved unequal to the job, our intervention was absolutely required, with no definite end in sight. Failure to do so would be highly destructive of our power and prestige, not simply because we failed to respond but because we failed to respond when we were quite capable of responding. Acheson nodded. Prestige, he said, is not to be overlooked as a fact of national life, for this "long shadow cast by power" is of itself a great deterrent.[17]

But the other part of Kennan's argument, after saying we must be ready to use force, was lost on some of those present, and on the whole of the American people. That was his saying that whereas we would go to war if necessary, the object would not be the punishment or even destruction of the North Koreans. All we ought to do, he said, is "to see that the attack failed."

From the capital city of Pyongyang came a proclamation, a de facto declaration of war. Thus ended Sunday, June 25, 1950, and the first National Security Council meeting on the Korean War.

Acheson met with the President early the next morning and offered a suggestion. The UN Security Council would meet the following day, and Acheson thought it a good idea if in the second American-sponsored resolution we called on United Nations members to give Korea as much help as might be needed to (a) repel the armed attack, and (b) restore peace in the area. This was a "we-win" policy, for in the event the Russian ambassador did not return to the Security Council (and thus be unable to veto the resolution), there would be clear sailing for our resolution. If he did return, and exercise his veto, Acheson said simply "we would have to carry on under the existing one."[18]

The President agreed, and the Secretary felt chipper.

Later the President issued a statement to his people commending the UN for its speed and determination. He added with a straight face that we would support the UN resolution.[19]

Monday evening, June 26, and the second meeting at Blair House commenced. By now it was obvious that American force, in some form, would be required if complete disaster were to be averted. The question was, what form ought our assistance take? Seoul would fall at any time, and the next natural defense was the Han River which curved menacingly to the south, in the direction of Pusan. Something had to be done, but what?

Two alternatives, or a combination thereof, were possible. Mr. Truman could order the half-trained, pitifully understrength divisions from Japan onto the peninsula. That would buy time, at the cost of much American blood, and would undoubtedly generate severe political storms. The psychological overtones of American infantrymen being slaughtered while defending distant rice paddies were undeniable. Besides, Japan would then be without protection. Ground forces, then, would be used only if all else failed.

Naval and Air Force representatives estimated their personnel might tip the scale, and urged the President to limit his Korean response to these two arms. It would be more "natural and normal" than slugging it out on the ground, the public would more readily accept this response, and as a trump card the President was advised that the use of naval and air power could be done more or less under the aegis of the UN—by "stretching" the Sunday Security Council resolution. So even a Russian veto would not change either our posture or the set of actions we were now commiting ourselves to.[20]

The discussion went on. The JCS stuck by their view of the strategic value of Korea (it was of little or no value, the body said), but agreed that Japan's defenses and American prestige were worth the gamble. Secretary of the Army Pace (as others) feared the Soviets would offer a counterresponse; that would, in turn, see the bursting forth of an angry American public, with its demands for all-out war. To Acheson, who would live to hear the ironic ring of his words, Korea and our conduct would show the very worth of a collective security system.[21]

The plan took shape. We would go in with air and naval warships. If events proved them insufficient, we would, to use a term drawn from a later war, "escalate." No ground forces at this time. Aid would be increased to the Philippines to help in their insurgency problem, and the President then ordered an accelerated program of assistance to aid France in her wretched little war in Indochina, along with a U.S. military mission "to provide close working relations with those forces."*

With a discussion of domestic political problems and hostile reaction again deferred, the second NCS meeting ended at 10 P.M., Monday, June 26, 1950.

While preparations were being made for an emergency meeting between the President and fourteen selected legislators, the results of the meeting were communicated to General MacArthur along with a mission statement: "Your mission is to throw the North Koreans out of South Korea."

The general was upset that he had not been consulted prior to this first decision, and first political goal, being formulated.

There was one other item of importance during that Monday eve-

*If we can believe his daughter's memoirs, President Truman had decided the night of June 25 before to send both planes and troops into Korea.[22]

ning meeting. Acheson said the United Nations would be kept abreast of what we had decided to do in Korea. Such consideration probably was required, since the Secretary added that it was the UN "in whose name (American action in Korea) would be taken."[23]

Such action as would be taken would flow from the contradiction already mentioned, the straining forces of which already were visible to the keen observer when Truman told us that as members of the Security Council we had to go to war. In the next breath he said that if Formosa fell, our Pacific interests would be directly threatened. He concluded by saying America would be doing certain things in Korea, and that our ambassador to the UN would tell the Security Council what we had decided.[24]

On June 27 the American people got their first solid indication of the drift events were taking. It was announced that American combat aircraft would now be roving the skies over Korea, engaged in the game of seeking out and destroying North Korean tanks and North Korean lives. They learned at the same time that the South Korean forces racing to the south along the coasts could expect the thundering armament of the U.S. Navy's guns to shred the countryside in the path and rear of the retreating force.

With that news the voter pondered and, for the first time in five years, thought he detected a promise, perhaps only a hidden promise, coming from the mouth of a wartime leader. The first rumblings of vague but powerful expectations had begun.

Mr. Malik still was absent when the UN Security Council met two and a half hours later. The UN Commission on Korea was present, though, and confirmed what everyone else had pretty well agreed upon: that a war was underway in Korea, launched from the north. The council moved onto new business, which amounted to the second resolution inspired by the Korean crisis, the second not only written by the Americans but, in the case of the second document, personally approved by Truman. Warren Austin, our ambassador to the UN, read the resolution, which recommended that UN members aid in repelling the invaders. Just what "recommended" meant would not be specified for several months.

By a vote of seven to one, with two abstentions, the resolution passed. It was now fifteen minutes before midnight, June 27. The vote came approximately twenty-six hours after the President and National Security Council had sent the order to MacArthur to throw the NKPA out of Korea, and approximately eleven hours after the American people had been so advised.

Thus ended the second meeting of the UN. As the delegates left there was still some question as to what "restore international peace and security in Korea" meant.

In the early hours of Wednesday evening, June 28, as the third major conference between the President and his advisers was getting underway, General MacArthur looked another time at the message containing the UN mandate. Where he was sitting, in Tokyo, Thursday had already arrived, and all that day's news from the front was bad. Resistance had melted. Troops streamed to the rear without rifles, helmets or boots. Glancing at the message a final time, he had a call placed to the Commander, Far Eastern Air Force. When General Stratemeyer answered he learned that the mandate from above was taken by his superior in the Dai Ichi building as being permissive not restrictive. The Air Force general was given immediate authorization to hurl his planes north of the Thirty-eighth Parallel. Without hesitation the order went out: "Take out North Korean airfields immediately. No publicity. MacArthur approves."[25]

And a second-order contest was joined, as a second possible goal pushed its way to the surface.

Five P.M. Thursday, U.S. time, and the fourth major conference between President Truman and those whose judgment and bias he demanded was on. The principal topic of the agenda concerned instructions to MacArthur. During the first three days of the crisis any illusion about a seamless foreign policy quickly evaporated, as the two centers of decision-making separated by half the earth operated by intuition rather than principle. The sum of the fragmentary instructions had now been made into a directive, so said Secretary Louis Johnson. This would permit MacArthur to bomb north of the Thirty-eighth Parallel if, in the general's judgment, such were necessary. The Secretary's directive followed the order to "Take out North Korean airfields immediately" by twenty-two hours.[26]

Then the subject of American riflemen was again raised, and Mr. Johnson said that a limited number of infantry were needed for the protection of the essential port facilities, and to aid in the handling of refugees.

This sliding commitment, and the oblique introduction of ground combat soldiers, disturbed the President. Men on the ground added an entirely new dimension to war.*

Russia's reply to the June 27 UN resolution was issued at 6 P.M.

*The President does not mention the discussion at this meeting of ground forces in his memoirs.

Thursday, while the President and his advisers huddled in Washington. Because of the Soviet absence, the reply read, the vote by the Security Council was illegal. By this time American munitions were ripping apart the Korean countryside and people and, faced with an accomplished fact, the technicality was in large measure ignored.*

Those men whose job it is to sit up each night at the Pentagon's message center were spared the usual tedium as the last day of June 1950 appeared. At three o'clock MacArthur's appeal, written in the most urgent of tones, finally came across all the lines and water and land, then found its destination. American ground forces were mandatory, now, if Korea was to be saved. The general concluded this after reconnaisance two days before of the area south of Seoul. Now, however, his argument for combat troops assumed quite a different form. Such troops are necessary, he said, to execute the President's mission of "clearing South Korea of North Korean forces." He thus made the execution of an order from the President conditional upon the receipt of American infantry.[28]

At five that morning, while most recruits along our eastern seaboard were stumbling from their beds, their most senior Army leaders at the Pentagon were hard at work, reacting to MacArthur's message of one hour previous. General J. Lawton Collins had been notified right away, and he in turn called General Omar Bradley and Secretary of the Army Frank Pace. Before the recruits had moved out to their last peacetime breakfast, the President had been notified. He, in what had to be a gesture of agony, granted MacArthur one regimental combat team, thus committing America to infantry battle. Still the President did not lose all hope, and refused the two division build-up in Japan. That would have to await study and, perhaps, a miracle. Nothing short of intervention either divine or American seemed likely to hold back the Korean attackers.

Hope at this time was in short supply, for it had been just seventy-seven hours since the optimistic decision had been made to commit planes and ships, in the hope that action would be enough.

Ground combat forces added a new dimension to more than the fighting front. Their introduction amounted to a stirring of the American's memory and imagination, the arousal of needs the satisfaction of which would require the subjugation of North Korea by force of arms. By committing infantry to battle the President made

*Presidential press secretary Lincoln White shortly thereafter made an interesting distinction by saying that though the voting had not been conducted in strict accordance of Article 27 of the UN Charter, the legality was unquestionable.[27]

his people a promise, even if he did not realize it at the time. He promised them that the American view of war would be upheld, that our recollections of battles of the past were not idle, that American battle deaths required not compensation but revenge. Finally, President Truman had promised his people victory, in the only sense in which that term means anything to us.

Just before noon that Friday, inquisitive and earnest reporters in our nation's capital were told that President Truman meant what he said, that U.S. troops would be used only to defend communication lines and supplies. American soldiers would not be committed to combat at the front.* Those representing our government who were speaking to these reporters said they had no idea just how many troops the President had committed.

The reporters, despite their studied cynicism, had about the same emotions as those to whom they would report the news. They also had about the same expectations, having heard the same implied promise.

As the news conference ended a Senator repeated to the press charges of usurpation of the Congress's war-making powers by the President.

Friday, 4 P.M., the United Nations. The universality of resolve and burden-sharing was not as yet overwhelming, as only five nations promised to send troops to Korea, and only thirty-three of the fifty-nine members chose even to support the Security Council resolution.[30]

Ultimately seventeen UN members would send men into battle alongside the Koreans and the Americans. That total would be exceeded, though not much, by American battle deaths.

And General Marshall remarked that India was trying to perform the rope trick.

With the Seventh Fleet deployed to keep Mao and Chiang from each other's throat, an offer of perhaps 30,000 Nationalist Chinese troops was made the United States. For reasons of economy and efficiency, because they might be needed to defend Formosa, and because such a move might be all it would take to send swarms of Red Chinese across the Yalu River, the offer was declined.[31]**

Amid newspaper headlines screaming, "Yanks are in it now," the

*"General MacArthur has been authorized to use certain supporting ground units."[29]

**Acheson also feared the use of Chinese Nationalist forces might have meant the withdrawal of the more efficient British soldiers, one battalion of which began moving from Hong Kong almost immediately. It was generally conceded that Free China's troops lacked both training and equipment.

national pulse quickened, as it always does at the first whiff of gunpowder. It would be a year before the scent became a compound of decomposing bodies and near-victory, frozen feet and stalemate. By that time it would be overwhelming.

But for now the President had the wind fully at his back, and as the initial commitment of one battalion grew to four, then five divisions, with the promise of more if needed, still the wind was strong and constant. As the furnace of a Korean summer scooped up more and more of our men, as one delaying action after another was crushed under the avalanche of mustard-colored uniforms, still the wind held. With August, and the first indication of the atrocities practiced by the North Koreans on our wounded and captured reached the voter, as descriptions of summary executions, disembowelings, and burnings alive arrived, the force was firm and steady.

And during August, the nadir for the American in Korea, 70 percent of the public stood behind Harry S. Truman.

While his public support was growing and firming, the first countercurrents were observed, not in the public but in the Congress. Back on July 3, two days before Task Force Smith engaged the enemy near Osan, the Secretary of State made a recommendation to the President, and the President had accepted it. In so doing American wars took on a nature such that two decades and more would be required to remake them. Congress was in recess, and the President would not call them back because he feared, rightly, that a prolonged debate would be the price any resolution of support would have to pay. In this decision Secretary Acheson concurred. But he went further and advised President Truman to ignore a solution, and simply tell the Congress, in a full report, what Truman had decided, and what Truman had done. This was another instance of Acheson's "we win" principle for, in the event members of Congress proposed a resolution, then he would provide those Congressmen with an acceptable resolution commending U.S. actions which could be introduced. However, if opposition arose, a resolution really was not required, Acheson argued, and the President could rest on his constitutional authority as Commander-in-Chief. Truman did the latter.[32]

The arguments Truman gave for our going into Korea were a ruinous blend of the defensive and the eschatological, although his prosecution of the war was actually political from start to finish. By saying that communism was acting in Korea "just as Hitler, Mussolini and the Japanese has acted" it is clear that we were opposing not a breach of the international peace but a brazen act of Aggression. Aggression is evil, by fighting evil we discharge our responsibility as a Virtuous People. Thus, the eschatological argument.[33]

Only in a tenuous, slippery sense could he argue that our national security was at stake, but such was necessary because of our being historically wedded to the defensive argument. By coupling the attack across the parallel to the lower case rendering of Aggression, by rousing the latent messianic urgings within his people, and by introducing something very much akin to what later would be the domino theory, he himself became greatly responsible for the ultimate spiritual breakdown.

The argument held well enough during the first scorching months of the war.

His other argument, clearly an afterthought, that "it was also clear to me that the foundations and the principles of the UN were at stake," proved as much a detriment as an asset to the President. The idea in its original form might work, since a collective security arrangement between ethical nations forges a link between the defensive and eschatological arguments. The problem was that some member nations, indeed a majority, took only the political conception of war to heart, and contributed troops and resources in direct ratio to their perceived national interests.

But for the moment, with seven out of ten Americans with him, a gifted Secretary of Defense again,* and a genius of a general ready to serve up a Caanae victory, the President could watch summer come to an end without serious misgivings.

THE SYMMETRY OF WAR

For two weeks U.S. Navy Lieutenant Eugene Clark held one of the world's most unusual jobs, and had fourteen days of experience than which few greater can be conceived. Put ashore on a scrubby island in Inchon harbor, Lieutenant Clark spent his days in hiding, his nights locating gun emplacements and suitable spots along the sea wall for an invasion.** His work nearly done, he tested a signal from atop an enemy lighthouse, then went to his prearranged spot to await MacArthur's grand arrival. Dawn, September 15, 1950.[34]

*Like a family embarrassment, tight-fisted Louis Johnson was dismissed and forgotten on September 12. He was replaced, after congressional opposition was smothered, by ex-Army Chief of Staff, ex-Secretary of State George C. Marshall.

**The assault had to be conducted not onto beaches but across a barrier designed to hold back the sea, for which purpose ladders had secretly been constructed in Japan.

The general watched the bombardment and wake of the assault craft and felt neither glee nor vindication as his superb piece of strategy unfolded before the incredulous eyes of Inchon's defenders. His emotions were those of quiet satisfaction, like those of the patient scientist whose hypothesis is verified in the quiet of a laboratory.

Those important persons who thought the two-phased landing over mudbanks and through a twenty-seven-foot tide a five thousand to one gamble—a gamble whose risks far exceeded the gains, people such as the Chairman of the Joint Chiefs and the Chief of Naval Operations, had to give MacArthur his day, as the Marines poured over the wall. Soon the Army's Seventh Division was ashore, followed a short time later by paratroopers of the 187th Airborne Regimental Combat Team.*

Even the forces of nature seemed to be at the general's command, as typhoon Kezia, with winds of 125 mph, diverted from the invasion fleet just in time to shackle North Korean spies who knew of the invasion.[35]

On September 18 Seoul's Kimpo airfield fell, and three days later Al Jolson gave the men of the Eighth Army a crusader's send-off.

On September 22, after six weeks of humiliation and death and bravery, the Eighth Army exploded northward, eastward and westward, showering the now-outgunned North Koreans with steel and death.

A classic of hammer and anvil, but with a crucially important difference. The idea was to slice into the enemy's rear, severing his lines of communications and forcing him into the waiting arms of the Eighth Army. But there were in effect two American forces, virtually independent of each other. Lt. Gen. Walton II. Walker commanded Eighth Army, and his soldiers tore north eager to play either hammer, or anvil, or both.

Inchon's invasion force was called Tenth Corps. MacArthur had created it especially for the thundering spectacle it had just performed, and now he chose to retain the divisions of that Corps, the First Marine and the Seventh Infantry, for the coup de grace, which would be his curtain call.

Just eleven days after the young Navy lieutenant signaled it was go for Inchon, General MacArthur told those around him that the destruction of the NKPA—always the general's goal—required one of two offensive moves. We could, he remarked in the manner of a patient instructor, attack overland and seize Pyongyang, capital of

*From whose ranks would emerge an aggressive and unrelenting lieutenant colonel named William C. Westmoreland.

North Korea. That would take some time—and lives. On the other hand, another amphibious assault, this time going inland from the Sea of Japan to the east, would sever the head of the fleeing enemy. The target city was Wonsan, which lay north.

By September 26, MacArthur had decided that he would breach the Thirty-eighth Parallel by a distance of some seventy miles.[36]

The next morning, September 27, Eighth Army and Tenth Corps linked-up at Suwon, south of Seoul. Defenders of the Pusan perimeter now drove north, by-passing a lot of irksome guerrillas. As these men continued the attack, the general withdrew his corps in preparation for the final burst of glory.

Back in July, as Taejon was being consumed by flames and attacking North Koreans, George F. Kennan and Paul Nitze of the State Department's Policy Planning Staff argued in the strongest language possible that MacArthur should not be permitted to cross the parallel if the North Koreans withdrew or were thrown back. The ultimate destruction of the enemy could not be the purpose of modern war.[37] This was not World War II. Our goals were not transcendent, but very, very mundane.

At this early date only a few officials had thought the problem through to the extent necessary to come down firmly one way or the other concerning crossing the parallel. But Syngman Rhee had, and in mid-July he said he would go north regardless of who might accompany him.

During July 1950 the mid-course was taken not by politicians but by the professional military planners of the Pentagon. We could cross, the generals agreed, but only if we had the muscle, assurance Russia would not come in, full promise of support via a Presidential-Congressional proclamation, and the belated imprimatur of the UN calling for a "united, free and independent Korea," with the pledge for U.S.-UN troops for as long as necessary.[38]

In time of war democracies are cauldrons, stirred by leaders and the led. Direction in the form of pressure can come from below—or laterally—quite as easily as from the top. On August 8 one of the most venerated ladies of our land stoked the fire. When the chairman of the National Citizens Committee for United Nations Day issued her organization's resolution which demanded a "free government for *all* Korea," Mrs. Eleanor Roosevelt exerted pressure she never had been able to while First Lady.[39] And our people listened, and liked what they heard.

Geopolitical lines within the State Department were drawn by late August, when Operation Chromite, the invasion of Inchon, was seen for what it was. There were just two positions; the question admitted only a yes or no: Should we cross the parallel? The first, which might be called the pure containment view, that of Mr. Nitze and Mr. Kennan,* said that under no conditions ought we to cross into North Korea. Doing so would inflame public passions and make the irreversible commitment—and promise—of unconditional surrender. Further, the Yalu is hardly the sort of obstacle necessary to protect us from the virulent neighbors posted on the northern shores.[40]

The other side was that of Secretaries Acheson and Marshall, both of whom favored an opportunistic approach. Our goal ought to be, according o Acheson, the destruction of the invader's force and the restoration of security to the area. This view, he said, was the correct one if "properly restricted." Just what this curious phrase meant never has been explained. 'Troops," the Secretary of State explained, "could not be expected . . . to march up to a surveyor's line and stop." Until the actual military situation developed further, he went on, "no one could say where the necessity for flexibility in tactics ended and embarkation upon a new strategic purpose began."

The Secretary then added that he was at a loss as to what to do after the NKPA had been destroyed.[41]

At this juncture there were two dimensions to the decision which required consideration. First, there were the military-foreign relations problems of Russian or Chinese intervention, of the worst terrain and weather Americans ever had been asked to fight in, impossible logistic demands, and so forth. These factors received considerable attention.

A second set of factors existed, which required but did not receive adequate study, and which ultimately proved more influential than the crush of Chinese infantry. All along President Truman had steadfastly refused to permit extended discussion of domestic political issues, and had largely ignored public opinion.** His mandate came from the state, not the people. At this time Russian entry into the war was seen as more likely than Chinese, and one of the Nitze-Kennan faction's arguments against going north was the public demand for all-out war in the event Russia came in.*** Both the Nitze-Kennan and the Acheson-Truman wings favored and practiced the political conceptions of war, with ethical issues playing no

*Kennan, ready to leave government service, played only a minor role in this major decision.
**For that matter, he had with impartiality ignored Congressional opinion, too.
***Clearly, the same argument applies to Chinese entry.

important role for either group. All concerned has long held the voter in contempt. But the former knew and feared public response, for whether events proved favorable or unpleasant, the tendency among our people is to polarize their demands. If our forces are "winning" then the clarion call will be for "total victory." If things go badly, the demand will be for evacuation.

The Nitze-Kennan wing lost a debating point, the debate, and control of U.S. foreign policy.

With the first day of September drawing to a close, and Operation Chromite just two weeks away, the National Security Council met again. The State Department was of the opinion that the UN resolution of June 27 was sufficient to authorize sending our soldiers plunging across the parallel, to ferret out and destroy the NKPA. How this could be argued with a look of sincerity was made possible just because the United States had long since decided to keep the UN advised, "in whose name such acts are performed."

September 11, Chromite minus four days. The National Security Council definitely wants the invasion through Seoul's harbor exploited, either in the form of destroying the North Koreans as a fighting force or, at a minimum, to throw them back across the "surveyor's line." Only one issue now remains to be resolved: the entry of either Russian or Chinese troops. Otherwise, the green light to the Yalu is on.[42]

On that same day, September 11, the President authorized MacArthur the unbalanced alternatives of either destroying the NKPA, or ejecting them. The inequality of the disjunction puzzled the general.[43]

There was no evading the question of whether to cross or not, and Hanson Baldwin remarked in his column of the September 27, "damned if we do, damned if we don't."

We did.

The communications people in Tokyo called the general. It was General Marshall on the radio. What he wanted from MacArthur was an operation plan for clearing and unifying all of Korea. Assuming no communist forces are likely to join in, let your soldiers camp on the banks of the Yalu, he said. And even if new enemies were to attack, it was the President's desire that battle not be refused on policy, but only if we did not have a reasonable chance for success.

The impulses of electrical energy which carried Secretary Marshall's message altered not simply our war aims, but the very nature of collective security alliances and the American experience of war. The essence of the former would hereafter be distrusted and misunderstood by our people. As for our view of war, it would, ironically, be so conditioned by the metamorphosis of the limited engagement we had officially pursued heretofore that all yearnings for World War II would be reinforced.

September closed to the words of Ernest Bevin, British Foreign Secretary, urging we "eradicate" the Thirty-eighth Parallel, to the hoisting of the flag of the UN's sixtieth member, Indonesia, and to the reading of the third U.S.-sponsored resolution before the world body. The resolution called for "A united, independent, and Democratic Korea," thus reviving the dormant UN plan of 1947 for unification.[44]

On October 7, ten days after MacArthur had been ordered across the border by his President via his Secretary of Defense, and seven days after the ROK Third Division raced up the east coast past the imaginary line, the General Assembly formally resolved that MacArthur had permission to cross over and unify the country.[45]

Years later Acheson would blame the JCS, and himself, for not recommending the front be consolidated along the Pyongyang-Wonsan line, where an active and vigorous defense could have been conducted for so long as was necessary. But the flush of victory was upon the nation, and its people, and its leaders; and so the ostensive UN aims of ninety days previous were jettisoned, the cry for unification and total victory went out, and our citizens, and soldiers, were given the news—and promise.

Our forces burst out of the Pusan pocket on September 22, joined hands with the invasion force on the 27th, then helped liberate Seoul on the 28th. After leaving that crippled, smoldering city, the Eighth Army went north, on the western side of the peninsula. On the other coast the Tenth Corps had to abandon the notion of invading through Wonsan, owing to ROK forces, suddenly in possession of leaders and backbone, who had already taken the city.

North they drove, with the First Cavalry Division maintaining the offensive and getting into northern territory on October 7. Four days prior to their rupture of the border, had they been in the proper position, troopers of the First Calvary could have heard India's ambassador to Peking tell of the threat of Chinese intervention if any troops other than Korean crossed the Thirty-eighth Parallel. But the troopers were not in position to hear any such thing. If they had, it would have made no difference. The orders were to go north, and they enjoyed chasing a defeated enemy.

Those who had heard Pannikar's words were not impressed, since his pro-communist leanings were a matter of record.

An ultimatum for total surrender, hallmark of the American at war, was layed down by MacArthur just as the last remnants of the First Calvary crossed into North Korea, October 9, 1950. The sullenness that was the enemy's response only proved a point, and further orders for his destruction were issued.

Pyongyang, capital of the Democratic Republic of Korea, fell to the Eighth Army on the nineteenth of October. At about the same time paratroopers of two battalions of the 187th ARCT jumped into the otherwise meaningless cities of Sukchon-Sunchon, in the hope of finding a train filled with American prisoners.* Instead they found scattered but ferocious resistance, and had two of their companies of airborne soldiers decimated.

They found a shallow grave of a hundred or so of their captured comrades, hands tied, faces blown off. An informal moratorium on enemy prisoners went into effect.

Heretofore there was some question about the wisdom of letting Americans and other non-Koreans enter the race to the Yalu, but as the final week of October got under way General MacArthur removed any and all such restrictions, then spurred his commanders on by directing them to use all possible speed, all possible forces, to get to the Yalu, to end the war.[46]

Parts of the Seventeenth Regiment of our Seventh Division would get there, clear to the Yalu, just across from the limitless top-of-the-world country of Manchuria. The village went by the unpronounceable name Hyesanjin. Someone would remark it was as cold as northern Minnesota. Another would discover he had no winter clothing. But that would be later.

By October 26 a full division of ROK soldiers were at the upper limits of the river, busily making their flapping right wing secure.

On the same day some members of the ROK Twenty-sixth Regiment were caught in a terrific firefight, and brought in some of the enemy that survived. The prisoners spoke something other than Korean, wore arctic-padded clothing, and said they had volunteered.

During the winter of 1944–45, U.S. Army air reconnaissance was able to detect almost every enemy build-up, weather permitting. That was one of the skills which had to be given low priority during the half-decade following the big war.

The loss of that skill was unfortunate, for it permitted 300,000

*After watching the paratroopers drop, General MacArthur said the war was over.

human beings to slip to the south side of the Yalu, hide themselves, and make final plans for the deaths of other human beings.

After the worst fears were confirmed, our State Department on November 6 asked for an urgent meeting of the UN Security Council. The Chinese were to halt their activities; such were our desires. The agency to bring this about had to be the United Nations. Besides, President Truman said the United States would huddle with the other members "in order to maintain UN support for any further action to be taken." The United Nations moved an inch or so closer to the spotlight.

Even before the troops in the field entered the meat grinder on the icy slopes, rifts were beginning, fingers being pointed, responsibility being denied. On the ninth of November General Omar Bradley, anticipating events, said MacArthur's move north was the execution of the directive the general received to occupy and hold elections throughout the whole of Korea.[47]

In fact, the worst fears were not yet confirmed, for the Chinese communists were still testing the waters. They launched the first phase of their offensive October 27–31, seeking out the more isolated, poorly supported ROK forces along the distant stretches of the Yalu. The ROK Seventh Regiment was strangled on the first day of the offensive, its vulnerability as a result of outrunning supporting units now evident. Then the attack in that region subsided, for reasons which were not clear.

As October closed, the U.S. Twenty-fourth Division, on the extreme western end of the line, was only forty miles from the vision, the Yalu, and the end of the war. Over on the eastern side the Marines were seizing the steel and electric sources, guarding the single road over which supplies and replacements for the steady casualties they were taking could travel.

In both east and west there were stories circulating about odd prisoners the South Koreans had taken, and apprehension struggled with biting cold for the men's attention. But our people held Unsan over on the west, very much north of the Chongchon River, the last such obstacle separating the soldiers from the thrashing Yalu, as it empties into the Yellow Sea. There were also obstacles separating the Tenth Corps in the east and the Eighth Army in the west—a range of wild and impassable mountains, which pulled themselves up and through the cushion of fog. Our plan was to consolidate all forces at the earliest time feasible.

A feasibility study on consolidating forces never was run, and the men of the Eighth Cavalry Regiment occupying Unsan as October changed to November never were asked for their opinions about consolidating or anything else.

Through the brittle-crisp night and through their own artillery fire the Chinese swept, probing, feeling, seeking a soft spot. Within hours it was clear that they meant to envelop and destroy the Eighth Army, and scenes reminiscent of early summer were replayed as Americans, once again the hunted, began withdrawing south.

By November 5 the Chinese attack ended. It was as if some massive animal, seeing its enemy too close to the lair, had attacked that enemy with the ferocity of an angered mother. With the enemy running away from its brood, the animal withdrew. Or so it seemed.

These attacks by the Chinese, separated by the distance of the mountain range and by one week, sent shock waves through Seoul and Pusan, Tokyo and Washington. On November 6 MacArthur, not being privy to the minds of the enemy who now opposed him on the field, assumed the attack was general and of long duration. He warned the Joint Chiefs of Staff that movement of the Chinese across the Yalu "threatens the ultimate destruction of my command." As the end slipped further away, the general made plans for the final, smashing stroke to save his command, his reputation, and his prize.

China had tested the water, and found it to her liking. The Koreans were not much, the Americans little better. As the fighting ebbed across the mountains of North Korea, two massive but completely hidden concentrations of Chinese forces gathered men and provisions together for the next phase of their liberation offensive. One mass was in the west, opposite the Eighth Army, the other not in the east but directly in the center of the country. The idea was to let the western forces smother the Eighth Army while troops in the middle sliced through to the port of Hungnam on the east coast. After that the garrot could be applied to the outstretched neck of all our eastern forces, at the leisure of the Chinese.

Those enemy volunteers who moved during daylight hours and exposed their position were shot out of hand. As a rule, there was little movement among the Chinese.[48]

After eleven days without major contact, MacArthur regained his sense of direction and told his superiors in Washington that in one week, on November 24, he would launch his final attack and drive to the Yalu. That would be just one day after Thanksgiving, a date especially appropriate.

Thanksgiving Day came and went unnoticed, save by those who

failed to get a hot meal. That day rumors of something big were in the wind, along with fearful hopes that this would be the last holiday spent away from home.

On the flight from Tokyo to Korea the next morning, the general put the final touches on his speech, and thought of the much greater audience that would be listening. Once on the ground he advised his subordinates, his superiors and the world that the Chinese were not coming in, and to show he deserved all the glory that was his, he ordered the Eighth Army to race to the Yalu.

It did, and ran headlong into a quarter million survivors of war with both Japan and Chiang Kai-Skek. The Eighth Army was permitted to cross the Chongchon, and when it did the trap sprang shut, and enemy swords were unsheathed. A series of slaughters ensued, and for the second time in three weeks the identical positions were turned over to the Chinese. Then the withdrawal of four divisions down a single-lane road was begun, and "ambush" was reintroduced to our vocabulary. Trucks, tanks, and artillery collided to form a hopeless mass as the retreat became a route, as Drew Pearson urged mothers to pray their sons were not at Kunu-ri, as a general who had tried to carry out orders he knew were senselessly dangerous saw his division, and his career, carved away.*

In the east, the First Marines and the Seventh Infantry held the left and right sides of the Chosin reservoir. They were flailed even more brutally than the Eighth Army and, like their comrades to the west, had but a single, primitive road over which to retreat. But there was a difference. The Seventh soon ceased being a vital fighting force despite individual acts of heroism, and some of its men had to beg Marines for a ride out of the trap, with the Leathernecks taking the necessary precautions for a retreat. They also took many casualties, but time and again cleared the ridges overlooking the escape route, even if doing so meant still more casualties.

Twelve CCF divisions were targeted on the Marines, whom they rightly considered the best fighting troops America had to offer.[49] That group of Chinese had the mission of annihilating the Marines, and they tried, twelve divisions strong, again and again, In the end a Chinese corps was no longer capable of combat, and one division underwent such carnage at the hands of the Marines that it disappeared.

Meanwhile, President Truman was assessing the magnitude of the "end the war" disaster, the "home by Christmas" defeat. He was unable to make a rational assessment, though. News in the early

---

*Major General Laurence B. Keiser was sacked. His division, the Second Infantry, was combat ineffective after this, with 4,000 men lost along with half its equipment.

days of the violent fighting simply could not be verified. He wondered how newspapers could make such categorical pronouncements.

Within a week of the CCF* November offensive the center of the UN line had plunged fifty miles. On the fifth of December Pyongyang was lost, where only a month or so earlier gleeful American soldiers had squashed plastic explosives around the vault door of a People's Bank, blown it, then scattered the strange money to the winds. Drums of gasoline were kicked from the backs of trucks and riddled with tracer rounds. Pyongyang burned.

With the aid of an untried division, the Third Infantry, Marines and survivors of the Seventh Division pulled out of Hungnam the day before Christmas 1950, along with the ROKs who could be grabbed up and 91,000 North Koreans who elected to leave their socialist paradise behind.

Hungnam became a pyre.

Our lines were well below the Thirty-eighth Parallel by mid-December, and still it could not hold.

With his command shattered and in full retreat, General MacArthur began giving press interviews, explaining the inexplicable, seeking revenge. Had he been given his way, he told us, the war would have been over long ago. The Chinese were bandits, international marauders, and must be treated as such. MacArthur's acts had been legal and in no way amounted to belligerency against the Chinese homeland, "in spite of the outrageous international lawlessness emanating therefrom."

The general wanted to end the war, as Americans always had. Doing so would require getting to the root of the problems, even if that meant general war.

Eighty miles below the parallel the Pusan perimeter story was repeated, as the primitive supply lines of the communist peasant army strained and frayed, just as our own shortened and again gained strength. Our soldiers ate their icy slabs of sausage from green cans, removed their boots to massage, or perhaps count, their toes. A respite the ground soldiers had to have was shaping up as artillery and bombs layed carpets of death to protect the exhausted riflemen. They started to rest and think of the climb back up the peninsula. Mostly they rested, as New Year's Eve arrived.

It was exactly at this time that the Chinese launched their third-phase offensive.

*Chinese Communist Forces.

ASYMMETRY

The Korean War was decided December 4, 1950, while U.S. troops were preparing to incinerate Pyongyang. It was ended not by decisiveness but by a question, not by American generals but by the British prime minister. For in asking the President of the United States the probable cost of a cease-fire, Attlee highlighted a question which, if not disregarded totally, had to be answered. An answer—any answer—would be an implicit approval, an incremental move toward disengagement.[50] The question was not disregarded. The President tried to buy time. The dilemma rested in the back of his mind, while dispatches from the front lines told of holocaust and disarray.

November 30 was a gloomy day in Washington, the darkness compounded by the partially verified fears of total disaster along the Yalu. At his press conference the issue of nuclear weapons came up, and with his usual candor and dispatch,* President Truman told us, and the Chinese, that he would not rule out the use of such devices, and had in fact always considered their use. After all, consideration of the use of a weapon is implied by the very possession of that weapon. He spoke from the Indian Treaty Room with some desperation that day.

United Nations support, heretofore absent but unimportant, now was needed—not for the troops they might give us, for that limit had been reached. Also, there would be no widening of the war. A disaster was in the making, the outcome of which was still very much in doubt. What was required to cover the worst eventualities was that the UN move, and move quickly, under the spotlight of public attention. By doing so, the United States might step partially into the shadows, at least so far as the people at home are concerned. Pressures, inexorable and absolutely predictable, were sure to rise both from the Dai Ichi and from the ranks of the citizenry. To give in to his people's polarizing tendencies to make Korea a war of opinion might well mean the destruction of the country.** Consequently, condemnation of the Chinese Communists by the United Nations and the appearance of broad support from afar would be desirable. Actual control of military operations and political decisions would rest, of course, with the United States.

*The President's friend and ally, Dean Acheson, said of the man whom he called "mighty Captain" that Truman's mouth was often faster than his mind.
**By his use of gnostic rhetoric over the years, Truman had made public response to blood-letting inevitable. The fuel made from Clausewitz and Jomini was preparing to combust.

His people's habit of clustering around mutually exclusive options permitted, in theory, a rush to the other end, away from the violence of the battlefield. Determined to keep such possibilities at the level of speculation only, the President resolved on December 5 that we never would voluntarily withdraw from Korea, regardless of public opinion. At that time the public unalterably opposed withdrawing. But Truman was aware of the fickleness of public opinion, so he ignored it, or tried to.

At the Pentagon one of the endless series of contingency plans was drawn up. The play was constructed so that the United States would be able to withdraw, in the words of the Joint Chiefs, "with honor." That particular balloon burst at ground level, as the State Department issued a categorical No![52]*

President Truman met again with Prime Minister Attlee on the 11th, a week after a cease-fire first was discussed. The package had too many barbs and hot places on its surface. The two men agreed neither country would go after a cease-fire.

Those pressures the President feared were churning now, as the general issued statements to the press on how best to conclude the war. Using an analogy MacArthur probably wouldn't have been pleased with, the President said the general would have rightly court-martialed any second lieutenant who expressed his disagreement in front of reporters. That was just one source of trouble. For the time being the general would keep.

Another source was the Congress, specifically the conservative element of the GOP. On December 13 Truman met with leaders of both parties. He reminded them the country was at war, and wartime is a special time, and the President needed more authority. Presidential discretion never was popular among conservative leaders, not even during World War II. As memories of the years of mutual distrust and occasional excess by the Executive welled up, Senator Robert A. Taft asked first whether full or partial mobilization would be requested by Truman if he got the extra power; the Senator then let it be known that he saw no reason for a declaration of national emergency. In the end the President was given a period of grace, and he declared a national emergency,** and irritated some Congressional lawmakers unnecessarily by requesting in the same breath military appropriations and aid for Yugoslavia.[53]

*However, at this time MacArthur was told his basic mission was protection of Japan.
**The declaration was made December 15, a masterstroke of poor timing.

Thirteen representatives from Asian and Arab countries were drafting a resolution to determine the basis for a cease-fire while the President and the Ohio Senator were arguing. On December 14 the UN General Assembly adopted the resolution; two weeks later China turned them down cold, knowing the wind was fully at the backs of her infantry.

Throughout December and early January discussions were held on the new military realities, and what the United States was capable of doing to change things for the better. Only those UN countries who had actually committed troops to combat in Korea were consulted. The result was not what Truman wanted so much as what had to be, and a consensus opposing risk of general war was shaped.

After the fundamental decisions had been made, the prime ministers of the British Commonwealth sponsored in the UN a resolution calling for a cease-fire,* to be followed by talks between the USSR, China, the United Kingdom and the United States. Even though Formosa's future was included in the resolution, President Truman thought he had no choice but to support it.

Shortly after the Commonwealth resolution was offered, Truman hinted that unspecified "industrial type production" might be targets for our atom bombs.

BACK INTO THE POCKET

Collapse along the front had been a repeat of November and December, but only for a few hours. Now, as battlegrounds in July and August were again raked with fire, our forces withdrew, true, but in an orderly fashion now, maintaining contact with the unit on either side. By giving ground during this first week of the new year, the Chinese were flung to the end of their tether, and after attacking through their own bursting artillery shells, then ours, their infantry lay bleeding and exhausted when they should have been exploiting.

Contact was lost toward the end of the week, while the Chinese pawed at thin air. It was regained by a strong reconnaissance probe by the Eighth Army on January 7. A week later General Ridgway, the new commander of Eighth Army,** directed that contact be made and maintained. It was, near Osan, site of the first American infantry combat of the summer prior. This was a time of caution, husbanding risks and casualties.[54]

Autumn's blaze of glory was gone, never to return, never again to

*Not surprisingly, this organization had committed the greatest number of soldiers to battle, aside from South Korea and the United States. They sent one division.
**General Walker died in a jeep accident December 23.

lure us on. There would be advance under Ridgway, but orderly advance, with phase lines and specific objectives, and less discretion left to his subordinates. And no victory.

On January 25, when his army started the powerful and cautious attack back up the mangled roads and trails of central Korea, the name of the operation, "Thunderbolt," seemed a holdover from the previous season. For by this time General Ridgway had made his own calculations of enemy and friendly forces. This general had come to the conclusion that the cost of again standing beside the Yalu would be costly, prohibitively so.[55]

In February and March they punched north again, broke out of a place called Chipyong-ni (which the Army would enshrine in an oil painting), and settled on a policy of death and destruction toward the Chinese who stood in their way. Artillery used in an abundance unparalleled even during World War II stacked up Chinese bodies like cords of wood. Operations no longer connoted total victory and unconditional surrender, but only surrounding and killing the opponent. Names such as Roundup, Killer, Ripper ushered in a war of attrition, a war of limited movement, maximum death for the enemy.

Before March ended, Seoul was passed onto its fourth conqueror in nine months. The rains of spring fell on a diseased and desolute city, where heaps of rubble pointed to what used to be buildings.

Before March ended, some JCS directives were going directly to Ridgway, thus by-passing MacArthur.

And before the end of March the general issued an invitation to the Chinese Communists in the field, an invitation which requested that the two sides agree to fight an all-out war.

MacArthur's press conference had a violent impact on Washington, where his relief clearly was required if the President was to limit the war. But a far-less visible impact occurred among the people, where the expectations of last fall were once again kicked wide, into which promise followed promise. From the point of view of the conduct of limited war, this, and not MacArthur's insubordination, was the legacy of the general's dismissal.

When his dismissal came on April 11, friendly forces were strung across the peninsula in a line generally above the parallel by a few miles. According to General Ridgway, most important geographical objectives had been taken.

President Truman could not have done a poorer job of relieving the general had he hired a perverse PR agency. The fact that

MacArthur found out about his firing after his aides knew was simply a matter of some bad taste and worse luck. In itself, it affected the life of the nation not at all. But by insisting upon linking MacArthur's dismissal with the reintroduction of limited political and military goals—the third such set the Americans had been faced with since the previous June—the President forged an irrational but unbreakable bond in the minds of his people between the regal person of Douglas MacArthur and the unsavory doctrine of no-win war.* Under the best of conditions it would have taken years of preparation of his people before limited war could be accepted. Under the conditions selected** the ugliness inherent in the idea was magnified to a point such that it never would be palatable. Thus those who came after Truman would have to lie, and speak the language of salvation, even as they pursued limited objectives.

It was not until February 1951 that the UN was able to brand Communist China an aggressor, all the more remarkable when one considers the speed with which North Korea was so labeled for invading the South. By February parity was being reached on the field of battle, and no additional UN troops were forthcoming.

On March 20 the general was advised that the United Nations wanted a political settlement of the war, and four days later he asked the Chinese to meet him in a contest of general war. MacArthur said more that day. He said that either we win or get out, even if winning meant war with China—which it probably would have.

His fiery temperament catching up with him, the President scrapped a message of intention he was to have delivered, a message saying we must continue to inflict battle deaths on the enemy until "satisfactory arrangements" had been made for ending the fighting. Truman concluded, with some reason, that he had been upstaged.

And then it came. MacArthur, selfless defender of the Far East, was out. The press conference during which attempts to justify limited war were offered collapsed of its own weight. Our President tried too much, protested too much. The Nitze-Kennan arguments had returned to haunt him. By the time he concluded the press conference he had unintentionally pulled the plug of public support.***

*At 10:30 P.M. of the day he fired MacArthur, Truman feigned hurt feelings when he told his people, "Now, many persons, even some who applauded our decisions to defend Korea, have forgotten the basic reason for our action."[56] In order to forget, one first has to know.

**A different selection could have permitted the separation of MacArthur's dismissal from the issue of limited war objectives. Clearly, the connection is at best psychological.

***The order in which the President in his *Memoirs* lists the reasons for relieving

MacArthur's removal had a negligible influence on the course of the war. General Matthew B. Ridgway got MacArthur's job, General James A. Van Fleet got Ridgway's, and our forces inched their way up the waist of Korea ever more cautious of casualties. In late April the Chinese launched their fifth phase offensive. Its first round had the usual initial success. Next month the second round of the CCF fifth phase got under way. Many friendly soldiers were killed, blinded or maimed. The line sagged thirty miles, but then the predetermined maelstrom of American steel and fire ripped the surviving Chinese riflemen to shreds, and hurled them back. By the end of May the Eighth Army was back on something called the Kansas Line, generally along the Thirty-eighth Parallel.

By late April the new commander of the Eighth Army, General Van Fleet, was fully aware that Ridgway was no MacArthur, and that this season was not Fall 1950. He could not advance north of Line Wyoming without the express permission of his senior, who now sat in Tokyo, and the Joint Chiefs of Staff, who now sat in the Pentagon vowing never again to give a field commander his head.[58]

Van Fleet was aware of another fact. Even had he been given permission to charge north at full speed, he simply did not possess sufficient forces to encircle and destroy the enemy. No major additions to his fighting force could be expected. At the same time, the longer he waited the tougher the enemy would be to dislodge, for with every passing day the defenses became deeper and more lethal, the holes being cut into the mountains by the other side less vulnerable.

With the smashing of the final major Chinese offensive on May 20, operations of a severely limited nature got under way, toward a line a bit north of Kansas called Wyoming. On June 15 the objective had been achieved. Eight days later Jacob Malik, Deputy Foreign Commissar of the Soviet Union, said the CCF and the NKPA would be willing to negotiate an end to the affair. A week later, with his command roughly where the "surveyor's line" lay, General Ridgway obeyed the orders of his commander-in-chief and broadcast to the Chinese our readiness to discuss an armistice.

The war of movement had ended, and limited war, for the American, was about to begin.

MacArthur are illuminating: "It was in open defiance of my orders as President and Commander-in-Chief . . . This was a challenge to the authority of the President under the Constitution . . . It also flouted the policy of the United Nations."[57] The United Nations had not even been consulted before MacArthur was removed, though he was United Nations Commander.

THE EXCLUSIVE DISJUNCTION: Acheson or MacArthur?

At home the big news of early June 1951 was of the "MacArthur Hearings," of the master of rhetoric and persuasion, the praetorian with the infuriating habit of referring to himself in the third person, mesmerized public and Congress alike. His reception was nothing short of cataclysmic, the public outpouring religious.

Soviet and Communist Chinese war-making capabilities were discussed, then deleted from the public record. The issue for the people was twofold: What are the ultimate goals in Korea, and ought the military be in charge of military operations?

When the former question was put to him, Secretary Acheson squirmed a moment and replied in his usual domineering manner that we went into Korea to stop the attack, end the aggression, and so forth. What about the UN 1947 resolution, and the Cairo Declaration of December 1, 1943, for a free and independent Korea? it was asked. With the agility for which he was famous, the Secretary replied, "I do not understand it to be a war aim." It ought, he continued, to be pursued not by violence but by peaceful means, "Just," now diverting attention, "as was being attempted before this aggression."[59]

One side no more wins a set of hearings than it does a limited war. The most one does is move a little closer—if the cost is not prohibitive.

At the outset of the talks the Truman Administration, like the Johnson and Nixon adminstrations, decided that only a defensive war would be fought, and it was with that truth in mind that Vice Admiral Turner Joy and his delegations began two years of negotiations on July 10, 1951, as men clawed at each other and at the ground beneath them for a naked hilltop, or plateau, or ridge. Ten-thousand battle deaths later the war would officially end, though late in 1969 an American stationed along the Thirty-eighth Parallel would be shot to death by North Koreans.[60]

WAR'S NEW GENERATION

By the time Commissar Malik made his speech both sides in Korea were unable to budge each other, save for an important but meaningless hill. A plan to fight all the way to the Pyongyang-Wonsan line was drawn up by a now-disillusioned staff in July, only to be thrown aside when it was clear no more troops were in the pipeline. Both sides were locked in.

Another plan, this time ambitious enough to imagine marching right back to the Yalu, was drawn up by the staff in November 1951. It, too was put into the files, along with General Ridgway's comments that it wasn't worth the cost in blood.

In the same month, Ridgway ordered Van Fleet to do what American commanders hate to do. But it was an order, and the commander of the Eighth Army in turn told those under him to cease all offensive operations, and go over instead to something called Operation Ratkiller. Van Fleet was stung when both his general and the President rebuked him for carrying out their orders. It appeared that the American people both demanded offensive operations and minimal casualties, or at least for the casualties to count. They wanted, in a word, final closure, final victory.

By the Spring of 1952 pressure to minimize U.S. casualties covered Korea like a great sense of guilt. The mothers back home were busy, writing their Congressmen about this senseless killing, asking why their children had been picked to go off to an unnecessary war while others stayed at home. And so the orders came down: no big operations, nothing bigger than company-size without the approval of higher headquarters.[61]

It was in this context that Operation Chopstick was planned in April 1952. On the assumption that Koreans should die before Americans in a war fought, presumably, for Koreans, someone had generated the idea of using an all-Korean force for a major attack. For administrative and logistical reasons it was called off, but the precedent of having Asians walk point, with Americans in the van, was set.

By September 1952 the word from the top was that we had done all possible, in the words of General Mark Clark, "without highly unpalatable personnel costs." Pressure from home was for no more blood-letting, no more false prophets, no more broken promises. Ugly little patches of earth still were being fought over, but by fewer men than before, and the strategy of "active defense" was irreversible.

Perhaps. A general was about to be elected. Maybe things would be different with a military man in the White House. And so once again the staff officers were ordered to come up with a plan, a really outstanding plan, to end the war. It had to be a plan convincing in every detail, something good enough for the ex-general to get his teeth into.

But when President-elect Eisenhower visited Korea that December it is not recorded just what he sank his teeth into. It is a matter of record, however, that he totally ignored General Clark* when "Ike" was offered a plan for a major offensive.[62]

The thirty-day acceptance of the demarcation line in late 1951 resulted in a *de facto* cease-fire, which lasted until October 1952. Knowing that the war was about to close, and understanding the inseparability of violence and political power, the Chinese assaulted friendly lines. Then, later the next March, they hurled their soldiers in a massive series of blows the next May, and struck one final time in July 1953 in order to provide themselves with better seats with which to view the signing of the cease-fire.

INTERJECTION

When the war ended apologies flowed. They fell into two classes. Democrats generally applauded President Truman's actions, and his stopping of aggression (or was it Agression?) They quoted approvingly the President's line, "We live in an age when hostilities begin without polite exchanges of diplomatic notes." Even his sleight-of-hand and the blurring, then blending, of contradictory goals was applauded.

Republicans generally thought that President Truman was right to go in as he did, although he could have been a little more considerate of Congress' feelings, and that Korea would never have happened had he and Secretary Acheson pursued a more aggressive foreign policy. Things worked out all right, though, because once again a Republican President bailed out a war-mired Democrat.

Thus, each side competed for approval rather than tell the people what both parties had done.

SCRUTIBLE AMERICA

A couple of weeks after MacArthur's firing, Senator Taft said that "Psychologically, no one will stand for it . . . the choice which this country has is between Acheson and MacArthur. That is the only issue."[63] He was quite right, save for his timing. For the statement could as easily have been made in 1945 or, for that matter, in 1965.

Long after leaving the office of the Presidency, Truman reminded us that "What a nation can do or must do begins with the willingness and the ability of its people to shoulder the burden." The people were willing, in the beginning. As for ability, that had to be scraped

*General Mark W. Clark replaced General Ridgway on May 12, 1952.

up and patched together and learned, as conditions permitted. Things went well, in the beginning, before contradictions surfaced, and before unrealistic promises generated unrealistic expectations.

One month before the eruption of hostilities in Korea a Gallup poll showed that most Americans expected war of some kind within five years. Thus, going into the Korean War the President had on his side the rising sense of danger within the public. Though not comparable to the atmosphere of those days just before Pearl Harbor, there was a sizable and manageable energy being built up. The slipshod manner in which we became aware of the breach of the parallel by the North Koreans did not compare with the bombing of Pearl Harbor. That was a major difference. Nevertheless, Mr. Truman had a lot going for him in June 1950.

Initial reaction to the President's decisions to commit our men to war was good,* and the people read with pride and approval of a tough old war horse from Vermont, one PFC Hun Toon, who at age fifty-two fought in his third war for America.[64]

But there were disturbing undercurrents. Within six months they would be undermining the pillars of public support. Before the year was over the entire structure would collapse.

On June 28 Acheson held a press conference to update the American people on the Korean crisis. He told his people that no U.S. action had been taken prior to the first meeting of the Security Council of June 25. "From then on," he concluded, "all action in Korea has been under the aegis of the UN." He underscored his conclusion, remarking, "That is a very important point."[65]

The next afternoon at his press conference, the President announced his release of air and naval units to MacArthur. Noting that he had received 1200 letters and telegrams, of which 90 percent favored his action, he then said, "We are not at war."

During the first year of combat in Korea, 21,300 Americans were killed, Public support was solid for most of the year. During the last two years of the war, 12,300 died,[66] and public support had dwindled long in advance of the final shots. The decline was inversely related to the popular conviction that a total victory was possible. There being no overall strategy either before or following the invasion of the south, President Truman tried to orchestrate and extemporize. On the battlefield he was more successful than he should have been, as weaponry and men were piled one atop the other in order first to

*By committing American forces the war became, existentially, a unilateral affair between the United States and Communist Korea.

slow, then to massacre the North Koreans. The dimension supplied by the intervention of the CCF field armies was simply too broad to go 'round, too thick to cut through. On the whole, he fared not too badly in combat.

At home, though, for several months it was denied that a strategy for public consumption was necessary, Secretary Acheson's repeated reminders that unanimity for what Truman was doing could not be expected to last, especially if there were serious reverses, were ignored. Nothing comparable to the careful planning which preceded the invasion of Inchon occurred on the domestic front, no systematic preparation of the people for the possible eventualities all those who stood at the center of power that summer understood. Given the flux of battle, the meaningless goals, and the hysterical language of *jihad,* the Yalu River soon became for us a coping stone. Thereafter, liberal opportunism was spiritually defunct.*

In 1950 a substantial number of our foreign correspondents were press veterans of World War II. Having left the worldview of that war behind them, some reporters cut their own independent path in war reporting, an independence that proved a constant irritation to the President. One week to the day after elements of the Twenty-fourth Infantry Division engaged and then withdraw before the enemy at Osan, Truman was complaining that the delaying action, a technical military action for troops in retrograde which trades space for time, was being falsely reported as a retreat by the American press. Making unverified and unverifiable statements about entire units being wiped out served only to create unjustified panic among our populace, a panic more widespread at home than among the riflemen who were trying to hold back the tide in Korea.

Still piqued, the President—in order to assuage Chiang—ordered MacArthur to Formosa for talks with the Kuomintang leader. Reporters immediately concluded that the President's policy of neutralizing the island had been rejected by MacArthur, who favored a more aggressive line.** When they got around to reading their papers that last day of July, Americans learned that a famous general with long years in the Orient thought his President too timid.

As far as the general was concerned, the rules of World War II continued in force, which meant not only must we fight to win, but

---

*Liberal apologists have long defended the notion that possession of the banks of the Yalu was unimportant. Strategically such defense would have presented problems. They would have been more than offset by increases in prestige abroad and moral capital at home.[67]

**In this the reporters were quite correct, as events were to show.

that we must fight as one people. To do so meant unity of purpose, which in its turn meant unity of attitude. It was with that in mind that he tried personally to issue official releases on the Korean fighting when August began.* During that month, as our casualties on occasion hit one thousand a day, as withdrawals became as predictable as the tides of the Yellow Sea, MacArthur became heavy-handed with the press. He had not learned that the world wars were behind him.

With Inchon and the smell of final victory permeating the Korean air, there was nothing but good news to be reported, and only good news was reported.

But with the debacle along the Yalu, and a genuine retreat on his hands, the general saw his strategy and his person under attack by those who a month or so earlier were hailing him as perhaps the greatest American military man of all time. In January 1951, while the howling masses of Chinese were lining up for the push that would throw the Americans into the sea, MacArthur came down with both heavy hands, and imposed World War II-type censorship —or rather, he tried to. The screams of Marguerrite Higgins and other reporters in the field reached Washington, and New York, almost immediately. The guiding document of World War II for censoring war reporting was discarded. Work was begun on a document which would incorporate and reflect the society's current values, and by year's end censorship was formally as much a thing of the past as it in practice had been for the war to date.

With the legality of interpretative, even impressionistic, reporting now established, the President lost one of the rudders for steering public opinion. After long years out of office he would reflect on the war years, and perhaps thinking of an earlier war tell us that "our means of communicating and consolidating public opinion—the press and the radio—emphasize the differences of opinion rather than agreements."[69] But the press did not create limited war.**

By the time Truman offered his *apologies* still another war would be on the horizon and the society would have taken on still newer values.

President Truman never forgave the press for their coverage of the events flowing from November-December 1950. The war had

*Though his headquarters in Tokyo denied it, many believed that he was responsible for the issuance of a news release for Korean morale purposes which held that U.S. troops would gradually participate in the fighting, with air power immediately available. This Korean-language statement was circulated the afternoon of June 27 (Korean time), many hours before Truman had authorized the use of naval and aircraft, while denying that ground troops would fight.[68]

**The decline of official attitude control is summarized in Chapter 7.

been turned around and inside out by the entry of the Chinese Communists. A reader or listener now followed not the churning of battle lines so much as the impact of the war on the domestic scene. MacArthur had told the chairman of the Joint Chiefs of Staff, General J. Lawton Collins, that the restrictions under which we were operating were the same as surrender. Given in private, the word was leaked, then sped across the ocean and into the living room. For the first time in our recent memory private citizens raised and answered questions of grand strategy. Some even talked of communists in our government.

Congressmen were demanding either a declaration of war or withdrawal of all forces from Korea, others saying we shouldn't have gone in in the first place. After the MacArthur hearings began, the public choice was between Acheson and the general, and Acheson was not the people's choice. The private and genuine choice was between Acheson and Acheson, for the disappointing, unsatisfying end now was irreversible.

The slow process of reaction, which had set in as the final days of 1950 were extracting their price on the frozen mountains of Korea, began an upward acceleration with the commencement of the peace talks in July of '51. This reaction, a tension stretching our people between the poles of total victory and total withdrawal, became taut as the election year of 1952 arrived.* Then a curious thing happened: the war became a non-war. Our people, feeling guilty perhaps over their economic well-being while there fighting was still going on, or perhaps seeking the semblance of finality, blocked out the war as an issue. Psychologically and spiritually the war had ended for the American, and had become merely a nuisance.

A nearly identical rejection took place on the other side of the world, where for what seemed an endless time soldiers learned to count days, learned to think of the war as futile and stupid, and the Army as futile and stupid, and the country as not much better. Toward the end, a medic would occasionally refuse to crawl up a hillside to render aid to someone who had been sent out "to let the Chinese know we're still here." Most soldiers started stacking arms six months before time to rotate out.

General Maxwell Taylor commented on the plunging morale in

*Desire by American voters for decisiveness in Korea, in whatever direction, doubled between January and November 1952, probably as a function of Ike's political commercials. At the same time about 70 percent of our people, the same number that supported Truman in the early days of the Korean War, did not really believe a settlement was likely.

May 1953, which applied as much to the folks at home as it did to the men of his command:

> Political objectives hold little appeal and are not highly evaluated generally by soldiers in battle positions, whereas a clearly defined physical objective constitutes a goal, attainment of which tends to hold promise of a cessation of conflict, physical hazards, and the other unpleasant facts of war.[70]

The citizen did not suffer physical hazards, nor "the other unpleasant facts of war." He did, however, suffer from "promise of a cessation of conflict."

Our President requires two sources of support in order to wage war under conditions of his, rather than the enemy's, choosing. He must have his countrymen behind him, and he also needs the backing of elected representatives. Mr. Truman had both in the beginning, neither in the end. And one was shaky from the outset.

When war broke in Korea the Republican Party had two distinct wings. Both groups generally applauded President Truman's action of sending our men into war, but there was an underlying conflict which, in terms of the outcome of the war, is best symbolized in the persons of Eisenhower and MacArthur. The latter group, clustering around Senator Taft, simultaneously advocated driving through for complete victory, and withdrawal from Korea. No slogans were loud enough to drown out the contradictory directions being given by the GOP during summer and autumn of 1950.[71]

The Republicans also were hostile to our allies in the UN, and the increase in their animus as the intensity of the war militated against the President's policies. When the piddling contributions of other nations became known, and when the Chinese fell upon our men, cries of "U.S. out of the UN, UN out of the U.S." were heard. The issue became, who runs the war?

At 10 A.M., on June 26, 1950, the President met with the chairman of the Senate Foreign Relations Committee. Truman asked Senator Tom Connally if he, as President, held sufficient authority to commit American forces without Congressional approval. Without undue reflection the Texas Senator made one of the most momentous decisions in our nation's history, when he gave the President his blessings. The power flowed to the President, Connally argued, both from his constitutional position as Commander-in-Chief and as a leader of one of the United Nations. It is not recorded if this jarring inconsistency was given much attention on that unseasonably warm morning.

Just before lunch the next day the President met with selected legislators. They were not asked for a joint declaration in support of his actions, as most had expected. President Truman and Secretary of State Acheson did not rush to tangle with Senator Taft. Thus, any discussion of the ultimate costs, and ultimate goals, of military intervention were side-stepped for the moment.

Before the meeting ended, the President solemnly pledged there was no plan to commit U.S. ground troops.*

On the same day, June 27, George F. Kennan took pains to tell some influential allies that the United States had no plans to occupy North Korea. Stressing the continuum of political and military affairs, which he continued to assume everyone accepted, he insisted that our intention was to localize—"contain"—the conflict. Elsewhere in Washington Secretary of Defense Louis Johnson reinforced the prevailing attitude of those looking on by saying that, in line with the President's statement earlier in the day, no American troops were to be used.

Overall Congressional reaction to Truman's decisions was one of fervor, with a few misgivings. The majority reacted very much the way their predecessors had at the news of Pearl Harbor, with tremendous excitement and shouts of approval. Others, knowing full well they had been ignored by the President, saw obligations get the better of rights, and voiced support while harboring grudges, knowing they were doing wrong.

Senator James P. Kem of Missouri immediately asked if this meant Truman had arrogated to himself the authority to declare war, thus asking what others wanted but were too fearful to ask. His question was answered, irrelevantly, by Senator Scott Lucas of Illinois, who ticked off the list of more than a hundred such interventions in the past. Senator Hubert H. Humphrey of Minnesota thought it might prove to be the greatest peacekeeping move of the twentieth century, though he did not elaborate.

Debate continued late into Tuesday night. The basic issue of warmaking was what counted, and everyone knew it. Citing precedent is beside the point in such questions as the fundamental divisions of government as set down in our Constitution. A few more Senators joined Kem in refusing to let the matter die. And of course it never did die, but instead bided its time.

*When ground troops were committed three days later the apparent inconsistency was explained by the logically correct argument that the statement "I have no plan to commit ground troops" is not the equivalent of "I promise not to commit ground troops." Few Congressmen were persuaded, thus displaying the limits of logic in time of war.

On Wednesday Senator Taft conceded, bitterly, that our treaty obligations to the UN had complicated the issue of constitutional warmaking. But Truman was behaving as if this confusion constituted justification. It did not, the Senator maintained, and the question of who had the right under the Constitution to make war demanded an answer. The President ignored that question as much as he did Congress. Unless he is stopped in his "complete usurpation," Taft brooded, Truman "will have terminated for all time the right of Congress to declare war." The expression "for all time" was not given proper play in the press, or in the minds of the citizens.

The same afternoon another Republican Senator, H. Alexander Smith of New Jersey, reopened the old wound by disagreeing with Taft, by saying there was no need for a declaration of war. Then he added that what he had said was so necessarily, since we would have no authority north of the Thirty-eighth Parallel; in this he was joined by Senator Connally. Even "China Bill" Knowland of California said no declaration was necessary. The rest of Senator Knowland's statement was ignored as approval for Truman's acts turned into demands for more, though his closing words constituted the issue which, next to Executive discretion, lay at dead center. Knowland insisted we should not be limited by any imaginary line such as the parallel.

Demands for more action and pleas from the Far East coalesced the night of June 29, and by the time the sun rose the next morning we had begun our descent into the bottomless pit of attrition warfare. Such concern as there was about committing American infantry turned more on the issue of United States versus United Nations sponsorship. A few words from the President to Senator Connally was all the assurance necessary, and the Friday morning meeting adjourned with the understanding the United States was involved together with the rest of the United Nations. The rush and noise of events pushed aside Nebraska's Senator Kenneth Wherry, along with the sole senatorial objection to Truman's most recent act of disregarding Congress. Even Senator Taft was caught up in the emotion. He said we had to go all out and win. There would be plenty of time to criticize the President later. Now the nation had a war on its hands. Win it, then blast the President—this was the GOP game plan.

This plan held up into August, while our forces were withdrawing into the Pusan pocket, and while plans were being made both to withdraw them and at the same time to rout the enemy by striking at his flank and rear through Inchon. Two issues arose during that month within Republican ranks, though, which would soon cause the game plan to be rewritten.

The day after President Truman committed American naval and air power to the Korean struggle, former President Herbert Hoover said the only way out was to win, and winning presupposes unity of purpose and action. Having said this, he made the prevailing GOP view explicit. This issue of the opposition party being obligated to do what was necessary to see a war through to the end was just below the surface, anchored by feelings of tradition and honor and patriotism.

A second issue, likewise purposely restrained in the early days of the war, was that of the alliance which presumably brought us into Korea. But before the first summer was over GOP leaders were asking why, if Korea was in fact a UN undertaking, there was no clear-cut statement of policy from the global body. The truth is most Republicans knew all along that the United Nations took a back seat, indeed, sat exactly where the United States asked it to sit. Some believed the fiction of a UN undertaking was a Truman-Acheson ploy whereby the issue of the executive versus the legislative branch *vis-à-vis* warmaking could be obscured beyond recovery. Despite the Republican National Chairman's statement in September that regardless of the Inchon landing, it was Acheson's policy that brought on the war, issues, like affairs on the battlefield, were held in check during the summer and fall of 1950.

Chinese infantry and MacArthur's dismissal removed the checks, and long-seething issues and feelings burst forth as the U.S. Army in the field was routed, and as the treatment of MacArthur became synonymous with "appeasement," "containment," "limited war."

By December 1950 Senator Wherry was no longer alone in demanding an accounting for sending American foot soldiers into battle. Truman's response was characteristic—to ask for more power and a declaration of national emergency. Wherry's answer was that such power was possible, but it had to be parceled out by the Congress, just as the Constitution said it should. Transparty unity now out of the question, the President said that many of the powers he had to have were necessarily discretionary. Truman couldn't have selected words better designed to infuriate the other side.

With the staggering reversals and the speculation about a cease-fire as a background, Christmas 1950 meant the end for the rhetoric of deliverance. So was broad Congressional support, though enough continued, stripped of all enthusiasm, as the summer of 1951 approached, along with the truce tents at Kaesong.

Shortly before the truce talks began, a few representatives on both sides of the aisle were saying that had the idea of committing US ground forces been debated in Congress, there might have been no such commitment. Still others, anticipating fifteen years and a resolution which gave Lyndon Johnson all he asked for, said that at the time they really didn't understand what the President had asked them to agree to.

UNLIMITED MORALITY FOR A LIMITED WAR

Moral issues during the Korean War centered around three surface phenomena: the relief and recall of General MacArthur, that faction of leaders (largely from the GOP) who demanded the war be fought "the American way," and the ravaging of a small nation and its people for putative moral reasons. These issues are related. In fact they are but three aspects of a single issue: the American trapped in a limited war.

After getting the news of his firing the General MacArthur filed Communique #850, his final report on the war. That was on April 11, 1951. The speeches and hearings which followed his ouster revealed old convictions and concepts, vented new feelings, and seared the nation's soul. But the men at the center of the controversy flailed at the air, and filled it with words of bitterness, and prevented the people from looking at the bottom of the pit we now found ourselves in. The Truman-MacArthur argument was not over the function of President and general, but the function of war; and what war is or ought to be; and what peace is or ought to be. Their clash was that of two irreconcilable symbols, symbols our nation was to use for its self-definition, in order to know its place in the world, in order to know its worth as a people.

In the end everyone lost. General MacArthur gave an election keynote address, then plummeted into obscurity, President Truman's party lost at the polls, and the American people were forced to look only at surface issues, and surface emotions.

A second moral issue was tied specifically to the issue of limited war, but here again the issue was muddled by the hysteria of the day. Following the MacArthur hearings the GOP issued a minority report, calling the war in Korea immoral and un-Christian. The schizophrenia that had characterized the Republicans from the outset of the war had become manifest.

Six days after MacArthur's relief, on April 17, 1951, there was a GOP resolution declaring war both on North Korea and on China. This was immediately followed by a motion calling on Truman to remove all our forces from Korea.[72] The party's anguish was much closer to that which the people were undergoing than the pragmatic considerations to which the Truman Administration addressed itself. The anguish centered on neither Christianity nor morality, but on underlying conceptions of peace and war. It was not immoral to kill, but only to kill without having some real estate and a broken enemy sword to show for it. The virulence with which containment and Dean Acheson were attacked can only be explained as a nation undergoing spiritual disillusion, a confusion compounded by the introduction of ethical issues into an amoral arena. Into that arena we sent negotiators with instructions not to discuss political questions, sent them to face people who literally were unable to distinguish military and political matters, whose conduct at the bargaining table was a perfect complement to their fluidity as against our position warfare on the battlefield.

Though given far less coverage than the first two issues, there arose in Korea the vague, almost undefinable problem of a tiny and very foreign country being overwhelmed by a nation there to render aid. Almost from the outset of the war Congressional critics pointed to the death and destruction of friendly people and land, and asked how long we could be regarded as saviors when we were ruining the people we set out to protect. Parts of Korea were fought over three and four times, each time grinding down the Korean people still more. As the war continued, and the casualties and the cost mounted and Korea's economy disappeared, a closer look was given to what we were paying for. A nation lay in waste. The leader was patently tyrannical. Even before the war, in March 1950, President Rhee—fearing loss of power—had postponed legislative elections and held them only when the United States threatened to cut off his flow of money. President Truman was appalled at Rhee's use of police powers to break up opposition political meetings and otherwise control the latter's enemies. In April 1951 the Korean president demanded thousands of guns for distribution to sympathetic youth groups throughout the country, the better to stay in power with. Both sides were over a barrel. Both sides knew this. In that tandem arrangement, we would by 1956 pump $83 billion into a land of sullen, alienated foreigners.

South Korea was a desperately poor country on the verge of annihilation, without democratic inclination or tradition. After dallying with representation, its government swung closer to reality, to a militarized bureaucracy.

Another portion of our legacy was a new vocabulary to describe an ally. In an incredible scheme to gather manpower our side once started a plan called Korean Augmentation to the U.S. Army—KATUSA. Illiterate Korean peasants were impressed, then doled out to American units. The mutual contempt which arose never has been forgotten, although our inability to be on intimate, working terms with utterly alien Orientals was.

Reflecting on the war, General William Dean, commander of the Twenty-fourth Infantry Division until his capture at Taejon, recommended that an American soldier never again fight for something he didn't or couldn't understand.[73] His recommendation was still under study when the United States Army went, 549,000 strong, into still another impoverished and alien Oriental country.

CLOSURE

After the shooting ended in Korea, what our nation so desperately needed was a careful examination of those three years. What was needed was a critical self-analysis on every level—social, economic, political, military. What were the implications of future wars for economic discomfort, of the fact that the draft was seen by a growing number at war's end as an obligation to find an excuse for not going, of military alliances, of the national leaders' innermost convictions about the nature of war and peace, of the military's ability to anticipate rather than react? Most important, we needed to ask ourselves about the spiritual cost to a nation that unattainable goals in time of war take from that nation.

Had we looked at the cost of pursuing the liberal vision, we might have changed our minds.

Instead, we changed Presidents.

IV INTERREGNUM

> But the principal failing occurred in the sailing,
>   And the Bellman, perplexed and distressed,
> Said he *had* hoped at least, when the wind blew due
> East the ship would *not* travel due West!
>   —Lewis Carroll

HISTORY IN THE REMAKING

Pushing and elbowing its way into the crowd of platitudes, "Peace Progress, and Prosperity" finally gained the position it deserved. By that date we were half way through the new administration. Times were pretty good. If the nation languished now and then at least Korea and the killing were far behind us. In fact, Korea no longer existed.

Occasionally a voice, muffled the way academicians voices were muffled during those days, would try to get someone's attention, try to resuscitate memories of the horrors of stalemated war, in the hope of rousing the American for his next predictable, required war. It was not just a matter of clarifying an issue in which a handful of experts have an interest. The distinction between foreign and domestic afiairs had long since passed, pushed from the world while the fetid Korean wind lashed the truce tents at Kaesong and Panmunjom.

So a call for leadership in something called "the urgent process of public education"[1] went out and, finding no listeners, grew bored and withdrew. And Korea entered the kingdom of myth.

General Marshall identified the way Americans choose to become manifest during time of war when, in December 1950, our soldiers were being crushed between two CCF field armies. We rush, he says, "from pessimism to jubilant optimism, or the reverse, over the results of a single campaign. . ."[2] During World War II, and the North African battle he was describing that day in late 1950, a sure and fiery conclusion to the world war already had been promised us. So, we could be permitted our tantrums.

Times changed, as did our enemies. Against the Communists in Korea the general asked us to be cold, calm, and calculating, not realizing the only thing we would calculate was the time required to end the war and its agonies.

After the "I will go to Korea" speech, and the election, Truman took note of the leap in national expectations, and with no effort being made to mask his feelings remarked so that Eisenhower could hear. The general "must have known that by making this statement he was leading the American people to believe that the day after he became President he would bring them peace in Korea."[3]

It took about six months to end the Korean War (though seventeen years later United States servicemen would occasionally still be killed in action there).[4] Shortly after the cease-fire it was evicted from the public consciousness. Afterwards the minority interested in Korea talked to only each other, as explanations of what had occurred fused with competing justifications for what had been done, and with what had been done. Some mildly applauded the President's charge that Secretary Acheson's speech of January 1950 about America's defensive perimeter in the Pacific had not been "gratuitous." A few members of both parties praised Generals Bradley and Vandenberg for their support of the shifting UN goals in Korea. Occasionally a truthful if sarcastic political theorist would ridicule what had passed for a collective security action, pointing out that member nations, for the most part, wished us well and sent along nurses or medical supplies.[5]

The barest vocal minority, speaking for the large though silent majority, sided with Generals Clark and Van Fleet and their "shoot the works for victory" view.[6] Thus was formed within the military the "Never Again" club, as high-ranking soldiers and an awful lot of civilians thought that victory had been denied us needlessly in Korea.

"The nature of the war itself had to be clearly understood if we were to attack intelligently the problem of bringing it to an honorable end"[7] was the way President Eisenhower put it. But "the nature of the war itself" was not some solid thing to be tagged. Instead it was a fluid series of forced decisions and brave acts, of perfidies and egos, illegal promises and dashed public hopes. The fundamental problem the President or anyone else would have in baring that war's essence was that the war had none.

Apologists for Truman saw our response on the Korean peninsula as the skillful application of NSC–68, that secret policy paper of early 1950. According to this school, policy-planners had decided well in advance of hostilities not only what would be done in Korea, but what acts would not be committed.[8] Senator Taft called this nonsense, claiming that the Truman Administration's violent response repudiated prior policies, policies which made us stumble and bungle our way into the war.[9] President Truman's soaring rhetoric, following the smashing success at Inchon, served only to flatter our people into thinking that we were doing God's work in Korea. His speech in San Francisco in mid-October 1950, the warm banalities there let loose ("The only victory we seek is the victory of peace"),[10] could have only riveted our eyes on the starry expanses above. As a result, "the true nature of the war" vanished.

To have done his self-proclaimed job of public education would have required we be informed of the bitter divisions within our government during that first summer of the war. It would have meant exhuming the critical decision to go north of the Thirty-eighth Parallel, a critical look at those in support of the move (such as Dean Rusk) as well as those violently opposed (such as George F. Kennan). It would have also meant a new appraisal of Korea's President Rhee, who said in mid-July he was crossing no matter what the United States did, of the unconditional directive sent MacArthur by the Joint Chiefs of Staff on September 27 ordering the destruction of all North Korean forces, of the general's bending of a strictly conditional order which specified those factors which would justify his driving north, and of the JCS decision following the Chinese invasion that their September 27 ruling was up for reappraisal.[11] A new appraisal would have meant, in effect, a jaundiced look at the goals we sent our soldiers out to secure, and the means chosen to secure them. It would have meant reassessing Eishenhower's early and vigorous support for Truman's decisions of June 25–30, 1950, along with the deception and ignoring of the Congress whose approval those decisions required; of the perfunctory role of the United Nations in all vital aspects of the Korean issue; and the impossibility of forcing a decision on the battlefield following the 1952 elections.

On June 2, 1952, General Mark W. Clark investigated the feasibility of acquiring two huge artillery pieces, guns with bores of 280mm. If available, they would help offset enemy artillery firepower. If available with special ammunition, they would help vaporize the enemy, for the guns had a nuclear capability. They were not ready until the end of the year, about the time of General Clark's discussion with the President-elect, while the "I will go to Korea" promise was being kept.

Actually, only part of that promise was kept, for the trip by a former general very clearly raised our expectation for a quick, decisive end to the war. It turned out after he got into office that there was no usable source of power available which would allow Eisenhower to escalate it any faster than Truman would have, had he been reelected. But the gigantic guns gave the appearance of power, and in the early Spring of 1953 complementary atomic weapons were installed on Okinawa. Then, according to official history, the U.S.-Communist go-between, India, was asked time and again to transmit our hostile intent to the Chinese Communists. The message having stuck, so thte story goes, the Chinese began to negotiate in good faith, the war ended, and at long last we had closure and finality.

The true story probably is lost forever. Prime Minister Nehru of India later said he remembered no such conversation with the Americans about the possible use of nuclear weapons in Korea and, in any event, he said he never would have sent such a message to Pannikar, his ambassador to the People's Republic of China.[12]

Eisenhower was able simultaneously to promise disengagement from Asia, the reunification of Korea, and the unleashing of Chiang and his Nationalist Chinese to storm the mainland. Such promises were possible because he was talking to Americans who had been promised the unattainable, by the man Eisenhower succeeded as President.

In the years since that election Korea was relegated first to the plateau of has-been, then to the valley of never-been. When Acheson later said that this repugnant type of war is the only kind we or anyone else can afford, a pro-Eisenhower writer bristled momentarily, then dismissed the remark by recalling the former Secretary's history of bad faith, and remarking that we must expect him to still be without the language of statesmanship.[13]

GOODBYE, KOREA, HELLO, DOW-JONES

The war was over for real, and we were free to burrow as deeply into domestic affairs as we chose. This established American custom was a long-awaited antidote to the years of having our nerves exposed. At our request, the balm was applied by our President and by the aura generated by a very good human being who, according to one of the seers of the advertising world, permitted himself to be sold as if he were a tube of toothpaste.[14]

Two years into office Eisenhower made sure the door to the recent past stayed bolted when he consoled us, retelling the story of how the useless Korean fighting had been stopped, of how through his effort realism had replaced the effeminate wishful thinking of bygone years, of our word being our bond around the globe. Most of all he was pleased with the freshness and candor of his cabinet, an honesty which insured the development of a new and hardy concert of nations to replace the flabbiness of the past.[15] "The traditional use of masses of troops is gone forever."[16] This truth, above all else, precluded our looking back. Or wanting to.

The image inherited from the Truman years had to be changed, along with the helter-skelter defense planning which had kept public sentiment on a roller coaster. On the very day Truman was to leave office his officials had recommended programs which, if approved, would have increased the already swollen budgetary deficit to $44 billion in just five years. That sort of reflex action, and the public mentality it fostered, had to go. It had to be replaced with the realism of, among other things, good business sense. With this in mind the new President announced just two months after taking office that his Secretary of the Treasury, George Humphrey, would henceforth attend the meetings of the NSC. The soothing effect the announcement had seemed justified, for defense is only a means to an end, and that end is the protection of the nation as a whole, and that requires military and economic considerations remain in their natural tandem.[17]

Therefore, we came to believe we could comfortably ask that four promises be fulfilled simultaneously. Two were negative, two positive. First, we asked that Koreas never occur again and, sensing that this already had been granted, asked that our taxes not pinch. Then we asked that the promise of the liberation of those under the heels of the Russians be kept, and, with that in mind, asked that our national will be spread around the world while, and in fact as a result of, each citizen pursued his own self-interest.

President Eisenhower's fundamental break with the practices of the past amounted to planning a long-haul struggle with the Soviet Union, fixing as our greatest source of strength a vast industrial and technological base rather than towering stockpiles of weapons and the like which, in any case, soon go out of style. It was this redirecting of national attention away from periodic crises which created a genuine spirit of confidence among his people. "Spirit of confidence" is not entirely accurate, for the paternalism radiating from the nation's capital through the rhetoric of "rugged individualism" carried an implied directive that we leave our destiny in the hands of those who know and care. And the one who cared greatly and knew the most had conducted the greatest crusade in our world's history. Thus, to question was to doubt, and to doubt was to revert to that timidity of the past which the general had so justly criticized during his campaign.

The sole issue was defense against outside attack, which meant an air-atomic assault launched by the Soviet Union. This problem leads to a dilemma which, Secretary George Humphrey candidly insisted, "simply means two problems at the same time." Even as he was constructing new rules of language the Secretary urged us to put first things first. And the very first thing was achieving a sound currency. Then, in their natural order, the solutions would follow.[18] Eschew as well those who doubt that our economy is the first line of defense: "no other purpose is worthy of us at this time in history, and no other purpose—material or selfish or partisan—guides this government."[19]

Secretary Humphrey spoke those words early and late in 1953. Our eyes remained glued on job and market indicators, and on the still overheated economy.

The bonds he issued were of the thirty-year, 3.25 percent variety. They did what Humphrey intended them to do, and money that otherwise would have gone into corporate stocks and mortgages was immediately mopped up. What he did not intend then followed. As the heat of inflation lofted upwards, the recession became more entrenched than ever.[20]

"If you can win a big one, you can certainly win a little one." It was one of those phrases George Humphrey excelled at constructing, then lending to his President. It was, in addition, self-evident.

In 1955, before the National Canners Association in Chicago, Humphrey conducted one of the most imaginative question-and-answer periods of the Eisenhower Administration. To offset some of the flak from commentators and other partisans, he used the occasion before the canners to ask himself pointed questions, which were then treated with adroitness. There really was but one question, which had been asked him a dozen times before. "Why has this Administration cut so much from the defense budget?" The answer was to be found in the proper construction to be placed upon "cutting" and "defense." Irrelevancies alone were being "cut," with the result that the nation is far better off than it was at the outbreak of the Korean War. Cut, too, is the old concept of fighting wars with masses of men.[21] The audience was preoccupied with other matters. Cans.

"The Marines," Secretary of Defense Charles E. Wilson pleaded, "not only want the $46 million we are withholding from them. "They also want the full strength authorized for them by Congress." Reflecting upon his long military experience, and reminding his defense chief of the ever-present luxuries tucked away inside all things military, President Eisenhower remained aloof and unmoved. In the wake of the Geneva Big Four meeting he then ordered Wilson to trim again, then again, and to reduce his and all departmental budgets by not 5 but 8 percent in that summer of 1955.[22]

By the time of this last reduction, just as the first balanced budget since his promises of Peoria and 1952 came into view, we were able to congratulate the President and ourselves, on the fact that since he had come to power Americans had increased the total number of cars and trucks by ten million. The conclusive proof was that we were then in position, were we of such mind, to line up our trucks and cars and busses on a road, leave a living space of only 700 feet between vehicles, and stretch that road from coast to coast. Highways equivalent to six sidewalks to the moon were planned.[23]

In the mid-1950s it was common for most folks to hug the middle of the road.

THE RECYCLING OF INDIFFERENCE

During his campaign for the Presidency, Eisenhower's public presented an unprecedented problem for the campaign directors. The stirring and name-calling at home, and the blood-letting in Korea forged a public opinion which clearly opposed Truman's policies and, therefore, demanded decisiveness. Simultaneous with this there were the muddled demands that we neither incur huge casualty loads (which a decisive offenisve would have required), nor could we accept defeat (which a decisive withdrawal from Korea would have meant).

On a still broader scale the logic of special pleading issued a general get tough, fie-on-Acheson demand. This was to be accomplished just while the mandated retrenchment was underway.

The contradictions were resolved by passing to a higher level of being, and campaign strategy. What our people asked was that a stop be put to the undulating crises which stretched back over a full decade, and it is in the bright light of this demand that the resolution of conflicting impulses must be judged. By focusing our attention upon, and by the unlimited investing of hope in, the honest soldier who asked us to bring our troubles unto him, the surface contradictions were overcome, or just vanished. What was being asked of the new leader was far more than extraction from a futile, immoral war. The subterranean plea was for him to present to us a stable, sensible world. And in his person we saw just such a promise embodied.

That promise was certainly kept. Cheered on to his second victory, Eisenhower could take comfort in the healthy stability of the 1950s.[24]

By the time of the second election the self-assurance and self-satisfaction the Administration urged had indirectly layed the foundation for the moral acceptance by the people of the President's "long-haul" plan, not regarding military expenditure but with respect to the strategic-political position our country was generating for itself.[25] Those who had won by slaying the containment dragon now revived it.*

But the center of containment strategy had always been the conviction that war, should it be forced upon us, most not be permitted to direct its own virulence, for force in itself is the antithesis of reason. Consequently, war has to be controlled, which is to say, limited. And force is worthless without the resolve to use it if need be. The problem was, the promise of peace everlasting was the result of a larger promise—that is, the promise of, with just provocation, destroying the enemy.

The two promises stood in separate compartments of the public mind, held apart by the overarching need for a world without worries, but a world in which America could nevertheless be self-assertive when it pleased her.

The compartments and their contents collided more than once,

*It was given a different name, viz., the "long-haul" concept.

the most disconcerting crash coming in early 1955 with passage of the "Formosa Resolution." President Eisenhower's accumulation of plenary powers at the expense of Congress was an issue that went largely unnoticed.

A month later, in March 1955, the Chinese Communists were again weighing their options. Now accepting advice long thought obsolete, President Eisenhower and Secretary of State John Foster Dulles announced something called "graduated deterrence" through tactical atomic weapons. Public sentiment aroused, the apologists were busy again. For example, "we know now that the administration's policy was 'new' only to the extent that the administration's critics had misconstrued U.S. strategy."[26]

A general uneasiness seated itself alongside the citizen for about one year, during which time the Orient lost some of its explosive force, and Chairman Khrushchev delivered his policy on coexistence as he stood before the Twentieth Congress of his nation's most prominent party.

Then Sputnik was launched on October 4, 1957.

A SECRET OF THE HEART

John Foster Dulles had spent a lifetime preparing for his position as Secretary of State. During the years of study and work he had come to the conclusion that all obligations are, at bottom, moral obligations; all lasting power is fundamentally moral; all national missions, too, in the end, are moral.

After assuming his post Secretary Dulles added a corollary premise, one which compressed all the earlier wisdom into an aphorism: "Moral strength in a free nation could be sustained only with a public understanding of America's mission in the world."[27]

In 1952 the only understanding desired by the public amounted to an assurance the future would be unruffled. Broad strategic issues such as those pulled to the surface by containment's floundering in Korea were not marketable items, for with the election of the new President the people had issued a mandate to oppose evil if necessary, but do so quietly and at a distance. Optimistic preachments were to replace war, preparation for war, fear of war, and all thought of war. As a result, Secretary Dulles, intentionally or otherwise, had seen to it from the very beginning that the conclusions he wished derived from that premise of a morally astute, understanding public would end up confused. In a word, we did not seek nor would we accept if offered an understanding of America's mission in the world. Nor its consequences.

Then there was that other matter. By the time of the Formosa

Resolution our cosmic mission, and the language used to express it, had been shelved.* The silent but italicized admission that this was and perhaps always had been the national doctrine was made following the joyous rape of Budapest by Soviet social reformers in late 1956. Consequently, a full, perhaps forced explanation of what we intended to do and the means at our disposal for doing it would have meant painful instructions being force-fed to a squirming, uncooperative patient who couldn't have kept it down anyway.

That is not even to mention the required reawakening and reliving of the Korean experience.

Shortly after the Hungarian uprising in 1956, Secretary Dulles was positively puzzled first at the abysmal level of his public's comprehension of foreign affairs, and secondly at the low ebb to which his public relations had sunk.[28] Clearly he had done his best to remain cognizant of how the average citizen felt; this he did by checking editorials and articles in a hundred daily newspapers. The despised Acheson may not have been totally wrong, Dulles mused, concluding that the job required that decisions be made in advance of firm public opinion. In any case, "often such decisions have to be based on circumstances so complicated it's next to impossible for the majority of our people to understand them."[29]

Dulles reread Kennan's "long telegram."

"Does public opinion feel that it has a right to be told how many atomic bombs have been produced by the Atomic Energy Commission?"[30] The man posing the question thought it was ridiculous, but in the process of raising the issue probed it was not at all silly. It was, in fact, a reopening of that fissure of essential secrecy stored at the heart of containment; a theoretical requirement had become, in turn, a political handicap and an existential impossibility. The AEC example above had been chosen for its manifest absence from a public's "right to know." In so doing the writer-apologist was able to convince himself there was no wider issue at stake. That there was something more fundamental at issue could have even then been testified to by Mr. Truman. After three more Presidents and another war most any preschooler would, after stating his views on the morality of American foreign affairs, be able—even eager—to articulate the problem of secrecy in government.

Opposed to big government by nature and training, Eisenhower got through eight years of the Presidency without having to relin-

*One could probably date the emerging of brutal reality from the attempted revolt in East Germany in late 1953, its disillusioned German patriots, and our demonstrable inability to do anything about it.

quish a single power of his office.[31] Of truly decisive importance was the manner in which he was able to add to the momentum which had first been given direction by FDR during the Great Depression and World War II, and which had then been largely retained and redirected by Truman to fuel our side of the Cold War. This unhealthy trend had been under attack for two decades when Eisenhower took office.* To the amazement of no one the general accelerated the trend.

One increment was added by President Eisenhower in a letter to his Secretary of Defense during the McCarthy-Army hearings. Using Achesonian language, stressing the need for efficient and effective administration, President Eisenhower told Secretary Wilson to order the latter's employees to keep quiet about matters in the Executive branch. This directive aimed to put a lid on the McCarthy hearings. But its long-haul effect was to establish another precedent for invoking Executive secrecy.[32]

The containment policy of the Truman years was largely neutralized by the 1952 elections, then slowly regained its ascendancy. Its recuperative cycle was cut even shorter than might have been expected. A principal reason for this was explained by Mr. Dulles in late January 1959, just three months before his death: "there are two ways in which the United States can assume international engagements. One is by treaty process, the other is acting pursuant to legislative authority which has been granted by Congress."[33] And the Executive is not willing to go beyond what has been granted by Congress. The idea is and has always been to make a request, spend or do as has been permitted by the Congress, then return for more if such is required. President Truman had failed to hew to this principle.

"All must agree that [the Formosa Resolution] is a broad grant of authority that would make a declaration of war unnecessary in case of Communist aggression."[34] On the one hand, as the President explained when another Formosa crisis erupted in September 1958, that resolution was permissive not mandatory. Neither it nor even the backing of both houses of Congress could bind his hands, since these might not apply to absolute advance commitments, nor could

*As mentioned in Chapter 2, a GOP phalanx issued an open invitation to Truman to battle over the alleged misuse of secrecy boards and government classifications. The emerging liberal press enlisted in these rightist ranks during the Korean War when Truman's Executive Order 10290 of September 24, 1951, centralized still more control over security information. It also radically extended the number of agencies and departments authorized to classify documents, withhold information and so forth. Eisenhower's Executive Order 10501, November 5, 1953, consolidated the gains for the Presidency even as it protected security information.

they cover every contingency. And, on the other hand, what was required in these times was to let the President use his judgment "according to the circumstances of the time."[35] And yet, he now had both feet sliding across the ice floe of containment. Quemoy and Matsu? "In modern war there might not be time for orderly procedures."

O! Dean Acheson, Where Is Thy Sting?

Detecting containment's nature more by scent than through reason there began among our people very early in the Eisenhower era rumblings of incredulity. It was not the specific disbelief concerning specific issues already noted during the Truman period—not the conviction the President was not telling all about our purpose in Korea, for example. Instead, there was heard the faintest murmurings of disbelief in general. In time the very short psychological step from disbelief to distrust was sure to be taken.

The proximate cause was the omnipresence of foreign affairs, the more distant and important causes being our habituation to receiving contrived if comforting answers to all problems foreign and domestic from FDR onward; and the slow, calculated and irreversible tipping of the scales in the direction of concretized yet limitless individual "rights." Neither was amenable to human control.

In his first State of the Union speech President Eisenhower hammered at the theme of the inseparability of Korea and the French agony in Indochina. Eight months later, in September 1953, Secretary Dulles reaffirmed the integral connection of those areas, thereby doing his honest best to educate his people both factually and morally. The President later admitted he and Dulles had failed in their mission. The "official character of governmental declarations," he agreed sadly, simply doesn't guarantee their penetration to all the people to whom they mean most.[36]

Against the rising waves of disbelief the President and his people in government were faced with what he himself saw as a genuine necessity: to assure every American (not to mention the people living in Indochina) of "the true meaning of the war." Committing the same errors of intertwining national self-interest with defense of the eternal as FDR had done (when such was fraudulent if harmless), and as Truman had done (when it was just as illicit but thoroughly harmful), and as John F. Kennedy and Lyndon B. Johnson would do (when such folly had become fatal), Eisenhower set out on his impossible course.

That particular journey ended abruptly, with the decision not to relieve Dien Bien Phu. Some Air Force technicians had been sent in February 1954, and detailed plans had been made for joint intervention by the United States, Britain, the ANZUS, and some Asian nations.* The reasons for nonintervention are many, one of which being the irremovable thorn in the side of containment: discretion by the President to slide into war, initially on condition there be no ground troops committed.[37] Wisely, the President refused.

After-the-fact explanations were a requirement of the time, and of the theory which guided those times. One of the President's chief desires was to secure from the Congress specific authorizations and monies and, as he put it, "return and ask for more if needed." That was, in principle and in fact, an impossibility. As he himself admitted modern war did not give the nation and her leader time to conform to Constitutional niceties.**

The ugly but unmovable facts of life were evident following the Caracas Resolution of March 1954, when, in order not to do something "contrary to the letter and spirit"[38] of the resolution we had sponsored in Caracas, we supplied two P-51 Mustang aircraft to an unidentified country, in order that that country could supply Guatemala, in order that Guatemala could suppress a bothersome insurgency.

Similarly, on April 24, 1957 the President declared Jordan's independence vital to our national interest and deployed our Sixth Fleet. A year or so later he ordered the Sixth Fleet to again steam east, and authorized the chairman of the Joint Chiefs of Staff to use "*whatever* force necessary"*** to keep Iraq from kicking over Kuwait.[39] During that same summer of 1958, using the same Middle East Resolution passed a year earlier, the Second Marine Regiment alternately terrified and irritated Lebanese bathers as the Marines walked through the warm surf and onto the beach. Ultimately, after alerting two Army battle groups in Germany and the 101st Airborne and Second Marines in the States, just under 15,000 troops made what the press called a "garrison move" into Lebanon.[40]

Fortunately for the future both of joint resolutions and the Presi-

*Likening the handful of troops the other powers would send into Indochina with the Korean affair, Eisenhower says a coalition nevertheless would "lend real moral standing to a venture that otherwise could be made to appear as a brutal example of imperialism." This admission was, of course, not at all what our people had been led to believe united fronts are about.

**For the President's views on the Executive and the Congress as regards war powers, see Eisenhower's press conferences for March 10, 17 and 24, 1954; and April 4, 1956. In these briefings he tended to downgrade the latitude his office required in order to handle foreign affairs adequately.

***General Eisenhower's italics.

dent's place in history, the Iman of Oman and the Sultanate of Muscat did not involve us in war, and by the fourth week of October 1958, all our soldiers had packed up and left.

HOLY WAR, AMBIVALENTLY: I

The heated breath of retribution lent its force to the campaign from the outset. Eisenhower had assured the voters that, if he were elected, Eastern Europe would be liberated. That mission, he said, had been taken up into and now formed a part of our national being: "The American conscience can never know peace until these people are restored again to be masters of their own fate."[41]

In October, the related question of Korea directed itself, he said, "to simple reason." The questions ended with the one drawn from the hearts of his people: "Is there an end?" The general's person radiated affirmation and optimism as, the words "I shall go to Korea" fell from his lips. His concluding line gave us a glance of the fiery side of the man and his administration as he asked us to rise: "In this spirit—humble servants of a proud ideal—we do soberly say: This is a crusade."[42]

That side—the servant of the everlasting—fought an eight-year struggle with another profile, one of prudence, utility, amorality. In the end the latter won, though without gaining a single concession from his partner.

One reason for the reluctance is that any direct admission would have meant abandoning the language and images which had come to mean so much, without meaning anything at all. Neither the speaker nor the listener could have adjusted to such colorless dialogue. By unanimous consent, then, we asked and he gave us what we both wanted and needed. The President's inaugural address was just what parties had in mind: "forces of good and evil are massed and armed and opposed as rarely before in history . . . freedom is pitted against slavery, lightness against the dark."[43]

More. We are told by his first Air Force Secretary that both before and after the inauguration Eisenhower spoke his ideal of an enforced peace, and of a new kind of war. It would be declared, total war, though not upon any human enemy "but upon the brute forces of poverty and need."[44] Before the vision could be realized, before all the "energies, the resources, and the imaginations of all peaceful nations" could be harnessed, the enemy across the borders had to be dealt with.

Principles for the remaking of the world into an acceptable moral affair had been set down by Secretary of State Dulles almost three years before President Eisenhower's inauguration.[45] Principles, to be intelligible and workable, have to hang together in such a way as to form a consistent, rational structure. This meant, as the President put it in his inaugural address, "a coherent global policy—one which did not put Asia first or Europe first or write off countries just because they were captive." And the urge for global symmetry was not aesthetic but thoroughly realistic: "As the Communist offense was one and global, the Free World's defense must be one and global." The trouble with his predecessors was their acceptance of the Cold War as a temporary truce. A promise was thus made to end the truce.

An observer might have pointed out that were all the stated objectives secured—peace and democratic elections throughout all of Korea, a total stop put to Communist China's fanning of the Indochinese and Malayan insurgencies, and "full independence of the Eastern European nations"[46] plus the continuous safeguarding of peace and the final destruction of poverty and need wherever these might be found—the list might require a lifting of the two-term Presidential limit law. What is more likely is that it would have committed us to perpetual war.

After listening to some of his public utterances it is hard to believe that Eisenhower was at heart conciliatory, but he was. This characteristic more than any other had secured for him the position as supreme allied commander in Europe. His handling of seemingly irreconcilable personalities from a dozen nations during the war years marked him as one for whom "compromise" is not something taken from Satan's lexicon. Hardly the same could be said for John Foster Dulles.

Throughout the campaign of 1952 Dulles had attacked containment as "negative, immoral, and futile."* Above all else, that doctrine was the acceptance of institutionalized evil as a permanent fixture of the world. He saw, as many before and since have seen, the Americans as a fundamentally ethical people who are true to their nature only to the degree to which they are practicing what they preach, and are exporting it around the globe, consistent with their implied moral mission. Digressions into sloth result from shabby, unprincipled leadership. He was now a part of the nation's leadership, and accepted the obligation not with glee but with pious resignation.

The best chronicler of the Eisenhower era sums up Secretary Dulles this way:

*Secretary Dulles' valuable assistance in helping the Truman administration conclude a peace treaty with Japan in 1951 was not overemphasized.

He was, in effect, the prosecutor assigned to the historic labor of arraignment, condemnation, and punishment of the Soviet Union for crimes against freedom and peace. Serving this solemn commission, how could he be less than morally outraged and politically uncompromising in his appeal of "liberation" of East European nations . . . And how could one "negotiate" some mitigation of the basic indictment . . . with a defendant allowed to go unpunished for such offense?[47]

Intellectual fabric and moral stiffening having been supplied, a net was cast upon all the seas of the world, its purpose being to save those who would stand with us. The result was the spiritualization of events set into motion in 1947 by the Truman Administration but, as President Eisenhower rushed to point out, the Truman Doctrine was not a part of a permanent network of defensive alliances "such as Foster visualized. As a result, during my administration, NATO was extended . . . SEATO was established, and CENTRO . . . was created." The final strands of the net were bilateral arrangments with Japan, Korea, and Formosa: "these treaties committed the United States to support the defense of almost every free area that was directly facing the Sino-Soviet complex."[48]

Fortunately, the words didn't mean what they said.

The opposition, principally apologists for the Truman years, delighted at the unraveling of the divergent strands of thought which constituted our foreign policy. Dulles' categorical statements of unalterable if unobtainable ideals were, for reasons never made clear, labeled "the new isolationism." His policies were a faithful continuation of Truman's Asian containment. But President Eisenhower just listened to and never implemented his Secretary's preachments.[49] Even in their condemnation and ridicule of the Secretary of State, critics revealed not only envy but ambivalence.

HOLY WAR, AMBIVALENTLY: II

Admiral Arthur W. Radford eventually became chairman of the Joint Chiefs of Staff. Many critics charged that the admiral was picked because his views concerning the value of strategic bombing were compatible with Eisenhower's, although Radford, earlier in his career, had been opposed to strategic bombing.[50]

One of the first tasks handed Admiral Radford and his staff was to examine our current might, then to project U.S. military needs for the next four years.

Simultaneous with this study another was being conducted, sponsored by the State Department.[51] There appeared to be three basic politico-military strategies open: a continuation of Truman's containment, deterrence through fear of nuclear annihilation, and the subversion and eventual liberation of the world's captive nations.*

The JCS study concluded we were overextended and, in the "never again" language of the day, argued that places such as Korea and Germany ought to be fought for on the ground only by citizens of those respective countries. If we were to be forced to go in it should be through American sea and air power. Also, and again in light of the barely ended Korean experience, these top soldiers wanted the President to give assurance that the JCS would be allowed to use nuclear weapons in future wars, should that seem to be militarily advantageous. In 1954 the President agreed to the request for freedom to hurl atomic missiles, spelling it out in NSC162/2.[52]

The study group which had gone in search of an overall strategy did so against the backdrop of another policy planning paper. This paper was one of the last holdovers from the Truman era, and amounted to an estimate of that point in the future when Soviet capability would coincide with Soviet desire to wage war. The year plucked from the hat was 1954, and with this date in mind the paper had recommended our systematic accumulation of weaponry and men sufficient to at least blunt the Communist attack when it came.

The Truman proposal had two flaws. First, the cyclonic changes which were even then being felt within the world of weapon technology could be guaranteed to make any gun or missile obsolete before it ever reached the stockpile. Therefore (or secondly), that recommendation could be counted on to knock the props from under a peacetime economy. Therefore, something new had to be tried.

There was one other factor which pushed in the direction chosen as the final string of defense decisions. Pressure was put on everyone concerned to reduce government expenditures. The JCS, far from being an exception, were a prime example (or, as some have remarked, were made an example of). In their 1953 study on our defense needs the military chiefs, seeing the money arriving ever more slowly, said that President Eisenhower had to make a basic policy decision as to the kind of future wars we would fight. Only if were they privy to that judgment could they tighten their military belt more.[52]

*In commenting on the eventual compromise as being inconsistent blending of containment practices and the language of incineration, it is often overlooked that Eisenhower in fact retained and pushed all three options, though very unevenly. He deployed a Special Forces Group, stuffed to the brim with ex-East European refugees, to Bad Tolz, Germany, a few months into office. He also soon had something working in Indochina. See below, pp. 138–139.

Assuming that the JCS paper exerted influence in the big decision there were, in total, three strains of conviction which forced the President to opt as he did. In addition to his Joint Chiefs (and the pervasive view throughout the services that future Koreas must be avoided), there were the major influences of his two principal Secretaries. The repeated advice and admonishment of Secretary of the Treasury Humphrey, and the implicit assumption that war and peace are never to be engaged in simultaneously, already have been recited. This second member of the trilogy was without question very powerful in influencing the Chief Executive,* and the interests he followed along with the image he helped create certainly altered the psychological climate sufficiently to permit the rapid shift in the public mind from defense to domestic priorities.

The third force, and a very strong one it was, was the combination of public utterances and private convictions that there had to be a clean break with the past and its morally decadent containment policies. Any pain resulting from the break would be worth it, as expiation usually is.

The spiritual cleansing accompanying this rejection of a policy, which was based upon shifting and indeterminate goals, would, in harmony with the mood of the Joint Chiefs of Staff and the fiscal soundness of Secretary Humphrey, permit our people to reassert the validity of their notion of time-as-blocks-to-be-placed-one-in-front-of-the-other, events with beginning and end, war's end as closure.

The President made the decision. The results were presented to the people a little at a time (since there were refinements made throughout the administration), and it was shown us a level at a time.

The first and more general level talked, as mentioned, of a "long haul," along with the creation of a basically peace-oriented industrial society capable of very rapidly expanding production should events force us into a war of long duration. For shorter affairs, we would instantly smite the Russian foe with a nuclear bludgeon.

At a second, more specific, and less interesting level the President did more than tell his military leaders that they should learn about and prepare for nuclear war. In giving them the guidance he did, President Eisenhower had in fact decided never to commit American riflemen again for purposes of limited ground combat.

The country got the picture. So, apparently, did our enemies.

*Dean Acheson is unequivocal on the point of Secretary Humphrey's influence, maintaining that the latter, not Secretary Dulles, was the architect of the new defense and, therefore, foreign policy.[53]

The positive moral force of the strategy was supplied by John Foster Dulles, the negative having been provided by some leading soldiers recently bloodied in limited war.

The ethic was set forth quite clearly in the weeks before the Republican National Convention, assumed more grandeur during the closing months of the Korean War as it foreshadowed, for our President, "the later unveiling of a change in American defense,"[54] then was sanctioned by law one year into the new administration. Speaking before the Council of Foreign Relations on January 12, 1954, the Secretary Dulles ticked off the foolish and self-defeating practices of the Truman years. There were two cardinal blunders. First, containment required we never take the initiative but, instead, always respond to aggression *when* it suited the enemy. Secondly, the ways of the past forced the United States to respond in kind— rifle for rifle, tank for tank, foot soldier for foot soldier. This second failure further required that we respond *where* it suited the opponent, that is, in "direct and local opposition."

President Eisenhower changed the rules, perhaps the game itself, as he ironed out basic policy concepts and handed them over to his Joint Chiefs of Staff: "The basic decision was to depend primarily upon a great capacity to retaliate, instantly, by means and at places of our choosing."[55]

Or, as Harry Truman might have put it, "If the Red bastards cross that line, Nuke 'em."

As the negotiators at Panmunjom were wondering if those across the table would ever decide to give in on the prisoner of war issue,* two obliquely related decisions were made in Washington.

The first decision was required by the major one—that we would fight *nuclear and only nuclear* war. This being the case, the President ordered, in turn, a "horizontal analysis" of our strategic requirements, and a reallocation of resources within the military bureaucracy.

A horizontal analysis "simply means to examine our armed might in the light of tasks which must be performed and the forces and weapons available to perform them, regardless of parent service."[56] That didactic adventure behind him, President Eisenhower then got

---

*The issue was the communist demand that we return, at gun point, captured NKPA and ChiCom personnel who preferred permanent exile to the socialist bliss from which they came. Both our Presidents chose honor above expediency, and refused the demands.

down to specifics. Nuclear retaliation was our first line of defense, the primary mission of the armed forces. Therefore, the term "reallocation of resources" could be more clearly defined. It meant, in fact, that now Korea and all wars like it had ended, the gluttonous Army must diet, perhaps fast. The Air Force would get all the sweets it could accommodate, including the eight-engine super bomber, the B-52. It's called "interservice rivalry."

The Army was likewise permitted to go atomic, stringent as its diet must remain. There wouldn't be much, but what there was had to be employed properly, which meant, among other things, a rewriting of some doctrine and the reconfiguration of combat units. This was entailed by another of Eisenhower's guiding principles for his generals: "Our armed forces must be modern, designed to deter or wage the type of war to be expected in the mid-twentieth century."

Therefore, doctrine and formal structures were changed so as to reflect the Army's ownership of nuclear-tipped shells and rockets. The most dramatic consequence of this switch was announced by the President during his budget message of January 1955. Army regiments were out; battle groups were in. Five battle groups in place form a pentagon, to house and protect the nuclear weapons. Incorporating both factors, plus our terrible compulsion for coming up with spurious labels, the resulting unit was christened the "pentomic" division.[57]

His other decision flowed first from the cash-and-carry environment created early in his mandate, secondly from a study completed by his Secretary of Defense and the Rockefeller Committee. Six years had passed since James V. Forrestal's compulsive dream of a unified defense establishment had first taken concrete and very imperfect form. During that time a war had been fought, a general elected, the nation's defense realigned. A reorganization was indicated, and Reorganization Plan Number 6 happened. "Greater management flexibility" was its secret to success.

Forrestal's National Security Council was refurbished through the addition of a Planning Board and an Operations Coordinating Board. It was situated halfway between the President and his principal officers. The Council's systematic, hierarchical arrangement made sure differences from down the line would be reconciled before being placed before the President. It was then up to Eisenhower to say either "yes" or "no."

Those who approved of the doctrine of massive retaliation were likely to approve the new staff system that would implement it.* Those whose public lives had been expended fashioning ideas antithetical to massive retaliation, persons such as Dean Acheson, let ridicule compete with contempt in denouncing the President's smothering of imagination, his outright silencing of opposition. To the latter group, "forced agreement" was the death blow to the NSC.[58]

Fiscal 1959 was to be year when massive retaliation attained the age of reason. The shift of events abroad had forced at least the hint of another strategic shift at home. A mobile, combat-ready strategic force positioned at home but ready for rapid deployment in order to squelch "small-war situations" seemed reasonable. The point of the lance was to be the Strategic Army Corps—STRAC—made up of two airborne and two infantry divisions, combat-ready, capable of coping with any brush-fire war. But shifts cost money, and as the President was learning what "interregnum" means in the American system of 1960 he was forced to leave to the man who would follow him a STRAC cut from four to three divisions, one of which was not yet fit for combat.[59]

The clutter of years in office now being tidied and packed, some of those charged with cleaning out defense records of the past probably came across the notes made by the Air Force chief of staff four years earlier, notes taken the day of an air show the Russians put on in celebration of their Air Force Day. Amidst the flapping of rotating blades and instant dust storms the Soviet helicopters landed precisely, disgorging an impressive number of impressive troops and weapons.[60]

That was in June 1956. A few short months later, as facts about the butchering of Hungarians by Soviets, and of North Vietnamese farmers by their own benevolent leaders,** were forced into the shadows of the mind by Suez, the British agreed that the Soviets had something in this new way to put troops into battle. A new era of war dragged the world inside as the first airborne-amphibious assault in

*They were not opposed to change, though. Five years after Reorganization Plan 6 took effect President Eisenhower accepted the recommendations of his second Secretary of Defense, Neil McElroy, and reorganized once again. The major emphasis of the Department of Defense Reorganization Act of 1958 was to attempt a solution to Forrestal's central problem, i.e., to state what the responsibilities and tools available were for the Secretary of Defense.

**Farmers in the provinces of Thanh Hoa and Nghe An, Democratic Republic of Vietnam, followed their own rendering of "democracy" and refused to be collectivized. They lost the argument to the forces of truth and righteousness. The moral sanctity of "agrarian reform" was preserved when, in the name of the People, 30,000 people were shot down.

history came off at Suez, when five hundred men of the British Forty-five Commando were lifted from the carriers *Ocean* and *Theseus* and let down onto the sands of Egypt.[61]

Dien Bien Phu fell to the Viet Minh May 7, 1954. In December of that year one of the President's aides offered a suggestion. With both sides about even in atomic weaponry, the enemy might decide to wage limited war and, in fact, might start several of them simultaneously. With this as a theoretical possibility, the aide asked, shouldn't we have a greater conventional force?

The question was deflected with one hand. What the young man proposed was, the President coldly reminded him, "the product of timidity." Secondly and conclusively, the whole idea was an "unrealistic solution," one with no friends in that era of realism.[62]

HOLY WAR, AMBIVALENTLY: III

Consequences of coupling the promise of a world of absolute security onto the frame of containment, then giving the product new ornaments and a coat of paint did not wait for an invitation before creating a public disturbance. Not even those in the driver's seat, who proclaimed through the rhetoric of earthly redemption the coming of a new time in the nation's history, were able to make it all hang together. For no sooner were the details of the Korean cease-fire nailed down than Senators William E. Jenner and William F. Knowland, absolutely consistent with one of the turbines now accelerating U.S. foreign policy, urged immediate war with China. Since Korea was an aberration, the result of timidity, etc., the call went out for total victory through atomic fireballs.[63] Few in the administration gave that solution serious consideration. Massive retaliation did not entail, it soon developed, preemptive or preventive war. It was a formula for the assured destruction of the Russians if ever they unleashed their atomic weaponry upon us. That was its primary purpose. Its secondary purpose was the prevention of future Koreas by letting us rather than them specify both *when* and *where,* giving us, that is, an alternative to limited ground warfare.

The *when* was Spring 1954. The *where* was Indochina.

Communist China had been warned by Secretary Dulles two months after the Korean settlement to keep hands off Indochina, told not to interfere, not to send troops, not to aid the Viet Minh. Should they disobey "grave consequences which might not be confined to Indochina" were sure to follow. Again in January and

March 1954 Dulles repeated the threats of death by burning to the Chinese, sending out at the same time a call for united action by those who felt as he did.

Most others felt either fear or ambivalence, or both.

On Saturday, April 3, 1954, President Eisenhower was at his Maryland retreat working over a speech he would give two days later. At the same time a conference was taking place, at the President's request. The issue was Indochina, the question was our air-atomic intervention to try and save the French outpost which stood guard across the hallway to Laos, a fortress without artillery support, with no roads for resupply, even its airstrip soon within the range of Viet Minh artillery. Clustered around the base was a series of strong points, each bearing the name of a love affair, an incongruity of which only legionnaires were capable. As Admiral Radford, Secretary Dulles, and the select representatives spoke of the feasibility of using the planes of our carriers, perhaps with some more aircraft from a base in the Philippines, the soldiers defending the entrance to Laos already sensed the ultimate doom of Dien Bien Phu.*

The crunch had come. On April 7 President Eisenhower gave the world a graphic way of conceiving what the effects on us of losing a nation to the Communists would be, with his "row-of-dominoes" phrase; on the 16th Vice President Nixon said if needs be we should "send our boys in;" and for the next two weeks Secretary Dulles had to ease us slowly away from that one, as a rider to prevent dispatching troops was stapled to an appropriation bill.[64]

The symbol belonging to the French commander, General Navarre, as well as his plan for all Indochina, was annihilated on May 7, when the survivors of Dien Bien Phu began their forced march into calumny and death as prisoners of the Viet Minh. By a miracle, though, neither the symbol nor the fact of massive retaliation suffered destruction, this despite the Administration's direct warning to the Chinese. On the contrary. The waves of relief which overwhelmed the American people after it was clear we were not going in strengthened the President's position at home. As for massive retaliation, it just sort of walked away, muttering to itself.

Three weeks after Dien Bien Phu had fallen to the Communists, our Joint Chiefs of Staff conducted a study, the results of which Admiral Radford transmitted to Secretary of Defense Wilson. Contrary to what the American people were later asked to believe, the

*Of all the Joint Chiefs of Staff, only their chairman, Admiral Radford, liked the idea of using atomic bombs to aid the French at Dien Bien Phu.

JCS were, as a body, unalterably opposed to involving the United States in another Asian war. Using words almost identical to those of 1949 when the peninsula of Korea was being discussed, the Joint Chiefs italicized their conclusion: *"Indochina is devoid of decisive military objectives."*[65] If ordered to go to war they would, of course, obey. But in that case they recommended hitting the logistical base of the Viet Minh insurgency: China.

Not ready to declare war on the Chinese, and not a man to dismiss the best judgment of his military advisors, President Eisenhower had been required to say "no" both to ground troops and to Operation Vulture—code name of the proposed nuclear strike.

He did this with the full knowledge that the French were even then pulling up stakes, that their Chief of Staff, General Ely, was probably right in saying we would, by our indifference, watch the whole area of Southeast Asia go over to the other side. He was also keenly aware of the latent anti-Americanism of modern Frenchmen, likely outbursts of which the French Defense Minister was still threatening for our failure to give him what he wanted a month after Dien Bien Phu was conquered. President Eisenhower glowed with something other than sympathy as he reminded Minister Pleven of the thousands of draftees we had sent to their deaths in Korea, where we had no imperialistic interests.[66] With that the debate ended.*

There were other reasons for the President's decision not to intervene, the most basic of all being the total absence of viable options. His people, his JCS, his cabinet, his promises all opposed to the use of ground troops.** Nuclear weapons were sure to sully friends for a long time, Asians for all time. More importantly, they could not have been decisive.

The first crunch in Southeast Asia had, so far as our world credentials go, been a failure. Air Force Secretary Finletter is unable to mask his envy of the Communist Chinese in describing their superb skill at running the war from a distance, at a time and place of their choosing.[68] As had been the case in Korea, and as would become the case in the Vietnam of the 1960s, the Chinese had likewise displayed

*By French law conscripts could not be sent to Indochina. Though the President's point was well taken so far as Americans were concerned, given the state of French public feeling at the time a change in their draft laws would have toppled the government. (During the last months of the French Indochina fighting her wounded had to be protected from spitting, frenzied crowds of French voters).

**Even had he desired to commit ground troops the US in 1954 was even less capable of quick troop deployment than we were in 1950, at the outbreak of the Korean war.[67]

the genius of keeping one hand on the American pulse, feeding an insurgency with the other.

In September 1954, four months after the moral collapse of the French, SEATO came into being in Manila. Its central idea was to insure that should Indochina fall the rest of the area could hold. It would resist through a combination of American aid and local forces. Our purpose would be to localize, i.e., limit any wars that might flare up in the southern hemisphere. Henceforth, it would take something greater than minor provocation to initiate massive retaliation. Just what was left unclear.

After that "Rollback" became passé. It was never repudiated, being held by the faithful to the end.[69] Its counterpart, "Massive Retaliation," was reserved for special public occasions, for the newest look at our defenses presupposed indigenous forces doing the initial fighting,* reinforced by our central mobile forces at home.

But the new had much of the old still in it, the breakthroughs in Soviet rocketry in 1957 forced still another change in course in order to catch up (and, in so doing, helped settle us into still another recession),[70] and so ground forces were put on still stricter rations, and drawn still more tightly into the heartland of the U.S. Self-exhortations had a way of becoming commitments, even if they tugged at us from opposite directions. Political commitments outran money and usable troops.

By the late 1950s Dulles had admitted that a seamless doctrine had been replaced by patch work—"vast retaliatory power" finally forced into compromise.

No sooner had the French pulled out of Indochina than the first shots of another revolutionary war were heard, this time ringing out from amidst the dust and squalor of Algeria. Legionnaires were committed instantly, French treasure was funneled into a bottomless pit, and the world's attention was riveted to the latest agony. Had events been different, it is possible we could have learned from the French experience in Indochina. As it was, we had to learn for ourselves, under cover of deception and secrecy.

It had begun four months before the death of Dien Bien Phu. On January 3, 1954, a group met at the President's request in Washington. The "Special Committee on Indochina" made its report.[71] The report contained the recommendation that we go in, but not in order

*In its purest form the new concept was to let Asians do the fighting, with the U.S. providing the weapons. A tainted but more realistic form was for us to commit our own STRAC forces if conditions demanded.

to help the French. They had lost. Instead it should be an oblique American move, for American goals.

At the request of Allen Dulles, director of the Central Intelligence Agency, one of the few genuine men of mystery America has produced, was selected to run the operational aspects of this oblique move. Air Force Colonel (later Brigadier General) Edward G. Lansdale took the job, arriving in the thick heat of Saigon on June 1, 1954. As part of the prior negotiations in Washington the scheduled MAAG chief in South Vietnam would be eased out in favor of another general, "Iron Mike" O'Daniel. General Navarre liked General O'Daniel.

Colonel Lansdale's organization took the totally neutral name, "Saigon Military Mission," or SMM. They had an empty office, a handful of men, and almost no funds. But they did have skill and a mission of high adventure. One team* was infiltrated into the Hanoi area and tried to create a resistance force up north. The results were marginal, the Viet Minh ruthless. A second team stayed south and enlisted in the local Viet Minh. The purpose here was to pare away from the Communist leaders of that front movement the many nationalists fighting against solely the French. A third effort was to try to woo, or buy, the backing of the bizarre politico-religious Cao Dai sect.

Other teams distributed black propaganda leaflets** wherever they could, the aim being the same dull goal it would remain throughout these wars: administrative control of the population. First the people have to be separated from the present government, and the confusion flowing from the leaflets was designed to force just this separation. For some North Vietnamese civilians the separation was complete, and the flow of southbound refugees tripled.

Counterfeit money by the truck load was dumped onto the stumbling North Vietnamese economy, an intentionally polluted fuel supply cost Hanoi all her busses, and an expert flown in just for one mission ruptured train service in the north for several months.

Both sides were at it, the other side doing considerably more than we. After SMM had been in existence about a year, skinny, teak-colored *montagnards* from the two northern provinces of Quang Tri and Thua Thien were being flooded with praise by those from the north, by people who spoke falsely of equality and justice, and truly of the racist views of most South Vietnamese. With the recent bombings of their long houses by the Saigon Air Force in mind, some *montagnards* went north. Three years later they were back, having

---

*The operational teams were Vietnamese nationals.
**Attributing a statement, usually a lie, to the enemy.

had their instinctive understanding of the terrain and people complemented by special training alongside a spartan North Vietnamese Army. Given special titles, these men began operating the crucial latticework of the upper infiltration trails.

During the last two years of his administration President Eisenhower learned of still others returning to south of the Seventeenth Parallel, the "regroupees," a class of faithfuls who had been ordered north by Hanoi following the Geneva Accords of 1954. They, too, had received special training, especially in border-crossing operations. By April 1959, those in the area told the President of the creation of the North Vietnamese Army 559th Transportation Group, hardly an exciting title even by communist standards. But this unit was in fact special, under the direct control of the Central Committee, and had been given the purest of missions: to insure infiltration into the south when the time came. During its first year the 559th saw about 4,500 like-minded citizens come back across the parallel.[72] Most of them were party members, with a handle on absolute moral truth, and were totally without conscience.

At this stage in the grisly game of revolutionary warfare, the other side was far ahead of ours.

HOLY WAR, AMBIVALENTLY: IV

It was not his job to point out theoretical inconsistencies and irreconcilable promises. It was his job to use his decades of service to the nation, his experiences as a paratrooper in Europe and as the replacement for MacArthur in Korea, in good times as well as bad, in the defense of the land he had sworn to defend. The mid-1950s were bad times, and General Matthew B. Ridgway so informed his President.* The retrenchment and reshuffling of national priorities and the faltering of the American spirit which was encouraged under the protective wings of massive retaliation had taken their toll. For rather than becoming Fortress America we had, principally through treaty arrangement, committed ourselves to the defense of half the globe, in most areas of which nuclear weapons either were politically anathema or otherwise worthless.

STRAC—the husbanding of swift and lethal conventional forces within the confines of the U.S.—was the law of the land, and General Ridgway would obey every order. But this strategic reserve, if it were to be either a deterrent to the Soviets in Europe or, if war came, capable of preventing the overruning of the whole continent, had to amount to ten divisions "in being," i.e., for real—trained, equipped,

*General Ridgway was Army Chief of Staff from August 16, 1953 until June 30, 1955.

and with deployment vehicles or ships standing by. STRAC (which, as noted, turned out to amount to a force in being of only two divisions by 1960) simply was not credible.

So reasoned General Ridgway. He lost the argument to General Eisenhower, but gained a reminder to reread those portions of the "new look" concept which stressed the Soviet atomic threat. The latter, Eisenhower counseled, was the "only kind of attack that could, without notice, endanger our very existence."[73]

But Ridgway would not accept the President's verdict concerning JCS support for his defense program lying down. His testimony before the Senate Armed Services Committee in February 1955 was simple and direct. First, he pointed out that the Soviet bloc never had attacked where U.S. troops had stood on the contested ground. Further, and at a more general level, the general suggested that in the "free world," the threat of aggression is inversely related to the number of American foot soldiers there.[74] He was referring at the time to the month-old "pentomic" announcement of our total commitment to atomic warfare.

On June 27, 1955 he tried again. This time he pleaded with Secretary of Defense Wilson for a semblance of military balance. Displaying a prophetic sense seldom found in our military leaders, the champion of limited war in an age of nuclear clichés told his superior, "no one knows when those ominous sight drafts may be presented for payment . . ." Permitting himself a judgment more properly made by elected leaders, General Ridgway concluded: "If military power is to support diplomacy . . . it must be capable of being applied promptly, selectively, and with the degree of violence appropriate to the occasion."[75] This was written but one year after the decisive test of massive retaliation had been held, one year since illiterate North Vietnamese peasants showed the idea to be bankrupt at the battle for the corridor leading into Laos.

After a few more tries General Ridgway resigned. Later so did two other general-grade paratroopers, Gavin and Taylor.[76]*

Korea had wrenched the U.S. Army from the apathy of garrison life. After three years and 36,000 dead Americans, the Army was half-permitted, half-ordered to resume its stuporous ways. With the knee-jerk thinking which follows every foreign war, our soldiers were sentenced to penury. Then, in an act of forced reconciliation, the Army was ordered to think small but atomic. It was deemed very

*General Taylor replaced General Ridgway on the JCS. Taylor gave up his job June 30, 1959. His role in the next phase of our Holy Wars would be without parallel. Continued in Chapter 5.

unlikely that another assault was coming but, if it should, the Army would be asked to be prepared.

But the assault already was well underway in 1955. It was neither an anticipated nor an orthodox one. Nor was it plotted. It just happened that the rapture which atomic thinking permitted occurred just at the time the British were half way through what they termed "The Emergency," regroupees were entering their second phase of training north of the Seventeenth Parallel, embittered and exiled French soldiers were holding a new inquisition in Algeria, and the brilliant, egotistical Cypriot Grivas was emersing his island in blood.

Then there was an even less visible assault underway, here at home, operating inside the uniforms of our troops. The attack came from mutually supporting quarters: the conscious hope that the individual soldier was in this day and age irrelevant, and the unconscious need that with the departure of those who thought as General Ridgway did about limiting war to accommodate fleeting political ends, the Army would restore itself to automaton status. For though Ridgway replaced MacArthur as senior troop commander in Korea, it was the architect of Inchon, the prophet of total victory, who spoke for the man with the rifle in his hands.[77]

These eight years served the people as a flotation device, permitting first stability, then a move to shore and at last a mooring. But the calm often seemed contrived, even when it wasn't. People began in the late fifties to assume first the right to ask questions, which are probably unanswerable, about war and peace and the perfect society. Misreading the signs of the times President Eisenhower in early 1958 ordered still another conference on how best to cope with the public demand for knowledge, not realizing that the real request was for the finality he and others had so often promised the people. The President asked Eric Johnston* to chair the conference.[78]

Another conference was held to investigate our people's goals.[79] A conclusion, not widely questioned at the time, was that we didn't have any worth mentioning.

And still another report was put together, the point of this one being not ideals worth pursuing but the prospects for our surviving in some recognizable form.[80] It was a stinging, uncompromising indictment of the tombs into which creative defense ideas had been sealed, of the criminal neglect which our plunges into the Absolute

*Mr. Johnston was ex-President of the Motion Picture Association of America.

had permitted, and of the quickly maturing "sight drafts" General Ridgway had spent his strength calling our attention to.

A final jab made in *Prospects for America* was a warning about "concealed wars," wars to which the term "aggression" truly does not apply, wars with which, the report concludes, "we are least prepared to deal." This and the other conclusions were made public just as the cadre of our North Vietnamese Transportation Group, and some misled *montagnards,* were checking out the terrain of the southern half of the DMZ, preparing to open the "armed struggle."

The badly needed rest which[81] Eisenhower's reign permitted turned in time to boredom, finally to sluggishness. As the nation's pulse searched for something, or someone, to quicken it, we were again condemned, as de Toucqueville had warned, to "soar impetuously," to once more permit our national spirit to burst its bounds in search of high moral adventure.

In the flush which a new challenge promised, the issues of secrecy, of Executive privilege to involve us in winless conflicts, and of unlimited ideals fueling limited wars, could find no audience. The year was 1960.

To lead the way back to greatness, the people were given a glimpse of what many would remember as a fleeting wisp of glory.

V THE BERETS ARE COMING! THE BERETS ARE COMING!

> Whether it be the heart to conceive, the understanding to direct, or the hand to execute.
>
> —Junius

STANDDOWN

Rain does not fall in Vietnam. It is hurled down by gods as violent as the land and people on whom it descends. To stand in the rain is to insult the gods, for which one always receives proper retribution.

For hours rain had been pouring onto the compound, with the force of waves breaking over a sea wall. Slowing to a fine, warm mist, it challenged the men to leave the buildings, for one final formation.

"We depart this battlefield with our heads held high, with dignity and pride in our accomplishments . . ."[1] Michael D. Healy, Colonel of Infantry and final Group Commander, was addressing his men for the last time. After almost a decade, and half a military career for some, the Green Berets were going home. All traces of glory were gone.

As the mist intruded upon the solemn occasion, some eyes blinked to deflect the rain while others skipped up and down the paved compound where only a year or so earlier the palms and white posts decorating the street had been outranked, if but for a day, by the blaze of flags and banners. On that day in late 1969 the Group had been presented still another unit citation, by none other than COMUSMACV.* It had seemed as if there were as many photographers covering that show as there were people providing for the physical safety of the visiting general. Jungle fatigues with starched, razor creases complemented spit-shined boots, both courtesy of young, well-paid Vietnamese house girls. Praises and declarations, compliments and slogans, and the general shook hands with the colonel.

Today, though, the general had decided not to come to give the men of Special Forces a send-off. So, around the corner from their very own chapel, where there lay a beret over which the commander each week read the names of those just killed in action, the strange departure ceremony went on. There were praises for exceptional acts of dedication and bravery, cooperation and patience. As the lecture moved on to other subjects, some in the ranks thought of the diseased and filthy natives of the mountains whom they had led out of the stone age, of the portraits of nude Vietnamese girls on silk who cast beckoning glances at the men in their clubs (until ordered replaced by pictures of boats and oceans by Colonel Healy), of friends killed long ago and memorialized with brass name plates inside Group Headquarters, of the venality of some Vietnamese counterparts they had been forced to work so closely with over the years.

Most of all they thought of themselves as special.

HEAD GEAR AS HISTORY

It cost $1.75, and the money had to come out of the pocket of each man who wanted one.[2] Everyone wanted one. They also wanted the silver emblem of a trojan horse and shield. That cost an additional $1.62, again to be dredged from the wearer's pocket. As the men of Tenth Group pounded through the snow of the compound just before New Year's Day 1955, they were trapped between the cold of the winter and the stunned expressions of those who saw the strange green headgear. Alternately proud and embarrassed, the men of the Tenth finally had what they wanted. Secretly it was admitted that the beret was as impractical as it was distinctive. Some wore them like a chef's hat, some like a coon skin. But it was their very own, and that helped them feel special. A Special Forces unit back at Fort Bragg, the Seventy-seventh, donned the new beret.

*Commander United States Military Assistance Command Vietnam, General Creighton Abrams. General Abrams was commander of all U.S. forces in Vietnam, replacing General Westmoreland in June 1968.

By 1956 the beret was everywhere. But not for long. The commander of the post reflected the displeasure of virtually all the rest of the Army at the thought of setting one group of soldiers apart—perhaps above—another group. The beret was banned in mid-1956.

BIRTH OF THE FORCES: CONTAIN OR LIBERATE?

Negotiations had moved from the village of Kaesong to Panmunjom several months ago. Now, in April 1952, the ritual of being insulted on a daily basis by the Communist negotiators and the wasted attempts to separate military from political matters were becoming routine for the Americans there seeking a cease-fire, or truce, or whatever.

By June 1952, Special Forces was a feeble if genuine operation. Tracing its lineage back through the Rangers and Merrill's Marauders and OSS to Francis Marion, the "swamp fox" of Revolutionary days, reversing by way of psychological warfare, the organization limped rather than sprang into existence.

Its predecessors are of interest, for their influence would alternate, as would the development and mission of Special Forces. In the main there were two traditions which pressed into this unusual unit. First, there was the direct action push, exemplified during our war for independence by Francis Marion who defied all rules of warfare by penetrating an impenetrable swamp to overwhelm an amazed and disgusted British opponent. In more modern wars ranger and related activities are examples of this tradition.

The other principal force came form the psychological warfare operations carried out by the Office of Strategic Services during World War II. This under-the-surface approach to war, where deviousness and duplicity are cardinal virtues, competed with the more dramatic influences handed down by those who scaled cliffs, blew up bridges, cut throats.

Eisenhower became President just seven months after Special Forces came into existence. It was not long before a genuine mission for Special Forces was created, for the talent of the men of that organization dovetailed perfectly with America's emerging foreign policy, with the evangelizing of the doctrine of containment. Within less than a year of its founding, the original eleven men who set up shop atop Smoke Bomb Hill had grown to a thousand rather zealous soldiers.

Orders were cut authorizing highly specialized training and a very peculiar structure for the new organization. Special Forces personnel were special from the time of joining the unit, and became progressively more so. All had to be parachute qualified, a prerequisite which substantially reduced the number of volunteers. Secondly, the fact that only volunteers were taken, and taken into what by traditional Army standards was a tiny unit, meant that the conditions for admission could be made rigorous. They were, to the inclusion of psychiatric examinations and classifying.

All members were to be specialists, in demolitions, communications, weapons, combat medicine, operations and intelligence.* The U.S. Government invested enormous sums of money in these and other schools, including scuba, underwater demolitions and high-altitude low-opening parachuting (HALO). This irregular unit received funds for running interesting and even radical training programs. Stories swirled among those outside the ranks of Special Forces of soldiers making parachute jumps dressed in civilian clothes, being hunted down by intelligence people, getting into fights when they refused to go along quietly. "Legs"—the rest of the Army—envied and resented the arrogant and loner attitude the new movement generated. The giving of elite status to one group of soldiers had always been anathema, and that tradition would not be jettisoned by giving in to the demand. Thus, the green beret was disallowed, by order of the Department of the Army.

Containment theory, given spiritual leave by Dulles, was twofold: massive nuclear retaliation in the event of an attack by the Soviet Union, and a permanent system of alliances. Part and parcel of these positions was the spirit of "rolling back communism." It was in the spirit of the latter that Special Forces received its mission after Eisenhower took office. Their mission was to become professional in the art of unconventional warfare (UW). In other words, they were to gain the capability of infiltrating hostile areas where guerrilla units friendly to the United States would be created and led. The assumption was that if the United States went to war against the Soviet Union, then the populations of those "Iron Curtain" countries would be unfriendly to the Russian soldiers, and, potentially, pro-American. Thus, by establishing guerrilla bands in these areas Russia would be fighting two wars at once, against friendly conventional forces to the front, and against guerrillas in the rear.

This meant language proficiency, which in turn meant either expensive and time-consuming language classes or the bringing into Special Forces of foreign-born personnel. Both paths were followed, and for the first time in its history there developed in our Army tactical units with a genuine language capability, by way of East Europeans thirsting for revenge.

*Additionally, they had to be willing to go anywhere, on any mission, without question. And they had to enjoy a good fight.

With a mission of vengeance and liberation* in mind, the Tenth Special Forces Group deployed for Bad Tolz, Germany in November 1953.

Following Korea there was a return to the atomic diplomacy of 1945–50, and with the predictable cuts in defense funds, personnel level for all Special Forces hovered around a thousand. This meager number of men, with their *hubris,* spent their days and nights either training, or preparing for training, or bragging about training. Hazards and impossible terrain were intentionally emphasized and over-emphasized.

After the Hungarian uprising of 1956 it became painfully clear there would be no rollback of communism. Incineration, perhaps, but no rollback. Nevertheless, recruiting continued, though at a leisurely pace. In 1957, when the Psychological Warfare Center was renamed the Center for Special Warfare,** there were still about a thousand men, though now without much of a mission.

MISSION II: VISION OF CAMELOT

A new mission was being precipitated out of the compound of the guerrilla and subversive elements which had been the twin driving forces of Special Forces. One tradition had been rather downgraded during the preparation for guerrilla warfare in Eastern Europe, but now was demanding its right to be heard. In June 1960, one of the other Special Forces Group (the Seventy-seventh) at Fort Bragg had a name change, becoming the Seventh Group. During the same month that unit's commander spoke not just of a mission of organizing and leading guerrilla bands in areas close to the enemy's home, but of "the training of foreign military personnel in counterguerrilla activities."[3] With the success of Castro and his promise of more of the same elsewhere in this Hemisphere, thought, though not much, had been given to inverting the original mission. Already there was mention of some place called Indochina. There were now three groups, and some expectation of more. Still there was no beret.

He didn't give it to them, but he did christen the green, circular prize. It was after the Special Forces people had put on one of their displays of weapons and radio, explosives and medicine, after some had over-simulated unarmed combat and shaken loose teeth and bloodied some noses. On Columbus Day 1961, after nearly ten years

*Their motto became, "Free the Oppressed," consistent with the new world-view of Dulles. It was also consistent with plans to support armed uprisings in communist-occupied nations.

**The title became the U.S. Army John F. Kennedy Center for Special Warfare four months after the President's assassination.

of waiting and training, waiting and wishing, the new President, John F. Kennedy, addressed the Green Berets.

On this band of men Kennedy would place a major responsibility for preserving the integrity of America. He had a plan for them, though not yet thought through, just as he had a plan for America, though that, too, had not yet been thought through. Both were still being refined on the last day of his life, when he spoke with an undisguised pride of "our special counterinsurgency forces," already increased 600 percent, already engaged in South Vietnam.[4]

Amidst an atmosphere of urgency he delivered a message before Congress in January 1962. The section of his speech devoted to national defense spoke of a comprehensive, enveloping system of defense, tailoring response to responsibilities. A key element, according to the President, was and would continue to be these men who could be deployed into a threatened area, soldiers we must permit to flow with the threat of communist subversion.[5]

Later that year President Kennedy couldn't pass up the opportunity to mention his novel force while campaigning for Birch Bayh in Indiana's Senate race. By that time Special Forces had quadrupled in strength, songs were being written about them, and new candidates for American folklore were trying to enlist. It wasn't clear just what they were enlisting for, but it was a unit seemingly hand-picked by the nation's leader for something big.

One week before his death the President addressed an AFL-CIO convention in New York, again not missing the opportunity to bring his Green Berets into the limelight.[6] A genuine mystique was permitted to develop around this band of soldiers, individuals who perhaps more than any other members of the armed forces symbolized Mr. Kennedy's surfacing world-view.

The world in which many of his Special Forces worked justified the mystique, and the exotic stories seem pale in comparison with reality. Within this world in which an American might find himself were tribal groups with names like Bahnar, Cua, Hre, Jarai, Jeh, Katu, Koho, Mnong, Muong, Rhade, Raglai, Sedang, Stieng.[7]* Some groups of natives cut off the nose of an adultress, some had a differ-

*As some indication of the complexity of the Montagnards, and the war itself, the 200,000 Bahnar language group is in turn subdivided into the Alakong, Alatanag, Bahnar Cham, Bonam, Boutes, Golar, Ho Drong, Jo Long, Kon Ko De, Krem, Rengao, Roh, Tolotenir, To Sung. The area is believed by cultural anthropologists to be the most ethnically complex in the world. Yet it was here that Special Forces probably did its best work, amid incredibly divergent peoples, among the Bahnar who were proud and warlike, and by skirting and not offending the VC-sympathetic Kohos. An undefinable affection developed between some United States personnel and the tiny hill people, in graphic distinction to the hostility which marked so much of the U.S.-Vietnamese working relations.

ent ethic. Some developed ulcers in their stomachs because of the copper decorations they wore on their teeth. Others cured gonorrhea by eating a special fruit from the steaming twilight of the jungle, thus inducing violent fevers and, hopefully, recovery rather than death.

And some, perhaps most, hated the Vietnamese. Of these none were more justified than the Rhade group. In 1964, some drew up the *United Front of Struggle for the Oppressed Race,* in response to "the Vietnamese colonialists." Six weeks later five hundred Rhade told their American advisers to take cover and stay out of the way for the next day or so, then attacked the Central Highlands town of Ban Me Thuot. Fifty Vietnamese were killed, and the radio station seized. Few Americans in the area at the time felt great sympathy for the Vietnamese.*

By 1966 there were 10,500 Special Forces-types around the world, half of them pushing through mangroves and rain forests in Vietnam. Many had been formed into Mobile Training Teams, then deployed according to a design to Iran, Nepal, Guinea, Pakistan, Brazil, Peru, Jordan, Nigeria, Venezuela, or the Philippines. Some were stupidly used, such as those who helped man untenable outposts along the Cambodian border in Vietnam. In late 1962 President Diem and his brother Nhu insisted their country's flag fly regardless of the realities of force. One such camp, installed to keep an eye on infiltration through "the trail," was Plei Mrong in the Central Highlands. One-hundred and fourteen weapons were lost when the perimeter was breached. Thirty-nine of the diseased, brown-skinned defenders were slain by the VC.[8] That was one of the less-publicized aspects of their job.

Advertising, in fact, is central to the history of Special Forces under John Kennedy. The President believed that they could go into unstable areas, especially Vietnam, without stirring up undue animosity either here or abroad.[9] It seems that at last there had come along a national leader who understood wars of opinion, and about American opinion, and about the limits within which the latter can be directed.

MOVING A NATION, WITH RESTRAINT

During his campaign for the Presidency John F. Kennedy spoke to a people who had temporarily lost its sense of purpose. The candidate spoke to an eager nation, a nation sated with the banal. He

*The province adviser, Colonel John F. Freund, was instrumental in preventing a still-worse situation from developing from the uprising.

flattered his audience by speaking of arousing an American's will to believe in himself, of implanting a goal to be struggled for, of a need to reclaim the title of a Choosing People, "a people who voluntarily assumes the burden and the glory of advancing mankind's best hopes."[10] He reintroduced the contradiction unknowingly.

Even after one factors out from this equation the aspirations the man held for his country's highest office there remains a statement with symmetry and with facts about the American character.

The problem he faced was not unlike that FDR had faced three decades earlier. America was not in the stranglehold of an economic depression in 1960, although the national economy had had its ups and downs during the Eisenhower Administration. The problem and the parallel with the 1930s was that of overcoming the indifference with which his people viewed the world, of forcing them to look at the bright and painful sunlight as it fell on faraway places. Like Franklin Roosevelt, Truman, and Eisenhower, Kennedy had to face the fact that his countrymen take a certain pride in their ignorance of all that does not influence their life directly. He was disturbed by reports that only two in ten were reasonably well-informed,[11] and he set about giving the people what he thought they needed to know.

But, and as was the case with FDR, he knew that the great melting pot could produce an explosive brew if conditions permitted. Whereas FDR permitted and encouraged this eruption, world circumstances had changed by 1960. Precisely because of the conditioning of his people by the "good guy, bad guy" approach of World War II it was crucial that one not be deluded into supposing history repeats itself, or that there ever could be another Pearl Harbor and the crusade that followed. With that, Kennedy mounted a crusade.

To arouse and direct his people, during the course of which understanding would be implanted: such were the stated ideals. It was necessary, then, to dampen the coals of chauvinism by pointing out, again and again, that enmities between nations, as between individuals, do not last forever.[12] Such statements alienated some, but he could afford to do without these best wishes. Suppression of chauvinism might permit a rebirth of nationalism, and the arousal of the long-dormant need to participate. Or it might confuse.

Participation is a democratic norm, an obligation self-imposed. Except in vicarious form it is as self-defeating as it is impractical when a democracy fights a limited war. During the very early months of the Kennedy Administration we eased into a very limited war, a conflict whose nature was not comprehended, one whose magnitude and participation had to be minimized.

But what of those who did not participate, those on the outside, those who make up the great majority? The horns of the dilemma were as forbidding in 1960 as they were in 1950, when an earlier President finally noticed that his people had noticed that a war was going on.

John Kennedy tried to go between the horns, by speaking over the heads of newsmen and to his people, or past Congressmen and to his people, or through fund-raising rallies and to his people. Occasionally he scraped against one horn and reacted by grasping the other, a few scrapes and bruises thus resulting. Throughout his time in office he seems to have had the promises-expectations continuum clearly in mind when Southeast Asia was being discussed. After his first year as President, Kennedy's exhortations became fewer and more subdued. As he gained an understanding of the military, political, and moral complexity of the war he aroused fewer and fewer expectations, made his promises less and less explicit. He died before his hypothesis concerning a democracy at limited war could be tested with any thoroughness. Five years later his experiment would collapse.

In May 1961 the President broke tradition by delivering to the Congress a special message on urgent national needs. His concern with the new aggression concealed inside the cloak of guerrilla warfare dominated the speech,[13] and he sought to stoke the coals, though ever so gently. Already he had learned that the task of education he had set for himself extended in many directions, and to be successful the course had to include as its students not only the voter but the congressman and the general.

In June the latest code words were "wars of liberation," an expression whose moralistic ring made the task all the more difficult. By this time Kennedy was trying to distinguish the new form of war from the Korea-type, and in so doing extract from his viewers implicit authorization for the actions soon to be taken.* To make the distinction clear he spoke of guerrilla warfare and wars of liberation, but that confused the public mind still more since the vision of guerrilla fighters still was largely a function of the silly and untrue pictures painted of the partisans of World War II. Now, it seemed the shoe was on the other foot, with the underweight, outgunned partisan taking on Uncle Sam and his protectorates. Matters were not helped by the communist monopoly on every usable honorific term, less still by our use of the same words.

*By this time some important decisions and actions already had been taken as regards the latest threat to U.S. security. In this regard President Kennedy was as one with his predecessors.

During his press conference of October 11, 1961, the President stated the problem nicely. "Our ambition," Mr. Kennedy said of Laos and all Southeast Asia, "is to protect our vital interests without a war which destroys and doesn't really represent a victory for policy."[14] His explicit statements that day were hints at developments, as he spoke of 44,000 M-14 rifles being produced each month, increased airlift capacity, and the multiplying Green Berets. Using the language of his predecessors, the language we demanded he use, the President spoke simultaneously of Aggression and vital interests, of the Geneva Accords and the Southeast Asia Treaty Organization, of a strategy not for war but for peace. To repeat time and again that we carried an unduly heavy burden by virtue of alliances which criss-crossed the world[15] he may have practiced overkill, but at the time the problem could not have been presented more clearly.* The confusion of self-interest and transcendent values was a necessity.

During his news conference on April 11, 1962, President Kennedy fielded reporters' questions in his usual manner of selecting favored newsmen. One not-so-favored got a question in, during the course of which Kennedy was asked what he was going to do about the American soldiers killed in Vietnam, the reference being to four men just recently slain. With disarming ease the President told those viewing that these four sergeants were in "that long roll" stretching back through Korea and both World Wars. Sliding to the next irrelevancy Kennedy thanked the men of the Wisconsin and Texas national guards for their contributions to defense of the nation.[16]

It was with the same adroitness that he approached the powder keg of casualties during his final State of the Union speech, January 14, 1963. Just as the major wars of this century had been lumped together so that the lesser conflicts of Korea and Vietnam might reflect some of the moral glow of the greater wars, on this day he told his people of an unstable world through which one must sometimes walk sideways, and of the hazards involved, and of the major who lost his life in the skies over Cuba, the young specialist recently shot dead in the snows of Korea, and of the sergeant killed by the Viet Cong.[177]He was hedging his bets, precisely as he insured our failure.

Kennedy's press conferences were a modern-day, animated version of the fireside chat of an earlier time. Whereas Truman tended alternately to fulminate and fumble, and Eisenhower refused to leave a cliché unmolested, Kennedy produced and directed his own performance. As he stepped before the cameras he began—always —with announcements and statements. The traditional give and

*This is because the problem—Vietnam—was not yet understood by any one in a position of authority.

take of his Democratic predecessors[18] gave way to a lot of giving, as the young leader used the openings to blunt in advance hateful questions and to allay fears. Resentment among reporters grew as the time left for questions on air time dwindled. The atmosphere of cordiality and warmth did not compensate for the opportunity for the parry and thrust the newsmen wanted.

One issue surfaced time and again, only to be submerged by the President. The flow of power to the Executive, and the consequent wall of classification, had pushed straight through half a dozen administrations following World War I, and JFK inherited both. During his press conference[19] of February 7, 1962, the President was asked about the right of the American public to know about developments in Vietnam. Asked if he could tell us what the situation there was, the President answered that there was a war going on in South Vietnam, that people get killed in war, and we are only living up to the Truman-Eisenhower commitments of old.

A few months later a reporter from *Western Aerospace* magazine complained of the closed-mouth profile of the Department of Defense, and asked how he might see an order that had been classified. Kennedy said he would talk to Arthur Sylvester, "without success, I'm sure."[20]

In a major speech before the American Newspaper Publishers Association on April 27, 1961 the gut issue of secrecy in our sociey, and of the newsman's compulsion to expose for sake of exposing, again popped to the surface. A totalitarian society, he reminded us, has tremendous advantages over an open society. He would not, of course, establish a new Office of War Information à la FDR to govern the flow of news, yet what is one to do? During our day and age there have developed needs which stand in absolute, irreconcilable opposition to each other: "the need for far greater public information . . . and the need for far greater official secrecy."

The President's speech concluded with a recommendation that the publisher reexamine his personal responsibilties, that he ask in addition to the question, Is it news? the question Is it in the interest of national security? All present were seated at the time, thus obviating the need to take their seats.

Two events followed rapidly upon the heels of his speech before the newsmen. First, as with Forrestal's plea of years past, there was a refusal to comply hidden within the flurry of editorials about the indefinability of "national interest"; secondly, the Bay of Pigs operation exploded. Mr. Kennedy's public popularity rose shortly thereafter, though the mutual influences of the events cannot be ascertained.[21]

The endeavor to educate (in his sense of the term) the public required the use of private media and the breathing, emotional, thinking humans who were in their employ. Most either resented or refused to be used, and a basic split within the press formed over the issue of Vietnam well in advance of the President's murder. With the lens thus distorted the scenes projected across the land already were couched in platitudes and invective, thereby revealing the nature of the newsmen far more accurately than the nature of the writhing, amorphous conflict in Indochina. There was one occasion on which the President might have averted, at a minimum, much of the invidious, unprofessional press work by both sides. To have done so would have been to gamble all on the unknown factor, the American voter. With less than a year in office he declined the advice of General Maxwell Taylor, his military adviser, after the general returned from a trip to Vietnam. A formal statement, a full articulation of what our long-term interests were in Southeast Asia, stripped of as many moralisms and clichés as he thought we could do without, might have made all the difference possible on subsequent history. Kennedy decided to keep his cards close to his chest, perhaps because of his conviction that one year in office was not enough time to wear down the moralisms and clichés accumulated over a nation's lifetime.[22] He probably was right.

ENCORE FOR KENNAN

Our military complex has never in its history had a better friend than John F. Kennedy, despite the false constructions some of his apologists have tried to place upon his name and, by implication, his acts. Were his speeches to be spoken in public today the speaker would be ridiculed as a Neanderthalic anti-communist. On the final day of his life his prepared remarks bristled with threats to that orbital string of countries whose very survival depended, in the view of Kennedy and the Joint Chiefs of Staff, on our continuing material and advisory support. The alternative, the President warned, was "the increased overseas deployment of American combat forces."[23] Those who would make of him an architect of everlasting peace could do worse than to reread his speeches and to reevaluate his acts. The peace he had in mind was not "the absolute, infinite concept of universal peace and good will of which some fantasies and fanatics dream," nor is peace a hopeless dream. The point appeared to be that peace is a dream, and possibly within the bounds of the possible.[24]

While running and struggling for the high office he hoped to hold,

Kennedy spoke of holes and runs in the nation's coat of mail handed down by the Eisenhower Adminstration.* Those who had followed Truman had moved from crisis to crisis, always in response to, never in anticipation of. This was because of two reasons, President Kennedy argued. First, there was no overarching strategy to guide and move the nation during the Eisenhower years. Secondly, our defense budget had been planned around money-saving rather than nation-saving concepts. All the while we had permitted the atmosphere we breathe to be permeated with a sentimentalism which, if unchecked, must inexorably push the nation toward either mutual incineration or a unilateral "slide downhill into dust, dullness, languour, and decay."[25]

The other-worldly critics who champion "negotiate" as the latest code word, the newest talisman for peace, are as foolish and dishonest as the boosters of a flatulent "new liberation policy." Fundamental causes of the Soviet-American conflict are to be found in the clash of basic national interests of the two nations, so there is little prima facie attraction to be discovered in negotiation per se. Similarly, Kennedy continued, with some uncharacteristic sarcasm showing, those who normally take their seats at the opposite end of the spectrum had found it desirable to scurry toward the center when it was learned there would be no freedom in Eastern Europe by means of dramatic or violent revolution.[26]

America's last "strategy of peace" was containment, forged just after World War II when Stalin was a genuine menace. That strategy was based on our monopoly of power both military and economic, and the Soviets had all but surpassed us in both. The result had been the unintentional acceptance by the United States of the role of voluntary fire department. The idea ought to be to prevent not extinguish, for which a new strategy is required.[27] In the development of these ideas and national aims let it not be forgotten who are the primary causes of world tension—the communists.[28]

Without admitting it fully, President Kennedy leaped back to Kennan and 1946, back to containment. The impetus for the quivering the world was undergoing, and would undergo, was the Soviet Union minus Stalin. This was his conviction during his final months in office when, in discussing Cuba and the missile alarm, he told his people he had seen "no real evidence that the policy of the Communist world toward us is basically changed. They still do not wish us well."[29] His strategy for peace would adorn itself differently from the Truman years, but its essence would remain unaltered:

*He was able to do this without attacking Eisenhower. This nifty trick was made possible by distinguishing between the President and his Administration.

> The center of freedom's defense is our network of world alliances, extending from NATO, recommended by a Democratic President and approved by a Republican Congress, to SEATO, recommended by a Republican President and approved by a Democratic Congress. These alliances were constructed in the 1940s and 1950s—it is our task and responsibility in the 1960s to strengthen them.[30]

That speech was made in May 1961, just while decisions of cosmic dimensions were in the making. The decisions were carried out consistent with this latest revision of containment, through the remainder of 1961, 1962, and ten months and twenty-two days of 1963. Toward the end of his Presidency, the allusions to Turkey and Greece and to Dulles' Caracas Resolution, and to the line through Asia and into CENTO, accelerated rather than diminished.[31]

If the combustion of the drive for communist expansion was constant, the specific outlets for the energy thus formed had undergone radical alteration. In his speech before the West Point graduation class of 1962 President Kennedy displayed his bitterness at the way in which our people had been misled by those who thought in clichés and acronyms. It is wholly misleading to call this the nuclear age, he told them. Thus, it follows that the nation's defense cannot rest upon such a magical ruse as "massive retaliation." Nor is it wise to rivet one's eyes too long on Korea, for there have been many wars in recent years which lacked the relatively clean lines of that war: Malaya, Greece, the Philippines. Algeria, Cuba and Cyprus, "and almost continuously on the Indo-Chinese Peninsula."

Graduating cadets should take heart, he confided, for this could well be the class the stars fell on.* In anticipation of that summum bonum, and in recognition of the new face of war, he implied they could do far worse than choose a stint with Special Forces.[32]

Our nation's defenses would make themselves malleable enough to conform to these most recent threats, all the time with the unvoiced premise that strength meant an ability to confine our response to nonnuclear weapons.[33] That means a broader, heavier spectrum of men and hardware, more and faster planes, a few thousand extra Green Berets. Those things can be bought or produced or recruited, though, and what was needed more than anything else was an idea, an idea supple enough to match the new configuration of a partially hostile world, substantive enough to hurt those "who do not bid us well." He went in search of an idea almost as soon as he took office, and failed.

*Thus, suggesting that many of those graduating would one day wear stars of a general officer.

A REPLACEMENT FOR "MASSIVE RETALIATION"

Chairman Khrushchev aided in the search when he announced to the incoming President in January 1961 that he and the rest of the Soviet Union stood committed to the support of communist wars of liberation. This total radicalizing of war, these "wars in the crowd," were virtually unknown to U.S. military theorists, save for the handful who had probed beneath the surface of France's Dien Bien Phu and Britain's "Malaysian Emergency." A clique of French officers, after retiring from Indochina, erected a Manichean metaphysics atop this form of warfare, only to see their philosophy and their politics go down alongside the OAS in Algeria.[34] Americans are not much given to speculation, or even to analysis; and to most Dien Bien Phu was a matter of unbelievable logistical and artillery feats by the Viet Minh, the terrible misplacement of a strong point by the French.

A few Americans had accumulated some experience during World War II with guerrilla warfare.* The analogy, which their experiences were to provide, had a limited foundation in fact. Orthodox operations had dominated World War II.** Nevertheless, there had been the OSS (one strain of which survive in the doctrine and activities of Special Forces), an Air Force colonel by the name of Lansdale who had racked up considerable experience during the Huk insurgency in the Philippines, and the memory of our serious fling at guerrilla warfare during World War II, the China-Burma-India theater of operations. One man who retained personal memories of the CBI Theater was on the President's staff with Research and Intelligence, Department of State.

The man who was warrior turned political scientist turned adviser was Roger Hilsman. During a meeting late in November 1961, the President put some serious questions to Hilsman concerning a speech by the latter just published by the *Marine Corps Gazette.* It was clear to President Kennedy that Korea was as unique as Pearl Harbor, that the contemporary threat of the amorphous, fleeting guerrilla was not only more subtle an adversary but one far more likely to require an American response. President Kennedy hoped

*For reasons to be explained, the term "guerrilla" within the context of revolutionary war is quite misleading, especially if one conjures up visions of the Maquis or Tito partisans.

**In defense of U.S. military theorists it has to be remembered the number of places throughout the world in which our military involvement was possible; thus, great expertise in the myriad forms of wars possible was not possible outside very limited circles. Secondly, the French and British experiences at revolutionary war were only partially applicable to the American problem. Also, reading can be tiring.

his expanding body of Special Forces could develop military tactics for use against the guerrillas which would keep up with the geometric growth of the Berets. He hoped that our side could come up with viable political tactics, too, for this new face of war had at a minimum a military and a political profile. As profiles they were aspects of the same being; therefore, a more comprehensive idea had to be developed which would make the hoped-for military and political notions interface.[35] At this point all the President had was a very large hope, in whose train several more hopes were carried. With the main idea providing the horsepower and also pointing the way, it was clear that without a genuine strategy secondary ideas were worthless.

At issue was not an idea but a strategy by which the United States could engage in war, in revolutionary war, in Communist revolutionary war on the side of the fledgling Republic of Vietnam.

Debate over an idea and, by implication, over the decisions to send men to battle and perhaps to death, raged within the Kennedy Adminstration until the day the President died.

SEARCH FOR AN IDEA: I

Back on April 6, 1954, then-Senator Kennedy had spoken of the "dangerously futile and self-destructive" consequences of dumping dollar after dollar, man after man, into the Indochinese jungles if victory were an illusion.[36] But China had stopped the Americans in Korea and, while counseling against adventurism, she nevertheless agreed to subsidize the North Vietnamese Communists partially. These two irreducible facts pressed the President from opposing sides, not as a baffling set of data might invite the attention of an academician, but as knives and clubs forming the edges of a guantlet the race through which had already been agreed upon. What was yet to be decided was the sort of defense to be offered, the best way to ward off the blows as they fell.

Hilsman thought this new conflict was an internal war, a subtle and complex interlacing of terror, subversion and ambushes—these essentially surface phenomena offering protective disguise to a political goal-oriented dynamism which churned beneath the visible. He did not represent a majority in his view of this most unconventional style of guerrilla warfare. So the search for the idea continued.

By the time of his 1962 State of the Union address the President, having dispatched many in search of the idea, had to content himself with offering statements of personal conviction rather than articulating doctrine. The independence of certain nations is simultaneously a bar to the communists' "grand design" and is the groundwork of our own policy, he told us that day. Beyond that he could say little other than hint there was some connection between Laos and Vietnam, and that we were helping. Otherwise the speech was not illuminating.[37] The crunch had been postponed.

By June the idea still eluded us. During a press conference a reporter asked if Walt Whitman Rostow of the State Department's Policy Planning Staff had done some planning on his own, rather than under instructions of the government. The President responded first by making the reporters laugh, then by admitting that we did not in fact know just what our military policy and force levels ought to be at this time. In an atypical stumbling over his words, Kennedy said we "are examining to see—guerrilla warfare, anti-insurgency—what should be our . . ."[38] At the time of his remarks it seemed clear that the scene in Vietnam was one of guerrilla warfare, but not of *real* guerrilla warfare, and that we were and were not engaged in putting down an insurgency, that we were and were not pursuing victory.

His search for an idea was conducted simultaneously while looking for a better-ordered defense concern, for more realistic (that is, usable) weapons, and for soldiers. Back during his campaign Kennedy took up the charge made by some retired generals* that the nation was imperiled because of our overreliance on nuclear weapons. Interestingly, the public deflected this charge (which was true) while accepting the dire warnings of a "missile gap" (which was false). The President evidently believed the former more than the latter, too, and immediately upon taking office directed his Secretary of Defense, Robert S. McNamara, to go to work refashioning conventional defenses. The Secretary did, giving the Army his greatest attention. During the first year of the new administration Army troops increased by a third (750,000 to 1,000,000), Army planners were thanked for redesigning their defense-oriented "pentomic" division,** and the US STRIKE Command was formed to bring under joint command the combat-ready forces of the U.S. Strategic Army Corps and the Air Force's Tactical Air Command.[39] Further, and based upon the conviction that the bluster of the Eisenhower

*Ridgway, Taylor and Gavin. General Taylor's book, *The Uncertain Trumpet* (1959), and its thesis of flexible response became central to the strategy of President Kennedy and Secretary McNamara. The general was military adviser to Kennedy 1960–61, and was brought back on active duty to serve as Chairman, Joint Chiefs of Staff, in 1962.

**Divisions now changed their composition to three brigades, each capable of handling two to five battalions in various mixtures.

years reflected fear whose intensity limited our military response to a nuclear holocaust, war material was prepositioned around the world in those places from which we could exert the level of subnuclear force required. To move men and munitions a massive expansion in airplane building was gotten underway, the intention being the radical upgrading of a world-wide airlift capability. Within two years we were capable of taking on the two-and-a-half-war concept.* It was part mystique, part strategy for peace.

It was the one-half war that helped spur the building of mammoth aircraft for carrying troops, made the President demand a smaller, lighter high-velocity rifle for the jungles, and got a handful of Americans interested in the meaning of "victory" and "defeat" in places like Vietnam. There was still a problem, though, in that the planes and Berets and verbal exercises took place without the benefit of an idea of the purposes to which they might be put.

SEARCH FOR AN IDEA: II

A basic difficulty in creating a concept which would articulate our response to the war was that rational thought presupposed an understanding of that to which we would respond. This, in turn, was complicated by three deeper factors: (1) the enemy in Vietnam did not at this time have either a fully engineered body of doctrine nor an established program of action. From 1959 to 1962 the Viet Cong spent the bulk of their energy and talent in the development of a superbly organized sociopolitical apparatus, playing things by ear when conditions demanded.[41] (2) During the first two years of the Kennedy Administration there was mass ignorance concerning the intricacies of revolutionary warfare, be its practitioners communist or noncommunist. (3) The existence of the Army's "Never Again" club.

As for the first of these—what the Viet Cong was up to—the President and his advisers and soldiers alike would have to wait and see, though the waiting need not be passive. If we could get the right people into the right spots it should be able, so it was argued, to learn the ways of the enemy. At a meeting of the National Security Council on April 29, 1961, after just three months in office, President

*Secretary McNamara also ordered a Planning-Programming-Budgeting System, complete with a five-year forecast requirement and cost effectiveness studies. This approach would in time be reflected in his Hamlet Evaluation System and, aided by domestic political pressure, "body count."

The Viet Minh-French war was described by the communists as "The Resistance," the upcoming battle with Diem as "The Revolution." The interim period was called "Special War," a term which apparently (and ironically, as things worked out) had nothing to do with the Special Warfare School at Fort Bragg (formed in 1957). The latter produced Special Forces soldiers.

Kennedy ordered the deployment of about 400 members of Special Forces, the first 52-man increment of which would leave immediately. They were to set up shop, and Group Headquarters, at Nha Trang. It would be five months until the President told those at Fort Bragg it was legal for them to wear the Beret, seven months before he queried Roger Hilsman on the status of guerrilla warfare theory, and much, much longer before a viable idea for prosecuting the war was hammered out. But, the Berets were coming, though minus headgear.[41] Their sub rosa Holy War was on.

When these men of Special Forces arrived they could plan on easing into a picture whose outline had been sketched in advance. There already was in existence something called "First Observation Group," described by General Lansdale as "a Special Forces type of unit," which had been created in February 1956. At the time of its formation a Korean-type invasion across the Seventeenth Parallel was feared, and an early mission of FOG was to prepare to wage guerrilla warfare in the enemy's rear should the invasion come off.* Blending with the circumstances and geopolitics of 1960, FOG began slipping across the borders of North Vietnam and Laos to see what could be seen. It was now the will of the commander-in-chief that these operations be expanded under CIA-military adviser sponsorship. The borders in Indochina were artificial creations which went unrecongnized by North Vietnam from the time of the 1954 accords. So, it was essential that they be kept under strict surveillance and, if necessary, crossed over if that should be the only way to get information on enemy activities and plans. During wartime it's called intelligence gathering.

Plans for resolving difficulty Number One were off the drawing boards and deep into the jungles and mangrove swamps.

Problem Number Two concerned ignorance—ignorance of ideology and war, and of ideologized war fought for the undramatic purpose of establishing administrative control over the 16,000 hamlets of South Vietnam. Just as he had said, "Let there be green hats," the President now ordered light to break upon his military planners, light which would take the form of theoretical constructs and political hypotheses, sociohistorical analysis and an understanding of the relative value of midnight kidnappings of VC "shadow government" officials.** To help fill the void of knowledge there were let contracts for the gathering of information that might be useful in understand-

*Special Forces' initial mission was to conduct similar operations, principally in Eastern Europe.

**President Kennedy created the interagency "Special Group (Counter-insurgency)"[42] on January 18, 1962. He tasked them with the creation of C-I doctrine and training, and the education of the entire U.S. Government vis-à-vis insurgency/revolutionary warfare. In the former they registered a qualified if belated success. Their second mission—education—ended in failure.

ing the elusive and successful enemy, for putting into book form ideas about this uncanny type of war, and for establishing programs of instructions for the soldiers who would, once the concept was shaped, be the visible, active agents for that idea's implementation. Universities were contacted, and some responded. Others, perhaps smelling government money, offered their services (for a fee) in the pursuit of the idea. Within a few years a great cluster of research organizations brought themselves into being, as close to government offices as possible, in the hope of either helping, or being well-paid, or both. Mostly it was for money.

About a year after President Kennedy took office the publications began rolling out, many relying on the French and British experiences. One such publication, written rather symbolically in summary form, says in its foreword "It need not be emphasized that a better understanding of the processes of revolution might well be of critical significance."[43] The times were again reminiscent of the early postwar days and George F. Kennan at the National War College, with theoretical papers being written in the Pentagon, CIA, Fort Bragg. Even a few Agency for International Development personnel contributed ideas. The ideas were thin and based largely on others' experiences. Nevertheless there was, in this flurry of theorizing, a new approach being shaped to the waging of war. The approach here was conditioned by the deep belief in the inseparability of political and military measures, though the relative weight to be given the two would not be decided during President Kennedy's lifetime.

SEARCH FOR AN IDEA: III

The USMAAG in Saigon had begun work on an idea for halting the communist flood even before Kennedy took office. Their *Counter-Insurgency Plan Vietnam* was completed late in 1960. Its main provisions were accepted by the new President one week after his inauguration.

The CIP was modest, inexpensive ($42 million), and without a genuine strategic foundation, a fact which bothered President Kennedy and some of his advisers. Some advisers looked to the past for guidance; others admitted they had to create their own precedent. Proposals were not long in coming, their reception mixed. An eager people quickened its pace and marched jauntily into a quagmire.

Hilsman proposed what was for the time and for the "rich nations, poor nations" fans heretical, when he argued that the existence of guerrillas did not mean the government was either popular or unpopular.[44] The implications of his remarks took years to penetrate the wall of sophisticated ignorance. In terms of the number persuaded it was a minor penetration at that. What Hilsman meant is that reform by a threatened government is not sufficient, perhaps not even necessary, for the successful control of an insurgency. Witness Hungary in 1956.

An idea similar to the one expressed by Hilsman in his *Marine Corps Gazette* article and to his President already was being advanced—on the other side of the world. In early Fall 1961 a career officer of the British Colonial Service was sent on loan by Her Majesty to the Republic of Vietnam. Within a month or so, Sir Robert Thompson had the situation sized up (which he called "an appreciation"), and offered a plan to President Diem for the pacification of what Sir Robert took to be not only the prize sought by an cncmy, but thc most sensible starting point as well: the Mekong Delta.

Copies of the Thompson plan were transmitted to Washington via General Taylor (who was visiting Saigon at the time). The concept embodied was a well thought-out confirmation of what a handful in the capital were convinced had to be the case.

During the winter holiday season of 1961–62 the Thompson plan was read, modified slightly, embroidered upon. By February 1962 the Thompson-Hilsman program, "A Strategic Concept for South Vietnam," was on the President's desk.

The drawing board was behind them, the quagmire lay ahead.

TRAVELS

In December 1962 President Kennedy asked Hilsman to make a firsthand report on Vietnam. He agreed and, as he left for the airport, felt his notions about the best way to counter communist revolutionary war threatened by a defect in the American character, a flaw too easily dismissed: just because at the time it was hidden by a uniform it has nothing to do with "the military mind."

Just a few months after assuming the Presidency, Kennedy told his Joint Chiefs of Staff to upgrade Special Forces training and give their general, William P. Yarborough, the support he required. After implying the generals should do some homework on guerrilla warfare, the issue of the man who would replace General McGarr, ranking officer in Vietnam, was raised. Hilsman and his faction preferred someone like General Yarborough, whereas the Army on the whole preferred someone more orthodox. The generals were not at all convinced there was anything special about this war that was underway in Southeast Asia; in April 1961 the JCS Chairman, General Lyman L. Lemnitzer, said his President was oversold on the importance of guerrilla fighting; and General Paul D. Harkins of the regular army not General Yarborough of Special Forces was named new U. S. commander in South Vietnam.

Just a month before Hilsman left for Vietnam in 1962, General Wheeler, Army Chief of Staff, delivered an address at Fordham University, saying although it was fashionable in some quarters to regard the problems in Southeast Asia as primarily political rather than military, "the essence of the problem in Vietnam is military."[45] The decision on the new military advisory general and General Wheeler's remarks represented a basic flaw in our national outlook: either/or, either fight or negotiate, kill or land reform, bomb or pacify.

Either/Or versus Both/And, MacArthur redivivus, win or contain: these were the two centers of thought as how best to approach the war in Vietnam. "Approach to war" means far more than a plan of operations or scheme of maneuver. What was at stake in these irreconcilable views was a fundamental appreciation for war as such, superimposed upon which was the self-portrait of the American at war. These basic attitudes, which can be summarized as *"Cry, 'Uncle'"* versus *"Sneaky Pete,"* the direct or indirect approach, were more than simple differences of opinion, for they constituted one of the major contradictions which coursed its way through the Vietnam War from start to finish.*

During those creative and frenetic first months of the Kennedy Administration, the President's people went in all different directions during the course of the search. Consequently, it was inevitable that they collide. Just before Kennedy ordered the deployment of the first contingent of Special Forces troops to Vietnam, Walt Whitman Rostow of the State Department paid a visit to their homebase of Fort Bragg. There he delivered a speech in which he gave a subsurface argument for seeking out the sources of aggression in this new kind of war and, therefore, an argument for bombing North Vietnam. He was convinced that sanctuaries and lines of communications were all-important in a guerrilla war, citing ex-

*With the onset of American retaliatory bombing for North Vietnamese provocations in the Tonkin Gulf and on our forces at Pleiku, "Cry, 'Uncle'" would show that it, too, housed two schools of thought: "Spiked Mace" (the JCS "sharp rap" view), and "Spanish Boot" (the "increase the quotion of pain" outlook of civilian dilettantes in government).

periences in Malaya, the Philippines and Greece as precedents to support his argument.[46] His speech must have been doubly confusing for his listeners, for their original guerrilla doctrine was indeed based upon such considerations as frontiers and conventional lines of communications (since World War II was their model, with a link-up with friendly conventional forces the goal for their guerrilla units). At the same time they had just received instructions from Mr. Kennedy to come to grips with revolutionary war (though it wasn't called by that name), to be truly unconventional, to devise new tactics based not on World War II but on Vietnam.

About six months later Rostow accompanied Kennedy's military adviser, General Maxwell Taylor, to Vietnam. That was October 1961, before the death struggle of "Uncle" and "Pete" had surfaced. Symbolic of the contradiction in the making was a third passenger on the trip, General Lansdale, who was selected for his expertise at doing the unconventional, the suspect.* General Taylor recommended the immediate deployment of about 8,000 U.S. troops, while General Lansdale was sent to study the problem of sealing off the Seventeenth Parallel across which a conventional invasion was presumed to be eminent. General Taylor's recommendations were in line with a JCS memo of five months earlier, which had urged we go in now (assuming the political decision was in that direction). To wait longer would be to invite a situation in Vietnam similar to that already existing in Laos, which is to say, a present, on-going combat situation.[47]

The cable the general sent his President from the city of Baguio, the Philippines, was only partially consistent with the request for U.S. troops made coincident with his trip by Vietnam's Defense Minister. He, too, wanted American troops to come, to be stationed along the parallel and in the Central Highlands.**

There the similarity ends, for Mr. Thuan, the Defense Minister, had not thought the problem through, whereas, given his premises, General Taylor had. The general admitted that a "bare token" was insufficient, and that there is no limit to our possible commitment if it is decided to close the frontiers (Seventeenth Parallel, plus the Laos-Cambodian borders). Were we to attack the source in Hanoi, he continues, then the number of troops required would be fewer. The

*Despite requests from General Taylor and President Diem that he be assigned to Saigon, General Lansdale was denied this post until late 1965. Distrust of the unconventional clearly is not restricted to World War II generals.

**The physical deployment of United States troops, once the decision was made, would be a running if hidden sore on U.S.-GVN relations. In general, the Vietnamese did not want our troops around populated centers. Moreover, they were pressured into permitting us free access of their country. This subject is pursued in the next chapter.

one point of confusion in his cable is the deployment of our men. They were not to clear the jungles and forests, and the border areas were not the place to engage them. On the other hand, American forces would engage in combat in self-defense, would back-up South Vietnam, and would be the advance guard if a U.S. buildup occurred. Understandable as the general's lack of conciseness is, he had unearthed, then packaged, in his report the makings of what was at best a dilemma, at worst an unconquerable inconsistency: American combat soldiers in an advisory role,* American advisers in a combat situation.

Thus, at the end of 1961 the search for the idea of how best to meet the challenge of revolutionary warfare as practiced by Vietnamese communists in their homeland was coming to an end. The search had started from the same geographic point—the President's Office —and had almost immediately separated into two groups to follow divergent and, ultimately, irreconcilable paths. On the one hand the more vocal, more numerous "Uncle" disciples reacted to the Taylor-Rostow trip by urging, as did Defense Secretary McNamara, "a firm, initial position," commiting the United States to the clear objective of preventing the fall of South Vietnam to the Communists.[50] In his corner were the Joint Chiefs of Staff, who said "Any war in the SEA Mainland will be a peninsula- and island-type of campaign" in which the U.S. had demonstrated its prowess both in World War II and in Korea.[51] It is not clear that the generals would have accepted Secretary McNamara's negative objective of keeping South Vietnam from falling to the insurgents, nor is it clear the Secretary would have equated all peninsulas. Just what "victory" should be taken to mean would be a recuring problem for those who shared similar emotional premises, as would the question of the precise form the fighting should take. These were decidedly not academic disputes; they went to the heart of the problem of America at war. One day they would convince our people we had lost a war.

In January 1962, Secretary McNamara and the Joint Chiefs of Staff submitted their memos on the conduct of the war in response to the Taylor report. At just this time Hilsman was getting read-into

*In his follow-up report of November 3, General Taylor recommended that the United States shift from a purely advisory stance "to something nearer—but not quite —an operational headquarters in a theater of war." We would become "a limited partner in the war."[48] The idea was unworkable from the beginning, as anyone who ever offered unacceptable advice in Vietnam will testify. Then-Vice President Johnson saw the problem quite clearly following his May, 1961 trip.[49] "First, any alliance-type action required clear-cut command authority; secondly, the presence of American combat forces was not wanted by Asian leaders, for the colonial experiences were still very much alive in their memory." With the introduction of Americans on a vast scale in 1965 the problem could not be skirted, was never resolved.

the current situation in Vietnam, having stopped off in Honolulu along with Secretary McNamara where General Harkins, U.S. military commander in Vietnam, was given the President's thoughts on guerrilla warfare. By all accounts General Harkins was not overly enthusiastic about the politicizing of warfare. Hilsman continued on to Saigon.

While in Saigon, Hilsman met with the master of counterinsurgency doctrine, Sir Robert Thompson. Sir Robert had been instrumental in breaking the back of the Communist insurgency in Malaya. His pacification plan for the Delta, built around the concept of strategic hamlets, had been accepted by the Saigon Government in March 1962. Again and again, Sir Robert stressed that his idea was a program and not a single operation. What he envisioned was the least dramatic approach to war imaginable, where the bulk of work and responsibility would be shouldered by the village policeman, the least by the commander of a maneuver battalion. What was required was the physical isolation of the insurgent from the population off of which the former necessarily leeches. This meant unending police and intelligence work, such that every individual inside the hamlet could be identified and, for all practical purposes, controlled. The social, political, and economic reforms which often were wanted more by those giving aid than by those receiving it could be commenced if genuine, round-the-clock security were a fact. To do otherwise would be to pump money and food directly into the hands of the Viet Cong, via conforming, terrified villagers.[52]

A difficulty arose immediately, for Sir Robert made the mistake of making his point more graphic by referring to an "oil blot" theory. Since most of the money to be supplied would be American, and since most of those administering any such program would be Americans, by applying such a title he made a blunder. A nation which prides itself on the manufacture of acronyms and labels could be counted on to grind down the sophisticated, time-consuming corners of any idea until it fits our homespun, linear mold. We did, though it took some time and required some help. The help required was supplied by some of our Vietnamese allies, and by members of the conscience-stricken press.

But there was a brief go at the idea, this strategy for developing a hedgehog of strategic hamlets which, if consistently applied, would force the insurgent to violate one of his axioms and fight on terms not of his choosing. Sir Robert's concept was integrated with ideas being developed in the United States, ideas which clashed with another set being developed simultaneously in other parts of the military establishment. Under the Thompson-Hilsman plan, a unified system of civilian, police and military operations would be made to mesh, the principal result of which would be the inverting of traditional priorities, symbolized by the police inspector giving orders to the soldier.* Giving orders from the top would be a proconsul.

President Diem approved the strategic hamlet program in March 1962, and immediately it ran into trouble. Sir Robert wanted to go into the wealthy and populous (but fairly stable) Mekong Delta for the first experiment, with the understanding that isolated, unsupportable attempts would not be made. General Harkins and U.S. Ambassador Frederick E. Nolting, Jr., could not agree, the careful integration and subordination of functions could not be brought about, and the overarching idea never was fully understood by those whose job it was to implement it. As a result, the shooting war was pursued independently of the "oil blot" theory, as in times of old.[54]

The American military advisors in Saigon who were hostile to the whole notion of meshing politics and war were aided by Diem's brother, Nhu, and by the *New York Times* correspondent Homer Bigart. Nhu permitted his creeping madness to overtake him as he ordered a hamlet established in the Ben Cat region,** which meant the forcible moving of unnecessary numbers of people into an insecure, indefensible area. Bigart said it was all an American idea, and that the idea amounted to the construction of concentration camps.[55]

In general, Hilsman concluded, there was no overall direction, Vice President Johnson's fears about lack of clear command channels had materialized, our military advisers had been hypnotized by the lure of large-scale operations and set-piece battles (though these were almost entirely illusory), intelligence work and small scale patroling ignored, and so forth. It was more of the same, with a program grown more massive and less controllable by the day, with no idea yet as how we might get some leverage on Diem.

At the same time, for all its misuse and miserable support, the strategic hamlet idea received the greatest flattery possible. The

---

*Neither Robert Thompson nor Roger Hilsman ever denied the need for a powerful military force in an insurgency, both insisted on long-range reconnaisance patrolling, both knew that many insurgents had to be tracked down and killed. Their principal point concerned the meaning of "source of the insurgency." If one gets a fixation on base camps and infiltration routes there must be a concomitant loss of attention given to the dreary but indispensable police and intelligence work at the village level.[53]

**According to Hilsman, "Operation Sunrise" began "for special tactical reasons,"[56] that is, because Nhu demanded it. Another ill-advised strategic hamlet was begun in May 1962, in Phu Yen Province. Saigon inefficiency and Montagnard hostility made the outcome inevitable.

flattery came in the form of mortar barrages and Chinese assault rifles, as hamlet after hamlet was overrun by the VC during that year of multiple, contradictory testing.*

A month before President Kennedy's death, Secretary McNamara, still reacting to the August 31 meeting of the NSC, continued to belittle the political side of an insurgency and to speak of the progress being made in the shooting war. By this time, his corner had won the argument and provided the fruits of the search for an idea; they would have won with or without Buddhist burnings, with or without the murder of two presidents. "Uncle" was preparing to move, to root our Aggression.

THE BERET: FAIR-HAIR TO PARIAH

During his press conference of February 14, 1963, Kennedy was pressed by a reporter to tell the American people the facts on Vietnam. The President went through the now-familiar litany of helping the Vietnamese, and so forth. He then admitted our people would, "of course, fire back to protect themselves." Deftly cutting the next question off at its source, he reminded his people and the world that we had not sent to Vietnam combat troops "in the generally understood sense of the word."[57]

As the President was speaking some of his soldiers were trudging through rivers and paddies with the time-honored purpose of seeking and destroying the enemy. Their Berets were back at camp, resting up for a tour of the local entertainment when this operation ended. In the field it was floppy, wide-brimmed hats with a circular bit of brilliant marker panel sewn inside, in the event someone wanted to signal someone else (say, for example, a rescue aircraft).

It was almost eight years to the day from Kennedy's February press conference that the final formation for Special Forces was held in Nha Trang. For eight years the men had moved through jungle and stream, or washed the sores of lepers, or taught the art of aiming a Claymore mine, or one of a thousand other lessons. After they had been given the mission of guarding the North Vietnam-Laos-Cambodian border area, over a hundred camps—tiny cities in replica, with all the administrative problems of small cities—had been built. Special Forces' initial mission—the rollback of communism in Eastern Europe—had been inverted as the men were sent into the misty hills of western Vietnam to draw from prehistory the

*In January 1963 Sir Robert saw some progress, though there was no end in sight and he resolutely ignored predictions as to when it would end. His successes are systematically overlooked by Diem's detractors.

tiny people living there, and to organize counterrevolutionaries from among them. A bit later Americans were joined with Vietnamese Special Forces, each man paring off with the person of like military occupation. Things seldom went perfectly at the grass roots level. Vietnamese Special Forces had been palace guards, personal assault troops for Diem's brother, Nhu, and too often took their title to mean they could extract as much money from the CIDG they commanded,* as much as the public would bear—and the public, having no place to go other than the route of desertion, could bear a lot. War lords are old hat in the Orient.

The Vietnamese learned the art of war quickly (many had fought alongside the French until 1954), and after a few years there was little for the men of Special Forces to teach. Toward the end of the war, with something like eighty camps to operate, a principal function was to impart the logistics to our allies. On combat operations the major role played by Americans was that of lifegiver to helicopter gunships. Still, morale remained very high, the *élan paler* if only because it was spread so thin.**

Only in the beginning, and only over very few men did the Central Intelligence Agency exercise control. In later years this arrangement, put together four years before the big American build-up, would be distorted and sensationalized for sake of a few headlines. But the legacy and rumors continued to the end, along with a profound distrust and dislike toward Special Forces by the rest of the Army. A tradition of unorthodoxy and individual initiative which had defined Special Forces from the outset had in fact continued through the Vietnam experience, and it never was accepted by "the legs." Besides, we lost.

THE ETERNAL CYCLE: "THE NEW LOOK IN FOREIGN POLICY"

Those who had been away for more than two years from Fort Bragg wouldn't recognize the sign alongside the drive leading to the Special Warfare Center. During the early summer of 1969, workmen had taken down the sign and put up another in its place. The work-

*Civilian Irregular Defense Group, though not mercenaries as certain "go-go" exposes have asserted (their average pay was $40 a month), the CIDG stood outside the regular South Vietnamese Army structure, were recruited with the promise of American medical aid in the event they got hit, and usually were able to keep their families close by or even in camp. It was not unusual for the wives to load weapons and carry grenades for the husbands when the camp came under attack.

**An important mission maintained to the end was reconnaisance and intelligence work. Conventional forces copied the former and respected Special Forces accomplishments at the latter.

men were concerned with personal matters and so didn't think much about the sign change. No longer was one bid a heroic and arrogant welcome to the JFK Center for Special Warfare. Now one received correct but bland instructions pointing the way to a center for military assistance. The museum with Communist weapons and the bust of the late President remained, and each morning the early visitor still heard the splendid martial sounds of the JFK Drum and Bugle Corps. There were still to be observed Green Berets, and the men who wore them, though their ranks had been thinned-far more by Presidential edict and a disappointed public than by the Viet-Cong. Those men who would talk to a stranger no longer spoke of freeing the oppressed. Instead they pointed to the very politic motto of the new Center: "To work ourselves out of a job." Some of the ranking officers who had thumped so hard for an élite cutting edge of America's foreign policy had long since departed to conventional units, long since divorced themselves from Special Forces, Special Warfare, counterinsurgency. The nation had been burned and badly in its attempt to forge an idea, and now it was time to seek more secure assignments. Some did, for career reasons. Most didn't, for reasons sufficient unto themselves.

A war they had all been a part of had turned very sour, for all of us, was considered lost by most and, therefore, immoral by some.

VI

DENOUEMENT

We will stand in Vietnam.

> —President Johnson

For many reasons it will always be difficult for modern democracies to put Clausewitz' dictum into practice.

> —Robert E. Osgood, *Limited War*

I asked you to get me out of here since this strategic nonsense isn't worth biting the dust for.

> —*Last Letters From Stalingrad*

The sour changed to bitter, disappointment turned into guilt, feelings of uneasiness became the conviction that we had lost. "Lost" isn't quite the right term, but words no longer seem to convey what we mean when the Vietnam experience is discussed.

Loss, or failure, or defeat for the American in Vietnam had its origin in Panmunjom via Washington; in Nuremberg via Montgomery and Berkeley; and in the impatient, punitive law of noncontradiction. A disintegrating society was part cause, part consequence of the experience.

The issue was decided in November 1965, after irreconcilable needs surfaced. The first was our desire to whip an enemy to his knees, to mount the head of a defeated general on a pike. This searing, driving force misappropriated from the deck of the U.S.S. *Missouri* as she sat in Tokyo Bay, pushed all other considerations from view in late 1965; it had done the same fifteen years earlier as the people cheered General MacArthur's race to the Yalu. Now it fueled a new campaign, one within the mist of the Central Highlands; it was the major force that hammered out the decision: the Americans would take the Ia Drang Valley by storm and would annihilate the enemy.

A second force sought release and satisfaction at almost the same time. Like the need for a defeated and punished enemy, this one too had been waiting since World War II. Our second desire was a demand: for finality, for closure, and for moral certainty in war. It burst its bounds as 20,000 Americans chanted outside the Pentagon, their ritual telling of an ineffable freedom, of the vacuity of traditional values, and of personal obligation to reach out and grasp, then implement, transcedent truth.

THESIS: FIND THE BASTARDS—THEN PILE ON!

THE LURE OF VICTORY

One of the ironies of what General Westmoreland described as the "bloody and classic campaign of the Ia Drang Valley"[1] was that this battle, which turned out to be a doctrinal model of counterinsurgency warfare, was initiated by a group of American soldiers whose heartbeats stood opposed to massive, conventional operations. But the handful manning the Special Forces Camp at Plei Me had their necks in a wringer. Three NVA regiments had surrounded the place, and the men, and were preparing to give the handle of the wringer its final turn. October 1965 was approaching its end. So was the camp at Plei Me unless some of the Cav's four hundred-plus helicopters could delay the finale.

They could, and would. A battalion of the First Cavalry Division moved into the highland city of Pleiku, faces and helicopters shining. A brigade followed. Back in Saigon an aide asked General Westmoreland, "Why don't you give Kinnard* his head? I think the Cav is ready." The general thought so too. Near the end of October, he issued his order to our first and only airmobile division: "find, fix and destroy the enemy forces threatening Pleiku, Plei Me, and the Central Highlands."[2] Operation SILVER BAYONET was on. The enemy was as new at helicopter assaults as the Americans were, so he stood

*Lieutenant General Harry W. O. Kinnard, at the time Commanding General of the First Air Cavalry Division.

and fought. Part of him was nailed into place such that his death could be at a time of our choosing. The exhiliration within the Cav couldn't be contained; nor could the larger and larger masses of American soldiers who piled atop the riveted North Vietnamese.

The smell of explosives and death and jet fuel hung in the air until November 20. By that time 200 metal caskets were being flown home. In the mire of the jungle, Army bulldozers tore holes from the earth's rotting crust, then nudged 1,200 decaying NVA bodies into their final resting place.[3]

It was a good approach to war, in part forced upon the U.S. command by our Vietnamese allies, in part the unfolding of the American will. A promise of the total destruction of the enemy was made good on the slopes of the hills. Prompt pronouncements of victory were made, the *imprimatur* of the press begrudgingly extended. The prototype was a success. From the time of SILVER BAYONET down to the hyperbolic COMPLETE VICTORY of May 1968, with the latter's record of seventy-nine friendly battalions piling one atop the other and the kicking all life out of 7,600 of the enemy, the scheme did not vary greatly. Success followed success. Techniques for racking up easier kills were developed, but the overall plan didn't change. It was an approach to war, a view of war, which nearly all Americans comprehend. More important, it was a notion found acceptable by the American citizenry, along with its implied promises, vicarious whiff of gunpowder, and visual coverage. It was all these things. At first.

After the words and exhortations and promises had turned to ashes, the plan was much criticized. It was criticized by well-wishers, such as Sir Robert Thompson, (who had counseled against the mass influx of U.S. troops for many years); and it was criticized by others, such as the journalist Ward Just (who, moved by a careful reading of an introduction to Clausewitz, solemnly yet obliquely denounced the attrition policy as "witless," as early as 1970).[4] Which only goes to show some of the forms disappointment can take.

In recounting the experience of the war the approach here will amount to a series of cuts, oblique views, and zigzags across the surface, followed by a penetration of layers of events. After the try at analysis and reduction, after searching for and locating where the core ought to be, we'll be disappointed.

America's performance in Vietnam was moved from the wings to near center stage in early February 1962, when MAAG met MACV, and the acronym race was on.* Two years later they combined; a few more months and MAAG was abolished. During 1964 Fifth Special Forces Group opened a splendid new headquarters along the beautiful shoreline of II Corps, just outside Nha Trang. At the same time two complete helicopter companies of the Army were setting up shop elsewhere.[5]

The Special Forces-types continued the program already set in motion by those who had made the trip earlier (and had received some fat per diem payments for their early efforts). The program was impressive and complex, ranging from the building and supervising of a string of isolated camps along the border—their jobs being rather like small-time city managers—to tromping through fecal streams with the diseased and primitive *montagnards,* to the grisly work of a midnite kidnapping or blowing away of a VC leader, to suicidal reconnaisance work. All this they did in America's first attempt to crush an internal war, or insurgency, or whatever the people back at Bragg were calling it then. The idea was to crush it from the inside out.

Special Forces and their kind from the inside, helicopters from the outside, the latter hurredly lifting Vietnamese soldiers, weapons and *nouc mam* from one hoped-for battle to another. Friends at helicopter school back in Alabama were getting assignment orders well in advance of graduation now, contracts were being let for more of the unnatural machines, aircraft which half-shuffle, half-grunt their way through the air. By 1965 the number of in-country choppers totaled 327, some of whose pilots were writing home about busing over 1,100 Vietnamese into combat in War Zone D north of Saigon, only to find there was no one there to fight.[6]

American advisers had by this time seeped down to the district level, and at the end of one war and the beginning of another, advisers and chopper pilots and the like were contributing to America's first go at internal war, or insurgency, or whatever it was the President had in mind. The idea was to gather enough weight in one spot so as to squeeze the life out of the cause of their discomfort, and to do this from the outside.

Those whose proper job it was to submit to the squeezing—the Viet-Cong—spent the year of Senator Goldwater's defeat insuring against their own. They also worked from two directions, with emphasis placed upon shoring up, then building from the inside out, lowest level first. Their infrastructure—in effect an unbelievably complicated shadow government—spread first down, always down,

*Military Assistance and Advisory Group versus Military Assistance Command Vietnam. Our ballooning presence in Vietnam and President Kennedy's acceptance of the dares from Hanoi, Moscow, and Peking required the change.

until it could anchor in the bedrock of the countryside, then curl upwards into the legal government of Saigon. West of the capital they were able in 1964 to put together their own division, the Ninth, selecting for their weapon the obsolete, cost-free and very effective AK-47 assault rifle. The Viet-Cong would work the surface as well as the interior. To give them aid and comfort in the surface work, when the "war of movement" against the Saigon regime began, the VC welcomed some twelve thousand supporters from north of the Seventeenth Parallel, then made preparations to greet three complete regiments of agrarian reformers from the north.[7]

Seventy-nine aircraft, stuffed with bombs, already were knifing through the clouds as the President spoke to his people early 1965, the year that the ground commander* in Vietnam called "the year of commitment." FLAMING DIRT, as the retaliatory destruction of North Vietnam was called, was waiting to be used a few weeks earlier, on order.[8] The order went out as soon as the mortar rounds stopped falling on our men at Pleiku, after the eight dead Americans had been identified. The enemy response was twofold: they tried to chop the stumbling republic in half between the Highlands and the coast, and, as evidence of their toughness, killed 23 more Americans by mortar fragments at Qui Nhon. They did this with the sure knowledge that more American bombs were on the way, and that more foot soldiers were bound to follow the 3,500 Marines who were then still shaking invasion sand from their boots at Da Nang.

They were right on both counts. FLAMING DART TWO obliterated some choice targets on February 11. Three weeks later the squeeze from without established its credentials with the programmed rubbling of the north by sprays of bombs, under the code name ROLLING THUNDER.

Weeks before the jets began bombing the suburbs of Hanoi, General Westmoreland was given the go-ahead on a request; thereafter any ARVN unit that was trapped, or thought it might become trapped, could rely on American airpower to save the day. Hoping to foreclose the possibility of VC traps entirely, "on-call earthquakes" were authorized. The B-52s responsible for those "earthquakes" were code-named ARC LIGHT.[9]

As we pounded from the outside the enemy bore from within. Amidst the fury of bombs and planes and helicopters the enemy made final plans for bringing people's justice to the soon-to-be liberated strip which linked the Highlands with the coast.

*The terms "Ground Commander" and "MACV" will refer to General Westmoreland unless otherwise noted. Similarly, CINCPAC refers to Admiral U.S.G. Sharp.

In late March, General Westmoreland's superiors in the Pentagon digested the general's "Commander's Estimate of the Situation." The document was as grim as it was direct: seventeen American battalions were required almost immediately if outright defeat in the south was to be averted. To hold onto the Highlands meant committing our singular airmobile division. Thirty-five battalions as soon as possible with nine more standing by was his estimate of what would be required to stabilize the area around Pleiku. After suppressing the outbreak there, serious thought could be given to the systematic destruction of the main force VC and NVA troops who were now openly marauding through the countryside.

Thus within the folds of that force level request of forty-four battalions was carried the overall plan of action: search-and-destroy.[10]

Instead of fourty-four battalions, he received two from the Marines and, after some squabbling, a brigade of paratroopers. The scales continued to sag in the wrong direction. In late May the ARVN Fifty-first Regiment was clawed to pieces along the northern coast, its relief column then flailed from front, side, and rear in a perfect ambush. The relief force ceased to exist. With catastrophes daily, General Westmoreland was informed there would be no more new ARVN units put into the bin for the foreseeable future. Losses in existing units whisked up every recruit Saigon could lay its hands on.

On June 7, the general informed his immediate commander, and the man responsible for the air and naval segments of the war, that either we go in fast and hard or the first domino collapses. Secondly, if we go in it will be to win. That means our troops will defend for no longer than necessary. Their mission is to get on and stay on the offensive.[11] Admiral Ulysses S. Grant Sharp, Commander in Chief Pacific, agreed. One month later their President was convinced, and ordered the flood gates opened.

What followed was more a heavy trickle than a flood. The important point is that it had been turned on and would flow faster as the situation demanded. The President himself proudly announced the deployment of the lone airmobile division (the First Air Cavalry) in September.[12] A month later the First Infantry Division sailed, as did the remainder of the Third Marines. They constituted the first part of Phase I of the overall strategy, which is to say they would soon be "arresting the losing trend."[13] The Marines killed 700 in August during OPERATION STARLIGHT when a Viet-Cong force backed into a cul-de-sac on the Batangan peninsula. They thus antedated the success in the Ia Drang by the Army. About the same time the enemy was evening matters back in the troublesome Highlands, where the muddy and isolated Special Forces camp at Dak Sut was swallowed. Eight of the twelve Americans got out alive: only fifty of the two-hundred and fifty shrunken *montagnards* walked away from it.

At year's end the enemy had been stopped though. Contrary to the fearful, 1965—the year of commitment—had been a success, we had found the secret: the hammer outside and anvil inside. Press from inside out, smash from outside in. And pile on.

Success was piled upon success during 1966, as another division of Marines and nearly four more Army divisions moved into the war zone.[14] This was the second phase, designed to hold back the enemy, conserve and build our own strength, and prepare for the decapitation of the enemy.

Even in this year of our husbanding of forces the successes were anything but minor. In a six-week fight the First Cavalry and some ARVN and Korean friends dispatched 2,389 of the other side in our first major thrust into the Viet-Cong recruiting area of Binh Dinh Province.[15] That operation (called MASHER/WHITE WING/-THANG PHONG II) was followed by equally successful ones with such titles as UTAH, TEXAS, COLORADO, PAUL REVERE, I, II, III, and IV, and so forth, whose successes read, respectively, 623, 632, 674, 546, 809, and so forth.

By year's end the Binh Dinh area had been raked over four times, the Pleuku region three times, five other lanes from the northern reaches of Saigon to the dust factory along the DMZ swept clear. Three and a third Communist bodies lay alongside each friendly corpse, as the year of the offensive, 1967, followed.[16]

The new year promised finality, as still more Marines and soldiers disgorged from air-conditioned commercial airliners, and prepared to enter combat. In January a few of our Marines moved through the slime of the Mekong Delta, our first troop commitment there.[17] The kill ratio increased to nearly four to one in our favor, as Binh Dinh and Pleiku were again hacked at. Results were impressive: PALM BEACH (conducted, appropriately, in the Delta,) 570; JUNCTION CITY, 2,728; MACARTHUR, 4, 944. PERSHING, 5,401.

As the pounding from outside and above by the hammer continued its successful ways, and as the anvil from within did its part through such Viet-Cong extermination programs as Phoenix and the Provincial Reconnaissance Units, ever more imagination was required to maintain the kill records. New things were tried. There was Road Runner and County Fair, Rome Plows and Leaping Lena,

Bushmaster and Eagle Flights, Recondo and Sniffers and LRRP, Seals and Igloo White and Cobras and Black Hawks. And we had thirty-six tracker dogs killed in action, while 16,000 pages of intelligence per day flooded Saigon.[18]

The result was the successful destruction of a generation of North Vietnamese males.

Almost a year and a half after the first battle of the Ia Drang, our Fourth Division was back there committed to the teeth. Admiral Sharp received the message saying that enemy forces were increasing and had to be destroyed. Not only in the Pleiku-Kontum area, but in stiff-necked Binh Dinh, too.[19] The other side expended human lives the way we do bullets, and slowly it was realized that fighting this particular enemy is like mowing the lawn: one has to do it every week, with the depressing assurance it'll sprout back up as soon as the mower is put away.

As the world's first partially electronic-mechanized battlefield was being crafted, as names on death lists of confirmed Viet-Cong had heavy, dark lines drawn through them, as the Cambodian border and the DMZ generated an ever greater target for the operators of the meat grinder (who were killing only about eighty-five of the other side per month per battalion) "success" asked that it be supplied with a less painful meaning—or any meaning, for that matter. As with General Ridgway in early 1951 (at the end of one war and the start of a new one) under a new commander, continued success would translate into 1,300 dead Americans per month.[20]

At-tri-tion (a-trish'an), n. (Latin. *ad-*, to+ *terere*, rub) a wearing away by or as by friction.

The ground commander realized his dilemma. On the one hand, if he stayed close enough to the population to provide them with protection, the uncooperative NVA (it was all their show by 1967— at least on the surface) would be able to plan major, coordinated strikes. On the other hand, to hit these bases meant withdrawing support of pacification. To explain the problem the general drew on a simple analogy of a boxer who simultaneously defends (pacification, protection) and attacks (major enemy unit destruction or, if they've gone, tearing up their base areas).[21] We needed more men to fill the unoccupied space, to finish up within a specified time. The well finally went dry, the request for more men was refused. Infiltration from the north promised bigger and better lawns.

All along the object had been the administrative control of the cynical, undernourished peasant, who was a citizen of no nation, for whom "allegiance" was like as not willingly given to whomever held the gun at his head. If enough of these people fear for their safety in enough places then a central government does not exist. If enough are willing, for whatever reason, to protect or even permit members of the competition government to move within it, at enough levels of society, then "space" and "time" in our enameled sense of those terms become enemies more formidable than an enemy rifle squad. We do know how to deal with the latter.[22]

LEARNING WHILE DOING, OR THE PROGRESSIVE EDUCATOR AS THEORIST

Within the defense establishment the early sixties were characterized by an unparalleled confidence, if not to say arrogance. Books eulogizing an emerging "flexible response" spoke with optimism of South Vietnam, citing as evidence the contingency plan for putting 100,000 men into Cuba, for doing whatever had to be done. The intonation in 1964 was majestic: "multiple options with a vegeance stood ready at the President's hand."[23]

Officially the same humility prevailed. We were strong and flexible enough "to respond quickly to any type of aggression with whatever degree of force is needed." A term of office later the same Defense Department publication was written with anonymity: we had "readied and deployed a substantial number of additional forces to Southeast Asia, conducted wide-ranging operations in Vietnam, and maintained forces in various other areas of the world."[24] In that "year of the offensive" another U.S. Government publication which chronicled our other go at limited war concluded, "It would indeed be unfortunate if the hard-won lessons learned in the Korean War, both on the battlefield and in the negotiations, should be ignored or forgotten because of the absence of victory."[25]

In truth, the "hard-won lessons" of Korea had been lost on all of us, partly by design of elected officials, partly by something approaching genetic default. All along the attention and the rhetoric clustered about two major events: Harry S. Truman's unilateral commitment of our forces, and Dwight D. Eisenhower's campaign promises. It required a foreigner to drag the Korean issue partially into the contemporary limelight. General Grivas' rapier cut: what would have happened, he wonders, had the guerrillas in South Korea been given massive support by the Chinese, thus obviating the invasion of June 25, 1950. Under such circumstances would intervention by us have been possible?[26] Such questions were not answered because they were not asked, they were not asked because they are damaging to pride, destructive of preconceptions and liberal visions.

During 1967, "the year of the offensive," the Department of the Army issued two pamphlets. One was magazine size, very well written, and told our troops what they wanted to hear. About those remote enemy base areas it asserted that "to find and smash each, one by one, is an essential task, a prime object in conclusively successful campaigning."[27] This was read by nearly every young officer destined to hump through the boonies of Vietnam.

In the same month there was released another Army document, also called a "pamphlet." This one had the stature and raciness of an out-of-town telephone directory. It spoke not of combat assaults and the ripping apart of base areas but of the gossamer and serpentine People's Revolutionary Party*—its history, methods, and fabulous organizational vitality.

The second document briefly mentioned its smashing military victories. Succumbing to such a seduction as that sort of solution demands "allows the party to continue with the activation of new elements or, at best, buys success at the sacrifice of economy . . . The only way to stop this insurgency is to crush the PRP beyond any hope of recovery."[28]

Roger Hilsman was one of those converted to the cause of "internal war." He resigned less than four months after President Kennedy's assassination. In his last memo to Secretary Rusk, the advocate of Sir Robert's "oil blot" theory and of a secondary role for the military, bade farewell. With a visible shrug he remarked that to fight a guerrilla's war we must adopt his way, that we use conventional operations only against the insurgent's conventional weaknesses.[29]

Two days later the President received a memo from Secretary McNamara, in which the Defense chief revealed his boundless faith in our commitment in Southeast Asia. The controversial "oil spot" or strategic hamlet theory demanded our support, for it is "now fully accepted both on the VN and US sides."[30] He likewise counseled against our taking over command of the Saigon forces.

During that Spring many spoke warmly and sincerely of victory, though the term even at that time offered the consistency and satisfaction of cotton candy. In his parting shot Mr. Hilsman used the

*The various hues and subtleties of which are forever preserved in the TV commentator's incisive expression, "the political arm of the Viet-Cong," Thus confusing the *PRP* with the *NLF*. It's called creative journalism.

term, though he didn't say what he meant by it.* The Joint Chiefs of Staff used it, and they didn't say exactly what they meant by it. Nor did they need to. They, among all principals in the war in Southeast Asia, were totally consistent from beginning to the big national turnabout. Their advice to Mr. McNamara on that raw January morning was that we put aside many of the self-imposed restrictions, and do some things which might entail greater risks. Some of these restrictions: "keeping the war within the boundaries of South Vietnam and avoiding the direct use of US combat forces." There was one other which even the new chairman, General Taylor, apparently believed should be lifted. We should "induce the Government of South Vietnam to turn over to the US military commander, temporarily, the actual tactical direction of the war."[31]

"WAR IN THE CROWD"

In one of the few irrelevancies of which he ever has been convicted, Sir Robert Thompson said the sorry end to which we came in Southeast Asia was partially because the Americans were not trained to conduct long-range jungle penetrations, and likewise were not trained to work within populated areas.[32] One of the miracles of the war was the chameleon-like way those Americans who were so instructed adapted to the ways of the jungle animal. Some did outstanding work "in the crowd."

The trouble lay elsewhere. It lay in the fearful combination resulting from arrogance shielding ignorance. Empirical and moral complexities were blurred or ignored. The source of the complexities overlooked bore the names partisan warfare, guerrilla warfare, brush-fire war, civil war, rebellion, insurgency. "Victory" and "defeat" no longer held their traditional meanings.

An early U.S. Government-funded project to secure a name for the Vietnam involvement argued that the Hanoi rulers were "considerably more tolerant toward middle-class elements than are Western Communist countries." Its report referred to the repressive Diem regime, of the great need for land reforms, and concluded that "Ho Chi Minh seems prepared to unify Vietnam by force."[33] No mention was even made either of the NLF or the PRP, each of which had by that time (December 1962) revealed its mission to the world. This report was flatly contradicted by another study paid for by Washington. The latter detailed the "flowing tolerance" of the Hanoi rulers.[34] Our Left calls it "a no-nonsense social policy."

*He had written much about what "victory" might mean in the Southeast Asian insurgency several times, and was under no obligation to become pedantic at the last moment.

We sent money in opposite directions which paid for studies likewise aimed at irreconcilables (probably because the authors were afflicted with contrary motives). One result, and one center of thought, is symbolized by the first of the two studies just cited: "Let us win their hearts and minds."

Those who are ignorant about government say: "Win the hearts of the people." The Chinese sage—or cynic—who offered this comment three centuries before Christ saw through land reform and unlimited goodies long before either was practiced. We have yet to learn, although we invented both under guise of burrowing from within the crowd, while in fact offering to buy off each person within it. That ancient's advice for social control was taken up by others who followed him, then transported to Vietnam when it was largely subdued. Later ideas for keeping those below in check were refined. They included mutual responsibility, mutual surveillance, and mutual denunciation.[35] There was also the tool of pacification. But the programs, like the dynasties they helped support, tended to ossification.

The surge of dynamism was supplied by people who live a Trappist austerity. Their precision work is fired by a Jesuitical enthusiasm, tempered only by a sense of patience unintelligible to the West. The two reinforce and feed upon each other, the better to do Satan's work.

Vietnamese Communists never had difficulty defining "victory." Its meaning was rolled out by applying the ageless principle, "We win."

One year before a few thousand of his people had to be killed off to make the vision of collectivization a reality, Ho Chi Minh created the Fatherland Front of Vietnam. Its aim was guided by "We win." The country would be unified by whatever means necessary. That Front* was succeeded by another, just two months before John F. Kennedy was elected. The Secretary General of the Lao Dong Party, Le Duan, simultaneously called for and announced its creation before the Third National Congress of his party. About the time President Kennedy promised us sacrifice and heroism, the entity Le had in mind came into being as the National Liberation Front. Steel-

*The term "Front" as used by Vietnamese communists is misleading, as it was designed to be. In democratic parlance a front is a group of organizations which join together to do common cause as, for example, different political factions might do during wartime. To insure control by the Communist Party, the NFL was formed as a command and control instrument. Organizations throughout the South were then put together (farmers, youth, etc.) and satellited onto the pre-existing control apparatus. It's called "spontaneous nationalism" by the American Left.

like leadership was assured by the presence of persons holding dual membership in the NLF and in the People's Revolutionary Party as well.[36] (The PRP disclosed its existence New Year's Day, 1962).

Their ideology was an opportunistic, bastardized Marxism, an ideology whose physical expression was experimental—one whose message appealed more to the peasant's greed than to his need for spiritual sustenance. Ideas would come later.

Until the murder of Diem "We win" demanded the NFL remain principally an agency of social control, making even this level subservient to the fundamental purpose behind it all: the administrative control of the population. Such military operations as there were (the purifying of known enemies of the people such as mosquito abatement personnel, for example) always reinforced a political teaching point. The NLF army was only another force, behind which a political officer inevitably stood.

Viewed externally the social and political phases lasted until the death of Diem. Bullets and satchel charges would thereafter become more common, so common in fact that many lost sight of the fiery agitation-propaganda team leader buried in the jungle who explained, between each dancing act of his female partners, the moral necessity for each bullet, each satchel charge.

The competition government constructed by the Viet-Cong almost defies comprehension and certainly explanation within the brief space allotted here. Its organization had great and mysterious features. As the mysteries were penetrated, schools of thought concerning the best way to defeat the Communist barbarism from within developed. The results of this theorizing were complementary. They were also pretty much ignored.[37] What attracted all this attention was the flowing, self-perpetuating fury of which the VC-controlled areas were capable; and the elusive and elaborate network which ordered, supervised, rewarded and punished in the name of "people's justice."

Direction and control always precedes communist agitation and organization. This was consistent with the slow but systematic destruction of non-communist nationals in the north. Soon the puppet National Liberation Front materialized—its strings were the People's Revolutionary Party, its puppet master the Communist Party of North Vietnam.

We have great difficulty grasping the notion of parallel hierarchies and the rest of the communist paraphernalia which control the lives of the people under their dominion in South Vietnam because of our overfamiliarity with our neighbors, and because of our compulsion to superorganize. Neither condition held in the Republic before the NLF. Much of the Mekong Delta's inhabitants thought of themselves as either free spirits or Cambodians; Cambodia (now the Khmer Republic) in turn lay claim to hundreds of miles of unmarked border land. The Hoa Hao and Cao Dai sects definitely *were* free spirits. Chinese and Indian merchants regarded themselves as userers, which they usually were. Career military officers thought of themselves as war lords, which all too often they became. Th thirteen language groups of *montagnards* thought of themselves as targets for low-land Vietnamese savageries, which they definitely were. The hamlet-dwelling farmer thought of himself as being strictly on his own, and he, too, was quite correct.

The communists decided to change all this to the party's advantage. The interest clubs or groups (fishermen, students, disenchanted war veterans, for example) were created and given recruits after the Front was formed. These associations were the horizontal element. Just as we, for example, have at the lowest level of that organization Boy Scout Troops, or members of labor unions wthin a given city, and at ascending levels continuations of Boy Scouts and labor unions in the form of representatives, up to and including the national level; so too did the NLF's groups. What distinguished the communist effort was the omnipresence of the People's Revolutionary Party (PRP). The Front is the series of horizontal, functional organizations. The Party runs not left and right but up and down: up with information on the progress of the Front and the war, down from the leadership in Hanoi with commands as to what to do next.

Communists are traditionally prudent. The Vietnamese types are no different. To make sure the people work the Party's will in accordance with the eternal vision, not only is a Party presence felt at each level of the Front, with the former paralleling the latter; but there is a central committee at the very top of each organization. The top NLF committee is made up of representatives from student and other groups. The top PRP committee is made up of, unsurprisingly, dedicated members of the Communist Party. Hedging its bet even more, Hanoi saw to it that at this highest level a select few wore two hats, and were members both of the Party and of the Front.[38]

Quality thought-control assured, penetration first of remote and unimportant villages was undertaken. People, perhaps planted years ago by the Party, now living inconspicuous lives as farmers, did not rush to greet the agit-prop leader as the ceremony unveiling a new era was announced. A strict compartmentalization of persons and activities kept the risk of compromise at a minimum. With one village reasonably secure the process of "stringing the beads"—the creation of underground cells which would later tell the Party of troop movements and of traitors to the people—went on.

It went on not just from village to village but at the level of the Saigon government. This "invisible government" of the communists was able to instill fear among the lawful government and among its supporters in the villages.

For Freud the human conscience is irrational, since it punishes the person who carries it within himself for breaking rules, rules which are themselves silly. He held this irrational judge in awe. Once an individual had it—or it had him—father and society could rest easy in the sure knowledge that with the breaking of a rule there automatically followed guilt and self-recrimination. It was, in Freud's view, an invisible and inflexible instrument of family and social control.

In an analogous fashion this is what the communists tried to do with their endless organizing of peasants and their untiring flow of communication. There were differences, though. The rules which the Viet-Cong chose to instill in the peasant's conscience were hailed as the transcendent become immanent, moral truths which pass historical man by save for a chosen few. Those so favored stand prepared to implement trans-historical goals, one of which is the remaking not of the world but of man himself. This requires teaching by the anointed, and submission-become-participation on the part of the suppliant. On occasion it also requires that a school girl who rides a government bus against orders have her hands chopped off.

The first difference, then, is that for the agrarian reformers the conscience is rational and benevolent so long as the proper rules reside within.

Secondly, not only do the communists think a properly-molded conscience desirable, they further believe that honest people have nothing to hide. This includes the structure of an individual's conscience. Through a range of techniques sliding from psychodrama, criticism/self-criticism, and the ultimate in sensitivity training, up through a program which gives a constant read-out on a person's political maturity and heroism in combat, on occasion the Viet-Cong showed themselves capable of producing the ultimate in social control. An individual who had been properly processed had seen the vision and, in the process, had turned his conscience inside out.

The hard core of the VC movement was always small; few were properly disposed spiritually and intellectually to be properly processed. They would be placed at the extreme end of a normal curve which distributed all VC and the civilian sea through which they swam as well. But the unmovable core stood as a standard, or archetype.

Around and beneath this standard developed the most politicized system of communication ever devised.[39] Through this *apparat* energy was generated, acts were induced. The raw materials were fashioned according to specifications sent down the PRP pipeline from Hanoi.

Supervision was the job of the NLF. Their job was to have, at a minimum, a society whose members would not turn them in to the Saigon authorities. Anything above this apparent indifference was a bonus. If the proselytizing went well, if active, controlled participation by the masses could be counted on, then theirs was declared a combatant village, and no one got out. The movement was designed to self-generate and to spread vertically into the roots of the village, and horizontally across the dikes and paddies into the next village.

Participating did not have to mean slipping through American barbed wire and dropping a sack of explosives into an enemy bunker. Just as the entire spectrum of persuasion was used, from a courteous gesture to a hamlet chief or sack of rice for a hungry family up through the burning alive of 200 unreliable *montagnard* women and children at Dak Son, so was peasant help modulated. It could be as simple as the driving of a few nails through an impaling board by a ricketed old man, or the recounting of the day's events by a tiny child who spent his life on the back of a water buffalo. Lenin's thesis concerning conspiratorial activity was proven absolutely: involve everyone in something, no matter how seemingly trivial. In time there must be a diverting of traditional loyalties, a generating of new expectations. Finally, there would be a self-perpetuating, self-regulating social force, a servo-mechanism in which ideology plays a negligible role. When these conditions hold within a given region, revolutionary war can pass from its initial stage into "the armed struggle." The base has been secured, the communist system of priorities (cadre first, then the people, and only lastly the opposing armed force) had been vindicated.

When U.S. soldiers and Marines were committed to combat in Southeast Asia, they were responding to the legal orders of our elected leaders. They made mistakes in the performance of their duties, stressed military operations above other kinds of acts, and ignored the warning "You cannot win the game merely by changing the rules."[40] Our people became disillusioned; their support dwindled.

Without help of either the public or the bulk of the press, the U.S. armed services, left with an insurgency on their hands, admitted:

> Any plan which seeks the destruction of the insurgent machine must concern itself primarily with the breaking down of an organization, not with the infliction of casualties . . . the insurgency ends, not with the disappearance of the guerrilla, but with the destruction of the *apparat* which spawns the guerrilla.[41]

The Army conceded that the decision "to take the fight to the enemy if pacification was ever to succeed" had been overstated.

The notion of a strategy suggests calculations made by a combatant power, such calculations resting upon what is taken to be rational self-interest, aimed at securing fairly specific political goals. We assume that a strategy is similar to an equation: the left side corresponds to anticipated efforts by us and by the enemy, to the right of the equality sign lies victory. If victory is not achieved it is because the equation was formulated improperly, which is to say, the wrong strategy was employed.

Amidst the anguish of our extraction from Vietnam, it is acceptable to argue that the whole affair was immoral and that we shouldn't have gotten involved in the first place. But if we had to go in we should have complied with the rules of revolutionary warfare and expended our efforts from the inside out, adopted the insurgents' way, and fought an internal war. That would have been the correct equation. It might even have made the thing moral.

This criticism ignores issues more basic than conceptual models for waging war. The option implied assumes that we possessed a sophisticated understanding of the enemy, and that with this knowledge in hand we could have fashioned a rational plan of action. The latter in turn presupposes the formulation of intelligible political goals by us, around which a plan of action or strategy could be developed.

The first assumption is unjustified because there was concerning Vietnam and her people a vacuum rather than knowledge when we went in; and the enemy threat was never a static, rock-like thing to be picked up in its finished state for our examination.[42]

The second assumption is unjustified because the curse of any limited war fought by Americans lies precisely in the impossibility for our President, even assuming he is supplied the proper advice, to formulate resolute goals. (It should be recalled that President

Truman pursued three quite different goals within a six-month period during the Korean War). Again, goals in our limited wars cannot be everlasting for two irreducible reasons, reasons whose force drives from opposite directions. The enemy may be uncooperative and/or love to negotiate; or he might have some friends who have a say in the matter. Also, liberal messianism and the American character will in time assert themselves. With that the parameters will have been concretized.

Since our destruction never is a sensed possibility in a limited war, the "correct strategy" is not our physical survival nor the defeat of an enemy, but the satisfaction of our citizens. The liberal compulsion makes this impossible, and the contest between Clausewitz and Jomini thus is fought between unequals.

AMERICAN STRATEGY, OR SOME DIFFICULTIES ENCOUNTERED IN ATTEMPTING TO ADJUST A SPANISH BOOT WHILE UNCLE WAS BAD-MOUTHING PETE

The boosters of "Sneaky Pete," those influential civilians and soldiers who argued for a strong internal emphasis and direction in our conduct of the Vietnam War, were objects of, in order, icy tolerance, suspicion, and banishment by the "Say, 'Uncle' " people. Those who wanted to change it from the inside often talked too freely and irresponsibly of pacification, police, and psychological operations.

In general, those who subscribed to the "Uncle" view had the destruction of VC/NVA units as first priority. The matter probably runs much deeper than this, for the "conventionalists" share a perception of war's nature which is largely irrelevant to the question of selecting priorities in a counterinsurgency. The obsession with racking up ever-higher kill counts even as the Viet-Cong infrastructure was undergoing cancerous reproduction among the people can only be accounted for by much more basic considerations.

Likewise, and again in general, those who accepted the Pete theory of Sir Robert Thompson and Roger Hilsman and fought a long delaying action for their interval view, saw the Vietnamese people, not the armed enemy, as first priority, and the creation of a viable Saigon government and republic as their definition of "victory."*

The definitions started early and have not ended as of this writing. In August 1964, four days after the adoption of the Gulf of Tonkin

---

*They also believed adamantly that local police and security, and grassroots intelligence, were not defensive but offensive considerations. This follows from the idea that the smelly little village rather than the remote base area is the frontline.

Resolution, William P. Bundy gave some thought to what it might mean if Hanoi were to do our bidding. He recommended that someone give some thought to a definition for "getting out" over the coming months, thought of bombing the Viet-Cong's infiltration routes and petroleum stockpiles, then concluded "beyond these points it is probably not useful to think at the present time."[43]

Those were peripheral issues. A rapid move toward the center was made two weeks before the President's commitment speech of July 1965. General Goodpaster, assistant to the Chairman of the Joint Chiefs of Staff, got a memo from a Defense official. It quoted a question put to the Chairman earlier that morning by Secretary of Defense McNamara. General Wheeler had been asked to respond to the following: "If we do everything we can, can we have assurance of winning in South Vietnam ?"

General Wheeler said there was no apparent reason to say "no," if such is our will, "and if that will is manifested in strategy and tactical operations." General Goodpaster was then asked to "produce a clear articulation" of a strategy for victory, "tough as that articulation will be."

The JCS study group concluded that if we can destroy the enemy forces and bases areas, we would be on our way.[44]

A year after the dropping of the gate our ambassador in Saigon, Henry Cabot Lodge, told his President that as far as these words are concerned, "In truth we do not need to define 'victory' and then go ahead and achieve it 100 percent." He said we should think more of a "psychological victory."[45]

On it went, through insurgency, buildup, Tet, phasedown, extraction. As Vietnamization was coming in, Herman Kahn and others still were wrestling with the term, the strategy it implied, the view of war which forged the basic definition.[46]

Our paucity of understanding of what we were getting into was recognized more by the internalists than by their opponents. That fact, and the lure of federal money, gave rise to a vast social and behavioral research community in and around the Washington area. Some of the research was truly awful, some excellent, most mediocre.

The most ambitious research operation ever undertaken along these lines was something funded by the Army, and appropriately named Project Camelot, perhaps in deference to the President who directed the Army to become experts at countering insurgencies. The idea was to construct a massive, systematic study of internal war potential. In a letter dated December 4, 1964, and sent to scholars believed to be interested, it was admitted that the highest levels of Defense realized their ignorance of insurgency dynamics. With luck we would be able "to predict and influence politically significant aspects of social change in the developing nations of the world. . . ."[47]

Chile's leftist press and a piqued professor were able to kick the blocks from under the proposal, and it lasted less than one year.* By that time our Marines were carving out an area of operations around Da Nang, "special warfare" already was losing its lustre, and preparations were well underway to get the war out in the open, onto the surface. Special Forces personnel were being recruited in ever-increasing numbers, but by the summer of 1965 the center of mass was on the surface of the Vietnam battlefield. Tremendous pressure still was being applied internally, though not with the long haul in mind, by those who applied the pressure. Immediately after the Tonkin Resolution emerged, McGeorge Bundy was reminding the highest echelons of Defense and State that:

> The President reemphasizes the importance of economic and political actions having immediate impact in South Vietnam . . . The President emphasizes again that no activity of this kind should be delayed in any way by any feeling that our resources for these purposes are restricted.[48]

A few months before this memo was written General Westmoreland had visited Malaysia to study the "oil-blot" tactics of Sir Robert. In June he proposed something similar to that program to Secretary McNamara. There was a difference, though. The general didn't like the uprooting of civilians and some other features of the "oil blot." He was sure "the two situations were only superficially similar";[49] failure was sure. So in September 1964 he started his version of a coordinated political and military effort called "Hop Tac." Progress was to radiate out from Saigon in concentric rings of security, and so forth.

It ended a year later, and the general admits that "Frankly, it did not accomplish all that we had hoped it would."[50] Two years later he would try again, this time using the strategic hamlet approach embedded in the "oil spot." There were major resettlements at Ben Suc and Edap Enang, and in May 1967 U.S. aircraft whisked 10,000 civilians up from the DMZ, setting them down at their new home at Cam Lo. The whole strategic hamlet program was bloated and des-

*Chile had been excluded from the list of participating countries, but the issue of "nation-building" and all it implies was and is so sensitive an item the program had to be dropped.

tined to collapse from the outset, not because of the concept (the Viet-Cong saw this as a severe threat and mounted attacks when the first ones were built); but because of the natural desire to please, a desire grown to supernatural proportions among Vietnamese functionaries. But having been burned, the decision was made to weight the offensive now raging on the surface. Other internal programs were launched, though never with more than public enthusiasm. With the aide of a team of Chinese Nationalists an ARVN political warfare department was put together with morale, loyalty, and political education as its primary purposes.[51] To date it never has received much more than lip service either from the South Vietnamese or from official Washington. As often as not the POLWAR cadre became personal servants or entertainers of senior ARVN commanders.

One of the other rallying cries of the internalists, local police and security, likewise was drowned out by the crash of our shells. A government-sponsored study report of 1966 urged in no uncertain terms that the civilian police and the paramilitary Regional/Popular Forces be given priority treatment.[52] Instead they followed tactical operations both in terms of assets and attention, the consequence being that in 1968 the police force was still at a peacetime level and the bulk of the ARVN casualties were taken by the poorly armed and largely untrained RF/PF.[53]

Efforts to put these paramilitary forces under the national police were pigeonholed, though a few continued to stress that the rural Vietnamese equivalent of the cop on the beat is the best source of local intelligence.[54]

The stress was consistent with the desires of "Uncle," and he held the power. With his usual facility Sir Robert illustrated one of the consequences of staring in one direction too long:

> It proved impossible to get across the maxim that, if the intelligence organization is targeted on the infrastructure, you will get the order of battle as well but, if it is targeted on the order of battle, you will not get the infrastructure.[55]

Only among one group, in one area, and for a limited period of time was the subordination or at least integration of military and political matters tried.* The Marines in the northern reaches of the Republic saw the twin foolishness of sweeping an area only to find

*When Robert W. Komer was sent in 1967 to take over the fragmented pacification program he was to have the title of ambassador. The ground commander's chart showed Komer's position by a dotted line opposite that of General Abrams, assistant to Westmoreland. Mr. Komer was deputy *to* COMUSMACV.[56]

they had created a vacuum for the VC to refill, and the attempt to dispense unlimited freebies in place of providing physical security for the villagers.[57] Even that came to an end with the Tet offensive, for the trust of the countryside was gone.

The battle between Pete and Uncle never amounted to more than a minor skirmish, and its outcome was obvious: the internal war proponents never had a majority, and after President Kennedy's assassination they were without anyone in a position of power to argue their cause.*

It was in the campaign waged between the conventional military, those who wanted to hear the enemy say he had had enough and, failing to hear those words, deliver a fatal blow to the enemy, on the one hand; and civilians within the defense establishment, on the other, that the blood flowed with vigor. One would have to guess that the wounds inflicted are deep and long-lasting. The importance of this internecine violence is the manner in which it forges ahead into the future, affecting our defense posture.

After Secretary McNamara had let it be known in October 1966 he was soured on the Vietnam involvement, the principal military figures reflected on what had happened to date. In describing the air campaign to those under him in April 1965, Admiral Sharp called ROLLING THUNDER "a precise application of military pressure for the specific purpose of halting aggression in South Vietnam."[58] ROLLING THUNDER was a carefully controlled list of targets in the North we were authorized to strike, and the admiral admitted this was not just another war with the objective of inflicting maximum damage. At the same time CINCPAC had a war on his hands. In the Defense Department language of the day, the "political signals to Hanoi," which the adding and dropping of targets from the list as well as the total bombing halts amounted to, were sometimes difficult to swallow. This was especially so when the modulated violence was being accompanied by an uninterrupted flow of exhortations and demands, promises and expectations from the White House.

In his account of the war Admiral Sharp is together with General Westmoreland on one count: the meatgrinder strategy presupposed powerful arms turning the handles, 24 hours a day, 7 days a week, whirling ever faster:

---

*This is not to suggest that President Kennedy was a total convert to the Hilsman-Thompson thesis. But he was closer to this approach than he was to the meat grinder theory, regardless of his motives.

It must be noted that the principle of continual and steadily increasing pressure was basic to the concept of ROLLING THUNDER and thus to the achievement of our purposes through the use of air power. This principle has not been held to in the RT campaign.[59]

The bitterness underlying these words was conveyed by the Admiral to the Chairman of the Joint Chiefs of Staff early in 1967. Two months later the ground commander in Vietnam said the same: "The MACV objectives for 1967 were based on the assumption that the CY 1967 force requirements would be approved and provided expeditiously within the capabilities of the services."[60] They were not provided; the objectives were not met. An unhealthy number of people are convinced there is a causal connection between the two, which is how the "Never Again" club was initially franchised— after Korea.

In 1967 "Uncle" gave up. Thereafter he continued along his stoic way, making more troop requests, asking that the attacking pilots be given more critical targets. By this time neither the admiral nor the general thought they had a ghost of a chance of having it their way.*

"Their way" probably had been ruled out a year or two before our troops were disgorging from helicopters into rain forests and paddies. President Kennedy's Special Group (Counterinsurgency) had been charged with coming up with ideas and approaches which were unorthodox and which cut across departmental and service boundaries. The emphasis was to be upon low-profile, undramatic programs, programs of the "Pete" variety.

In May 1963, the Joint Chiefs of Staff directed Admiral Sharp to work up a covert, "nonattributable" plan of action for South Vietnam. The program which resulted from this combined military-CIA effort was completed one month that December. It received the innocuous title of OPLAN 34 ALFA.

Lyndon B. Johnson, now President, directed the Marine general who headed up the interdepartmental committee** to study it and to make proposals. The first phase of the 2,062 possible acts was ordered into action by President Johnson on February 1, 1964. Admiral Sharp, Presidential advisor W. W. Rostow and, significantly, General Krulak's committee, thought it wasn't enough, that we

*Similarly, Westmoreland was assured in advance that his request for 200,000 men after Tet would almost certainly be denied. The possibility of a larger "Never Again" club is clear.
**Major General (later Lieutenant General) Victor Krulak.

would be spinning our wheels. Only punishment or attrition would do the job.[61]

As the moment of decision approached or, as Walt W. Rostow would shortly phrase it, "As we come to the crunch in Southeast Asia," the contradiction could no longer be contained. By April 1964, the Joint Chiefs of Staff were convinced that only immediate, remedial military operations—swinging the spiked mace—would get us what we were after. Those in State and Defense (especially those concerned with international security) were conjuring up scenarios the better to dramatize our commitment.[62]

Writing a drama which would draw acclaim was a problem. The problem was there were many eager playwrights and only one play to be produced. Later the executive producer (President Johnson) would enjoy simultaneous staging.

From the Far East wing of the State Department in September 1964 William P. Bundy wrote up a "tit-for-tat" story, one in which we would, with provocation, retaliate.[63] Or something. The famous "search for options" was on.

During and following November 1964 scenarios continued to be written. Writing the Defense Department view of the moment, Assistant Secretary McNaughton layed before the interested the options or routes we might follow: continue to march, perhaps with a heavier step but staying largely within the South; take the Uncle approach, grab the North by the throat and give it a "fast, full squeeze"; or settle on a plan of "progressive squeeze-and-talk."[64]

That was November 6. The next day William Bundy rewrote his staging effort, and choreographed how the Boot would look in operation. Progressive squeezing and talking was out in front.[65]

A week or so later a life-long liberal who would shortly be vilified and exiled to the South by his conscience-stricken brethren on campus set down his own script for Secretary McNamara to look over. Walt Rostow saw the drama moving away from the retaliatory, tit-for-tat business of the Tonkin Gulf response. When we hit them it should be as limited and unsanguinary as possible, just to let Ho know that the punishment we handed out would not be on a one-for-one basis.[66] The principle, not the act, was important.

The flurry of creativity within the ranks of the proponents of the Boot continued through the Holiday season and into the new year. "Tit-for-tat" was pretty much discredited by now. The need was for broader thought, something more comprehensive. This was supplied by the other Bundy, McGeorge, in February, one month before the ground commander would have some Marines on the ground to command. "It would be important," he set down, "to insure that the general level of reprisal action remained in close correspondence with the level of outrages in the South." Not tit-for-tat, but "a policy of *sustained reprisal** against North Vietnam."[67] That ought to do it.

Then we committed ground combat forces and, without being shown the script, "Uncle" thought he had been give his head, thought he had been commissioned to write, cast and direct his own show.

The other pure group, the disciples of "Sneaky Pete," knew that with the tramp of infantry boots across Indochina they had lost out. Not so those who wanted to thrash the enemy with a mace until he said "Uncle." The civilian advisers to the President never persuaded the military leaders that this would be an orchestrated war, ranging from loudspeaker appeals to the enemy up through hunter-killer teams and single bombs capable of blowing down half a national forest. The consistency and tenacity of the military is thus understandable. So, too, would be their seething when they were made to feel humiliated.

Meeting in Honolulu with General Westmoreland and Admiral Sharp two months before the Tonkin Gulf Resolution, the Chairman of the JCS asked their views about the "increase the quotient of pain" formula for success in Vietnam. With the exception of ex-General, now Ambassador, Taylor, all present thought it a poor idea, and called for *"positive, prompt, and meaningful military action."*[68] They never wavered from this position.** The proposed bombing halt for August sent out a signal to Hanoi, but an indecisive one. So said the admiral.[69] The entire body of military seniors was shocked at the pause, as they were with Ambassador Taylor's mid-August message urging caution: "The JCS consider that only significantly stronger military pressures on the DRV" will get what we want.[70]

These soldiers and sailors were especially appalled at the idea, one which dominated so many that election season, of tying our responses to specific enemy acts.[71] "Tit-for-tat" is a game, and we are in a genuine if undeclared shooting war. To announce such a plan with our Vietnamese allies, jointly and in public, would be tantamount to handing the script over to Hanoi and showing them the final scenes. As for the "cold blood" versus "hot blood" controversy, the Chiefs were not inflexible. But we have to go in and do it. Hard.[72]

*Italics in original.
**Italics in original.

Breaks in the air war continued to grate. "Offensive air operations against North Vietnam should be resumed with a sharp blow and thereafter maintained with uninterrupted, increasing pressure."[73] That January 1966 "sharp blow" statement became a code word, a rallying cry. It was stated and restated to everyone who would listen throughout the spring and summer: "fast, full squeeze," "sharp rap." It reached its crescendo of outrage as Secretary McNamara rehearsed his swan song in October; for they disagreed with virtually all his recommendations (stabilizing the air war, slowing down troop deployments, and so forth).[74] The generals lost, the Secretary turned to world banking.

An issue which goes to the very heart of limited war is the commitment of a people. There are many ways that commitment can be made. One method, one resource left untouched for domestic political reasons, still sticks in the craw of those top military people who made up troop deployment schedules during the Vietnam War. Operating within an "everything at once and get me a victory" environment, time and again the JCS were called on the carpet because they were unable to deploy the number of soldiers their civilian leaders demanded. Showing more political moxey than they are supposed to possess, the Chiefs asked for a call-up of the reserves. This would simultaneously give them a larger pool to draw from (and thus get the Secretary and President off their collective back), and would also commit the entire nation to war. It was their version of a political signal which flashed in two directions: into the face of the enemy and into the living rooms of America.

Political realities forced them to delete this along with their request for an extension of tours for people already on the ground in Southeast Asia very early in the war, just a few weeks after the battle of the Ia Drang Valley in late 1965. They tried again three months later, again in April 1966. It was hopeless.[75] As a result, our strategic reserve hovered around zero: Europe in fact became indefensible.

And then there were our allies to consider.

THE HYDRA AS THEATRE COMMANDER

Shortly after McNamara left the Defense Department, journalists Rowland Evans and Robert D. Novak painted a realistic word picture of what it was like to be working in Saigon, faced with prosecuting a war that defied orders. They spoke of the plight of the functionaries who went to bed each night knowing that with dawn's first light there would be awaiting them the daily torment of "the hot blow torch on our rear ends," a blow torch whose white flame spanned 10,000 miles in order to work the President's will.[76] He wanted victory now.

The issue was grasped and then spelled out with terrifying ease back in the early Kennedy days. It appeared, appropriately, alongside Roger Hilsman's influential *Marine Corps Gazette* article cited earlier. "The United States must of course decide whether it is ready to interfere in the political affairs and even in the administration of weak and often irrational friends, and help them—force them if necessary—to carry out the needed program."[77] The visionary, holy war mentality that prompted such arrogance was one of the motive forces that impelled us into this indecisive conflict. It is the same spirit that, at a minimum, condoned the murder of President Diem, the same messianism that would later take up the cause of the North Vietnamese, then come full circle by demanding we cut off all aid to countries which will not permit us to reshape them in our own image. It also deluded some important people into ignoring the problem created by giving someone responsibility without corresponding authority.

With the Tonkin Resolution just a few days old, General Westmoreland cabled his superior in Hawaii that operations across the border into Laos were necessary in order to know what the enemy was doing. Further, "it would be essential for U.S. advisors to accompany CIDG, ranger," and so forth. He concluded that he would try to build in U.S. controls, but once the operation got underway our control might be "marginal."[78]

Time and again the proposal was made to create a single, combined command, similar to the various theatres of operation in World War II. The ground commander (and many others) consistently rejected the idea, arguing this would stifle growth and acceptance of responsibility.[79] Another consideration was the fact that xenophobia is endemic in Vietnam. Korea was no problem (at least during the first year). President Rhee had asked General Walker to accept under his command all ROK forces.

The problem in Vietnam never was solved, since the leverage available to us was inversely related to the scope of our involvement. In a word, we had each other over a barrel. The North Vietnamese knew it, far better than we.

An example of this approach is the attempt to use the pacification program as leverage. It was done by putting ever-more powerful men in control of an ever-larger, more complex operation. By way of Secretary McNamara and others the President indicated his displeasure to Ambassador Lodge late in 1966, just after McNamara asked that the war be ended. We had "to bring harder pressure on the GVN to do its job and to get solid and realistic planning with respect to the whole effort."[80] There was no push-pull remedy available, and the undisciplined creation first of the Office of Civil Operations was followed by an overmilitarizing of pacification when it all was put under the ground commander as Civil Operations and Revolutionary Development Support; later there came the hurried dispatch of Mr. Komer to deemphasize military control.*

John Paul Vann, the great soldier-turned advisor,** suggested a tactic as blunt as it was oblique when it became clear that warlordism was being spawned by pacification. He suggested that we simply remove our advisory team from a certain ARVN division, letting the GVN know how much we desired a coordinated civil–military operation. His prediction was proven correct almost instantly.[81] That was a singular set of circumstances only, and by 1967, when this brusque approach was made, there were ten thousand sets of circumstances, to which no simple formula would apply.

The problem of command and control and, more generally, our relations with the South Vietnamese themselves had an impact upon the strategy as the latter developed over the years far more significant than all the concocted scenarios thought up in the Pentagon combined. Long before the Tonkin Resolution U.S. pressure was building to get our advisors down to all levels of Vietnam that MACV considered necessary. The problem was, the temporary leader of South Vietnam, General Khanh, wasn't terribly anxious to have our advisors at all levels considered necessary by MACV. So the JCS asked Secretary McNamara to "induce" General Khanh appropriately.[82] General Khanh wasn't around long enough to make the effort worthwhile.

But others followed who were worth the effort. When, on April 17, 1965, Ambassador Taylor, "with grave reservations," concurred in the deployment of the first brigade of American paratroopers to Vietnam, he let Secretary of State Rusk know that goals were necessary, for "it is not going to be easy to get ready concurrence [from Saigon] for the large-scale introduction of foreign troops unless the need is clear and explicit."[83] Clarity and explication prevailing, soon our troops were on the ground.

*Also, it was feared the GVN would militarize pacification—which it did almost immediately.

**Colonel Vann was killed in action in 1972.

They were on the ground—a handful of Marines and paratroopers —with more anticipated. The question was what to do with them. In mid-1965 everyone was agreed that the VC were sharpening their knives in preparation for severing the little country in half, along a line from Pleiku in the Highlands to Qui Nhon on the central coast. The ground commander told Admiral Sharp he intended to put the hoped-for airmobile division in the Highlands. In the general's words, "For obvious reasons, I wanted to engage enemy forces as far as possible from populated areas."[84]

CINCPAC did not concur at all and sent back a testy reply telling the general, who was subordinate to the admiral, that the First Cavalry should operate in troublesome Binh Dinh Province, along the coast, and close to the war's object: the people. General Westmoreland rushed his reply to a reply, explaining, first, that the highway running from the coastal city of Qui Nhon into the Highlands is important, and would become more so if our people entered in large numbers. Thus, it would have to remain in friendly hands. Furthermore, he anguished about the South Vietnamese "fixation on the importance of Kontum and Pleiku." His hands were tied. We had to go into the Highlands.[85]

The issue ran much deeper though. When the First Cavalry Division landed and fired up its helicopters, the South Vietnamese agreed they should go into the Highlands. Our allies went further. They wanted *all* deploying U.S. forces to be concentrated in this sparsely populated area, to try and hold down civilian casualties, hold up the value of the piaster, and to prevent their society from being ripped apart. The general refused. An Army requires maneuverability. We would maneuver into the populated areas around Saigon and along the coast.[86]

Eventually, it was deemed important that we send our troops into what was, for Sir Robert, the major target of the war: the Mekong Delta. To provide for the eventual move into the Delta the general announced that a base already had been prepared at My Tho "just in case." The ARVN commander who did not want us in the Delta was transferred.[87] Soon the Ninth Infantry Division was waging violent war, hip-deep in the mire of the river.*

All the apparent problems of Vietnam became irrelevant before they could be completely solved. In this culmination of perhaps insoluble issues, issues unique to the Defense versus State era, the awful difficulty of military and political considerations was recog-

*The Mekong Delta was the first corps area to be cleared of American ground forces after President Nixon's program of Vietnamization started rolling.

nized but swept under the rug until it was too late. An outline-understanding of Vietnam and communist revolutionary warfare was late and painful, but it was achieved. The proper emphasis upon large operations to seek out and crush the enemy, as opposed to the patient and systematic destruction of the Viet-Cong infra-structure, was decided upon later still—too late to permit some graceful and deserved retirements from the Army. A clear grasp and statement of American political goals and the implied problem of maneuvering Saigon so that its leaders would help pursue them is yet to be solved.

Even had these matters been understood and acted upon intelligently from the outset, unless the war could have been concluded within a year's time it would have made little difference. Three decades were claiming their reward within our own country, as the basic American weaknesses of valor and impatience were first victimized, then exploited, by those possessed of a cold, ideological fury.

VII

A LONG SPIRAL DOWNWARDS

> In such a society the principle of liberty is bound to go
> to extremes—it will permeate private life and in the
> end infect even the domestic animals with anarchy.
> —Plato[563]

ANTITHESIS: THE CARTWHEEL FACTOR (CF)

CF₁: Noises From The Great Unwashed

"Possessed of" rather than "possessing" is correct. When 20,000 disheveled minds formed in attack echelon in Washington late November 1965, only a minority was capable of coupling more than four words in support of their conduct. On the testimony of a *New York Times* correspondent stationed in Hong Kong, the eruption of North Vietnamese flags—at a time the first battle of the Ia Drang was being celebrated along with a public outlook that permitted such—was seen by Hanoi as potentially decisive in the Southeast Asian war.[1] This fact may or may not have been known by some of those thrashing about in Washington that day. The motives of most of those who took the event seriously were drawn more from a lazy political leaning and boredom than from philosophical commitment. That demonstration, like all that would follow, is of interest from the point of view of psychopathology, nothing more.

Perhaps. On the other hand it is possible that, clouded over by the ravings and convulsive threats to the nation, there is, part residue and part germ, the promise of at least philosophic pretense. Those caught up in the joy of destruction—fixated like primitives upon the immediacy of the act—perhaps share more in common than bedwetting. There is *prima facie* evidence in support of this contention.* Let us review some of the evidence, spotty though it is.

Hanging above these frolics, there are the inevitable proclamations about a new era of rights, alongside of which trots the rest of the litany. Sources, derivations, and limitations are foreign to the liberated; in any case such considerations constitute negative thinking, and the stress is ever upon advance, progress, "Freedom Now." In their uncritical affirmation of the bland, the direction an investigation ought to take might be indicated.

For example, the spiritual atmosphere within which these moral certainties are claimed has all the buoyancy of lead. Or so life is interpreted by some noted spokesmen. We are told it is in the hope of generating enough power to burst through into the sunshine that drastic action is taken. Psychiatrists no longer bother writing up cases about the handsome and intelligent lad who suffers from no particular malady, cannot be classified as neurotic, but who nevertheless is constantly in search of comfort and assistance. Typically, he will have read John Stuart Mill's *"On Liberty"* and, multiplying by a factor of eighteen, conclude both cause and cure. The problem, the young man tells his counselor, is that the world refuses to get out of the way, to accommodate an updated version of Mill. Mill argued that each of us has his own space within which we are free to swing our arms—so long as we don't hit the fellow next to us who is busy swinging his arms, and so forth. The revised edition has it that proper self-expression requires there be lanes cleared, down which the liberated can turn cartwheels.

One of the stalwart supporters of cartwheeling and demonstrating is symbolized by the hypothetical** Ms. Fonda, darling of the military reservation, jetsetter via MIG airfields, epitome of the silk-stocking Left. Quite without warning she will attack warism, sexism, and racism indifferently, in each case marshaling identical acumen and moral outrage.

The issue (or rather, issues—the point is important) is in no sense

*At this point in reading this chapter a member of the Left will lick his lips and call his friends, telling of the newly discovered paranoid on the Right who sees a Marxist behind every beard. The great unwashed does not read; therefore it does not read Marx.
**If not to say unbelievable.

amusing. Ridiculous, but not amusing. Cluttered minds which insist upon fashioning connections where none exist and, in the process, arrive at the smug but senseless position that all is to be condemned out of hand, should be held up to public ridicule. (That is one of Mill's postulates which Ms. Fonda failed to jot down.)

Coursing through the diatribes and treasonous remarks one looks in vain for a workable premise. There is none to be found, and the reason is as plain as it is terrifying. Whereas the traditional liberal pretty much restricts himself to a lot of babbling, the underlying intentions are humane. What distinguishes the Left is their over-whelming concern for Humanity, next to which individual human beings count for little. At bottom, the Left, whether a withered academician who packs around a full-blown ideology, or someone of the calibre of Ms. Fonda, share this one characteristic: hatred—cold, unrelenting, and, given the wherewithal, utterly ruthless ha-tred. Knowledge is power.

Knowledge, for example, of the eternal principles of justice set forth at Nuremberg, principles which forevermore are here to be taken off the wall and applied to Montgomery, Alabama; to the University of California at Berkeley; to Vietnam. No special training is required in order to apply and, if done consistently, will so confuse civil rights and napalm and the freedom to shriek obscenities "simply because it feels so good," that one will have had a vision if not of the good then at least of first-hand evil. Ritualistic denunciation is in order, along with the arousal of unattainable expectations, which in turn fuels the cyclical demand for more of everything now, and please hurry. Thus, everyone is free and equal; I even more so.

CF₂: ODE TO A COSMETOLOGIST

Axiom. Our nation, founded on opinion, fights only wars of opin-ion, is incapable of fighting any other kind. Perhaps the basic error of Vietnam was the delusion held by those Defense Department individuals who sketched a scenario each night in order to induce sleep—that we could orchestrate a war. We cannot, for we are not a subtle people. Reasonably good soldiers, brave by Western stand-ards, but not subtle. That was the irreducible datum which doomed the Thompson-Hilsman "oil blot" theory to failure.

Corollary. The war making potential of the United States is a direct function of prevailing public attitudes. That potential is de-graded by the introduction of forces which disquiet public feelings, attitudes, opinions.

Our most recent war which most Americans believe we won was World War II. That war was general, world-wide, and was fought with very strict controls placed upon such forces. The most important type of control exercised was press censorship.

Virtually no one believes we won in Korea; the majority believes we lost in Vietnam. Both wars were limited, their overt aspects were restricted to Asian peninsulas, and there was negligible formal control exerted over the American press.

Fact. Those who argue bias in news coverage of the Vietnam war miss the point, which is simply that our journalists are not biased so much as devoid of imagination; not unpatriotic but instead unprofessional; not lacking in honesty but only in competence.

A Recounting. Army Field Manual 30–26, whose purpose it was to provide guidance to commanders in the field as to how to best use the press for the successful prosecution of World War II, survived the holocaust. It survived the war only to see action in Korea, for no one had thought to take it off the books after the World War had ended. FM 30–26 did not become a casualty until the Chinese had blitzed from two directions, not until General Ridgway was stabilizing the line in January 1951, preparatory to launching his precursor of the Westmoreland operations. Then, with a serious defeat of Eighth Army at the hands of the ChiCom forces a fact, with a third set of war goals billowing across the Pacific from the mainland, General MacArthur applied the document in question. Or tried to. The screams about repression were loud, immediate, and unrelenting.*

The press won that one a few months later, when a new rule went into effect.[2] Its most pertinent line said that news material may generally be released if it does not supply information of value to the enemy. With such a mushy concept, the regulation might well have been written by a member of the emerging advocacy press corps. That was December 7, 1951—a date to remember.

Eight months later control of the gauges regulating the flow of fuel which drives the American during wartime was handed over to the major opinion-molders with still another superseding document.[3] Its key paragraph stressed that under no conditions would censorship be imposed "upon the ground of anticipated adverse

---

*Censorship was not imposed earlier in Korea for the simple reason it was not necessary, that is, either we had a victory plan in hand (June to September 1950), or else MacArthur was demonstrating his ability to produce a victory (September to November 1950). Which is to say, reporters don't like to back a loser.

reaction by the American public." Further, there was contained the provision that censorship of all sorts be relaxed as soon as an active combat area became inactive; since by mid-1951 large areas were inactive most of the time, the will of an industrious reporter rather than combat action would determine where the newsworthy action would be—which is to say, one step ahead of his competitor.

Best of all, from this time forth America's public reaction to a war would become integral to that war, requiring exposure in the interest of a better informed public, professional awards, and bankroll— in reverse order.

For purposes of what is to follow it is desirable that a line from FM 30–26 be recalled. It promised punishment for any press reporter who produced anything "false in fact or by implication." It also prohibited anonymous interviews. It did one other thing. It helped convince a lot of people our side was winning.

But times had changed, and wars had to change with them. In what is otherwise a good and fair treatment of the subject a reporter who had eight wars under his belt wrote concerning the attempt to retain some control over the press in Korea. His sole motive for opposing censorship was the "firm belief that the strongest girder in the structure of American democracy is that of its free and unshackled press which exposes and reveals so that the people may know and remedy."[4] And the truth shall make you free, so long as "the best interests of the people and the Nation" to which he alludes are as simplistic as his phraseology.

Another journalist saw that Korea put our country at the crossroads, saw too the ominous possibilities inherent in the art of word pictures. Sensitive about his craft, proud of much of its tradition, he wrote soon after the cease-fire about the aesthetic sense of the young reporters, and it seemed to him that "some reporters out from the States were happiest when they had a devil to chase—when they could see a story in terms of someone's malfeasance." After citing an example he added: "I thought it was a perversion, or stylization, of the old spirit."[5]

Then along came television in a big way, and rewrote the rules of cross-modality summation; slightly happy words spoken by a slightly happy man as he stared into your living room gave you a very happy feeling. It also works the other way around, and if he's cranky plus not very happy about what he has to tell you, you may go away feeling glum.

With the passage of the Freedom of Information bill in June 1966, the concept of judicial review added clout to cross-modality coverage. Still it was not enough and, knowing that the best defense is an offense, someone ordered the attack launched lest there be public scrutiny. One result was the preposterous claim that our press has been the tool of the Cold Warriors. One such account supports his charges (of our venality in Korea, among other things), by citing as an authoritative source the Australian communist Wilfred Burchett.[6] As for our treacherous conduct in Vietnam the same author uses ironic quotes to describe "reputed" VC sanctuaries in Cambodia; then, after our push across the border and the seizure of tons of weapons made his argument sag, he described the operation as he might have the Nazi violation of the Lowlands.[7] Westmoreland said to maintain the offensive spirit.

On the other hand, the stupidity which engineered the entire JUS-PAO effort[8] infuriated a goodly number of decent journalists, and justified resentment.

Some things, however, not even the massaging of information by the U.S. Government can justify. A case in point is gross incompetence, best summarized by one of their own most distinguished scholars:

> The weakness of the correspondents' corps as a whole was the extreme competitive urge that led some to seek sensation rather than responsible reportage. Nearly all of them suffered from the frequently crippling ailment, endemic to journalism, that led the victim to conclude that whatever he wrote was gratefully received by a large and appreciative public and therefore never had to be repeated.[9]

A Retelling. On August 3, 1965, U.S. Marines surrounded the village of Cam Ne, near Da Nang. They took fire, returned it in an appropriate ratio for Americans being shot at, then proceeded to search the village. The heavily bunkered area and its spider-holes for firing into the backs of passing infantry made it clear the place was being used by the other side. The order was given to destroy the village by fire, thus denying its use to the VC and, because it is a tactic of the enemy to push or preposition his stocks out in front, reduce the chances for an attack. Not sensing the ethical distinctions in various forms of fire, one Marine set fire to the thatch roof using a cigarette lighter. Beneath the floors was an elaborate tunnel complex. Its prepositioning purpose was obvious.

CBS' Morley Safer worked himself into a genuine hysteria, the better to distort the facts. Safer: "The Marines then moved in, proceeding first with cigarette lighters, then with flame throwers, to burn...."[10] Marines do some crazy things, but never in their history have they assaulted an objective with cigarette lighters. Again, Safer: "Two Marines were wounded, both by their own fire, although this has been denied." Marine Corps records show that four Marines were wounded by the enemy.[11]

There were two important results of this shoddy reporting. First, the American people were witness to the spectacle of the Secretary of the Navy correcting Safer's falsehoods. Secondly, Safer was shifted to another spot for a time and was, after a reasonable period, promoted.

After the war was all over save for the wailing and gnashing of teeth, one of the great propaganda pieces of all time, purportedly a detailed analysis of defense untidiness, in fact a Goebbels-type masterpiece, was presented. Two aspects will forever be cited by chroniclers of the art of deceit. First, there had been a little editing done to a speech given in public by an Army officer. Or so it would seem. It turned out the colonel was reading some words spoken by Laos' Souvanna Phouma. No problem. The network, in its passion for clarity (and for forgiveness from a stunned and outraged Congress) did a rerun, admitted the true source of the statement, then went one step further. The sole point under consideration was the attribution of the speech. In the best tradition of the sophist, apparently anxious to justify the current disbelief by a third of the citizens concerning two-mode news; anxious, too, to support those who spit rather than speak the term "journalistic," they added an utterly irrelevant statement also made by the prince in the article. The network won, in the end, which dramatizes the distinction between argument and debate.

The second item: the picture of a beautiful child staring down the rifled tube of a cannon. It was outstanding.

Among the *montagnards* of Southeast Asia there is a brutal habit brought into play at fiesta time, in which a water buffalo is tethered in place, then crippled with a machete, and finally tormented with spears until he dies. In like manner, just six months before he was to retire, General Westmoreland made the mistake of being tethered before a CBS camera where, rather than knives and spears, reporter John Hart used questions in a witless display of advocacy journalism: "Was it not destructive to the Army to ask them to take less than victory out of Vietnam? . . . "Was that limited mission—the no-win mission—unfair on the part of an Administration to ask of an Army?"[12] Showing an unbelievable control, the general ignored the smirk of adolescence.

And then there is Eric the Vain who will, without provocation, subject any subject to an intensive analysis. The sole requirement is that the issue possess cosmic dimensions. He has been known to devote upwards of seventy seconds to such issues.

Finally, and to come full circle, back to the printed word as that vehicle has been punished during the past decade, we hear from D.J.R. Bruckner in the *Los Angeles Times*. We learn that the war is immoral, manifestly so, and can be shown to be merely by comparing desertion rates. He groans with the fatigue of one who has labored long and hard to educate his readers, and he must rest after writing this column. Desertion rates in the Vietnam War are twice those of World War II.[13] His burden is not due to the crush of facts.

The truth of the matter is precisely the reverse of Mr. Bruckner's reveries. If one compares the last full year of offensive operations in Vietnam (1967) with the last full year of combat in World War II (1944), the desertion rate during the latter was nearly three times what it was in Vietnam. It was not until fiscal 1971 that Vietnam caught up with World War II.[14]

A Resentment. Two-thousand reporters covered World War II. The Americans had a feeble understanding of the war. A third that many crowded into Indochina and demanded rooms at the Caravelle Hotel.

In the wake of the noble venture of World War II, a commission on freedom of the press was held. Its first order of business was, predictably, an oration against government interference, safeguards, and so forth. Then the move was to more substantive issues:

> the moral right of free public expession is not unconditional. Since the claim of the right is based on the duty of a man to the common good and to his thought, the ground of the claim disappears when this duty is ignored or rejected. In the absence of accepted moral duties there are not moral rights . . . There is no such thing as the "objectivity" of the press unless the mind of the reader can identify the objects dealt with.[15]

A Question. Why weeps Eric the Vain?

An Answer. He fell down while turning cartwheels.

CF₃: BRUCE, THE TENURED PROFESSOR: THREE ACCOUNTS

The First. Dead of night in a darkened, lonely city. More broody and lonely still is a resident of that city, a man tormented by eternal issues suddenly concretized in the fury of today's events. Stirring within that sea of anguish known only to those willing to risk everything, to lay it on the line, he reaches the searingly painful conclusion. His vows to know the truth and to be free demand and permit nothing less:

> After long reflection, I have come to the conclusion that the theory of democracy is wrong . . . The entire theory of government by consent of the governed rests upon the principle of majority rule, and that principle is utterly without justification.[16]

Having drawn this most fateful conclusion Bruce begins packing his bag, in no sense comforted by the knowledge he is right. He must seek a new home, having cut the philosophical underpinnings from the government, underpinnings he now sees to rest upon a lie. As he shuffles down the hallway for the last time he looks around to say a final farewell. His eyes drag across the floor, up the wall, and then stumble as they hit something rectangular and suspended by a nail. Jerked back into reality by the stumbling, and then by the sight of his diploma, Bruce realizes he doesn't have to leave, doesn't have to be afraid, doesn't have to even act responsibly. He has seen the truth, one which drags behind in its own brand of logic: "The world might be a better place if Presidents agreed not to send young men to war and professors agreed not to send them to jail."[17] But conscience supercedes consistency in such matters. "But not all wars are just, and no man has a duty to fight in those which are not."[18] Further, "we must answer that selective conscientious objection is the only sort of conscientious objection that makes any moral sense."[19] Thus the awful conclusion, the second such act of courage required in one day: "The choice is simple: if the law is just, obey it. If the law is unjust, evade it."[20]

With that wicked use of the term "simple" behind him, Bruce selects the next burning issue which requires resolution before the faculty meeting gets underway.

The Second. Even after a cheery, low-calorie breakfast, the problem of moral obligation is as grim and demanding as ever. One thing is for sure. Legal and moral obligations are distinct (who can ever forget the Volstead Act?). The distinction has to be retained if moral philosophy, not to say simple decency, is to be preserved intact. Otherwise, he muses, any person having "taxable income would be under a moral as well as a legal obligation to pay that portion of their taxes which finances the Vietnam War, CBR research, endless stockpiling of nuclear weapons, etc."[21] The distinction is crystal clear to me, Bruce, and to all right-thinking people; all, that is to say, except the neo-nazis whose sole reason for being unreasonable is so they can keep their immoral draft going for their immoral war.

Searching for a philosophical principle which will convince even those young Himmlerians out there, he thinks and, just as the perspiration on his head turns cold from despair, the incontrovertible truth erupts. The fascists are wrong, Bruce can now gloat, firmly clutching his principle. The consequences mentioned above are "counterintuitive."[22]

The beauty of this principle* is its ability to energize in both directions at once, proving our draft is venal, also proving that Israeli conscription is not venal. To keep a clear conscience, he mustn't say "the Cubans have no moral obligation to provide the armed forces needed to defend their society against a counterrevolutionary invasion by imperialistic neighbors to the north."[23]

The Third, and Very Last. His ten daily push-ups behind him, bed awaiting, Bruce feels an article-need sweep over him. It is a compulsion to study *that* issue, that hideous, twisted problem the complexities of which defy even the gods. Eyeing his diploma he accepts the challenge, prepares for the sprint through the gauntlet.

Then he senses the central question of modern war, the intentional killing of noncombatants as, for example, in the burning of Dresden. Pulse quickening he writes: "Should I wager this determinate crime against that immeasurable evil?"[24] To this rhetorical question there are already in stock any number of comforting answers.

An Indictment. Bruce isn't at all amusing, only ridiculous. He is the intellectual complement to Ms. Fonda, glorifying carnage in the name of the Eternal, using language appropriated from Scripture ("that immeasurable evil"). The fact that the British admit having started the strategic bombing offensive, and in fact built Bomber Command for this reason,[25] either is denied by the Left or, as in the case of the article cited, given an ethical tut-tut. The competing theories of Professors Blackett and Lindemann as to how many Germans should be expected to be killed by each ton of bombs, ** as well as their conscientious efforts to generate typhoons of flame the better to incinerate human bodies into stubs of charcoal,[26] are publicly dismissed as the cost of modern war; they are privately greeted with glee and a sense of moral certainty.

Not being given to reading the other side, not even enthusiastic accounts of the great crusade of 1941 following, his outrage at the

---

*He is making appeal to the metaphysical principle, "hocus pocus."
**Professor Blackett: "We should expect 0.2 (Germans) to be killed per ton of bombs dropped." Professor Lindemann: "One ton of bombs dropped on a built-up area turns 100–200 out of house and home." The former was 51 times too cautious, the latter virtually on the money, viz., 1.4 too high.

news we have used tear gas in Southeast Asia is understandable. Were Bruce to look at his beloved war closely, honestly, he would discover that, among other things, our nation gassed a good number of Japanese to death. It was all very legal, since the smoke and sulphuric fumes used were not outlawed. The beauty of it all was that the stuff is harmless in the open, but quite lethal in enclosed spaces.[27]

This and more Bruce could learn if he were open and honest; but in that case he would cease being Bruce.

Confidence Man as Conscientious Objector. The really crushing answer to those who say, "If we permit conscientious objection to a particular war, so many may refuse to fight as to endanger the nation," is this: "the danger is nil if the nation's cause is just; its citizens will not fail it in time of crisis."[28] This is Bruce's ultimate principle, except it isn't a principle. His revulsion at one war, thundering applause for the next, is available to anyone whose revulsion-delight is "based deeply and truly upon moral convictions."[29]

Thought runs in circles,* each time cutting the groove a bit deeper. Worst of all, though, the irrationality which undergirds this eschatological orientation clutches its ultimate secret: strength of conviction is not a but *the* test of truth.** Thus does the Great Unwashed hear what it wants to hear and, in the process, move another rung up the ladder of moral superiority. The top rung is a roost for the morally invincible, persons who appreciate the dark beauty of violence.

It is the selectivity with which Bruce would enjoy this aesthetic experience that is terrifying. His argument has the philosophical value of a choice between vanilla and pistachio, to paraphrase Professor Narveson. If he attempts to make his argument worthy of attention, that is, make it a position, it will collapse, writhing with contradictions.[30] But it is not his intention to argue, only to bellow, to chant, to squeeze the last sense from our language. This, too, the Great Unwashed hears, and mimics.

I do not refer especially to obscene language, employed by them as a mark of their defiance of accepted standards of decorum. I am much more concerned with vituperative epithets and the contempt for careful and precise distinctions of meaning. It is as though, in their suffering and unhappiness, they were using language as a weapon, analo-

*Bruce must equate popular wars and just wars. PR possibilities are unlimited.
**That this radical subjectivism contradicts the pretentions concerning his possession of truth universal is of no moment.

gous to pistols and bombs, without concern either for its flexibility or beauty. In their mouths language becomes a succession of slogans in the original meaning of slogan as battle cry or war cry. This marks, so I believe, a deterioration of mind and character that is attributable to long-continued indulgence in passion.[31]

The words of the humble, the fearful, the enemy of Bruce.* They describe the rage and fury and senselessness which result from man's cleavage of consciousness from the world of concrete things. There is a further consequence. In their estrangement, or disengagement, there are spawned and nurtured what have been described as "abstract emotions":

> As the VC held him, the once proud village chief turned into a raging, half-crazed father as he watched his two children multilated to death; then into a sobbing, broken husband as his wife died under their bayonets; then, with no will or strength left to resist or protest, he stood as the red and yellow Vietnamese flag that had flown over the village was wrapped about his head, soaked in kerosene, and ignited. The terrorized villagers were given clubs and ordered to beat his lifeless form.[32]

Our Left calls it "a no-nonsense social policy."

CF₄: PULL OF THE VISION

"In the aftermath of [Pearl Harbor], the years behind seemed to many a sort of prodigal period for the nation which had strayed from great vision and was, with destiny thrust upon it, recalled to the vision's fulfillment."[33] True. The question was, Whose vision? For more than a decade public visions were of enough to eat and a steady job. Our people thus obeyed the law that, until they are satisfied, the appetites rule.

It was during the period of harsh deprivation that the rapid flow of power to the Executive really got underway. The flow, soon to become geometrical and irreversible, was justified on the basis of the national emergency. For uncomplicated reasons not many of the citizens were too apprehensive about this bloating. Fewer still, for the same reasons, were overly critical of the goals being pursued, goals in terms of which the ever-greater Presidential latitude was justified. The opacity of the social vision which the President and his supporters were chasing during the Great Depression was created by millions of half-filled stomachs.

With the coming of the war a second vision burst forth. This was a twin view, the simultaneous picturing of means and ends, of what

*Additionally, Professor Gray is gifted, both as writer and as philosopher.

we were to seek as prize for all the bloodshed as well as the requirements for securing those goals. The latter proved difficult and, as
pointed out in Chapter 1, produced manipulation of domestic attitudes by Franklin Delano Roosevelt which were restricted only by
an increasingly angry Congress.* So our attention was switched
from unpleasant facts of the war to visions of the future. Aside from
simple fear campaigns, the bulk of the propaganda produced during
the war for direction against our own people was linked not to the
defeat of the Axis but to the end of history which such a defeat
would produce. In a famous report on the casualties our basic free-
doms had taken during the first year of the war, the American Civil
Liberties Union paused for an instant of regret for the Jehovah's
Witnesses doing penance in jail, then pushed on. Surprised at the
"heartening contrast with World War I in war-inspired issues," the
report mentioned the lack of organized resistance in 1942 (which
was true but trivial), then grasped the central reason: "the concentration of public attention not on attitudes to the war but on the
debate as to what kind of postwar world we are in the process of
creating."[34] The fixation of the hand-crafted symmetry of the world
of the future, the world of our own making, blinded us to the film
of blood which was then encasing the world of the present. One
result was the *ex post facto* affair at Nuremberg, another the attempted remodeling of the German character, still another the
widespread conviction that Humanity lived down the block and
Eternal Justice was being codified in Washington.

Visions continued. President Truman had his Fair Deal and Mr.
Johnson his Great Society. The latter was more exportable than the
former. It had help from many sources, including the powerful if
quiet hand of Dr. Walt W. Rostow: "We Americans are confident
that, if this process can be maintained over the coming years and
decades, these (developing) societies will choose their own version
of what we would regognize as a democratic open society."[35] And in
one of his more famous messages for the President's eyes, he wrote,
"I believe [LBJ] should hold up a vision of an Asian community that
goes beyond the Mekong Delta passage in that draft.** The vision,
essentially, should hold out the hope that if the 1954 and 1962 ac-

*In 1943 funds for the Office of War Information-Domestic Operations Branch were
severely cut. The money was restricted because of the knowledge FDR tended not to
limit his PR program to nonpartisan matters. At war's end the foreign outlet of OWI
evolved into the US Information Agency. With memories of FDR's brand of politick-
ing still warm, the Smith-Mundt Act of 1948 was passed. Contrary to what our current
crop of liberals say, the purpose of the act was not to keep USIA products from the
American people, but to prevent a resurgence of Office of Government Reports dishonesty.

**Reference is to a plan for the development of the entire Mekong basin, which Dr.
Rostow thought too limited.

cords are reinstalled, these things are possible: (a) peace; (b) accelerated economic development; (c) Asians taking a larger hand in their own destiny; (d) as much peaceful coexistence between Asian communists and non-communists as the communists wish."[36]

Apparently we have gone too far, though. For Walt Whitman Rostow has been banished to Texas, Lyndon Johnson, torn from his office, is now dead. The banishments were carried out, it would seem, not by fanatics on the Right but by the actors' own kind. This result seems contradictory, if all the actors were in possession of the same vision. Apparently, then, they were not, or not to the same degree.

The unprecedented scorn which professed liberals have heaped upon the head of the driving force behind the Kennedy civil rights package suggests they do not.

This and other facts suggest there is at some point along the spectrum (to pun) a quantum "leap in liberal being." There is, and we have described this new and higher being as the Left. The contrast between the "politics of joy" and the pale-lipped savagery of other visionaries hardly needs embellishing. It does, however, need analysis.

Members of both groups tend to bemoan the sight of social injustice, poverty, and so forth. Both groups are given to babbling. But there the similarities end. Whereas one tends to interrupt his rhetoric in time to take account of the practical realities of life, the other intensifies his singlemindedness when put under pressure. One might crack an honest grin the morning following a lost election; the other has fantasies of assassination and a popular uprising to root out all evil compromisers—the first on his list being the pragmatic, humane liberal.

In the early Kennedy days many who are now members of the anguished Left giggled with delight at the prospect of turning Vietnam into an American satellite, President Diem into a diminutive Jefferson. It was known in 1961 that there were U.S.-funded clandestine operations underway, liquidation lists being prepared, and so forth. It was only when Diem proved himself as chauvinistic as he was unpliable that the hate mail started pouring in. So long as there was the chance of Vietnam being a laboratory for growing visionary cultures there was calm. In a word, when that country's leader refused to take orders about the remaking of Mandarin Vietnam into an upstate New York, his luck, and life, ran out.

In a parallel way, so long as it was thought that the nationalistic LBJ would take orders he was left pretty much alone. It was when he put national interest above slate-grey ideas that the decision to pull him down began to germinate.

Within the next few years, Harry S. Truman, heretofore the darling of liberal foreign policy, will also be pulled down, in order that the seamless intellectual fabric of the Left remain untarnished. It will be untarnished, cold, and given the wherewithal, utterly ruthless. It is the latest instantiation of Mani, or Marx, or both.

CF₅: GNOSIS

Sir Robert Thompson raises the question whether the mania of revolutionary war is part of a consistent policy or whether it is partly a natural symptom of our times.[37] At a more general level of discussion, J. Glenn Gray suggests the continuing explosion of violence and anarchy as being due to the *Zeitgeist*—the spirit of the times.[38] The answer proposed here is a combination of these explanations. There is no inconsistency in arguing that the times themselves are partly responsible for making people more susceptible to arousal and violence, and that those countries which do not bid us well both contribute to and take advantage of a world in spiritual crisis. Furthermore, evidence suggests this answer.

As suggested earlier, the type of evidence which argues for this position is contributed by those who populate the left end of the political spectrum. The hysterical and almost animalistic hatred felt by the Left for their more moderate brothers is a fact which refuses to disappear, and demands that it be looked at again.

This vital dogma is the source of the "liberal evangelism."[39] Those are not the indicting jabs of the Right but of the Left. The proximate cause of Professor Goldstein's outrage is a view put forth by Arthur Schlesinger, Jr., according to which unpunished aggression will lead to more of the same, and so forth. The fundamental reason lies, superficially, in the two men's disagreement over what "aggression" means. Peering a bit deeper it turns out that Schlesinger's use of the term within the context of Vietnam was done with little rancor, that his motives were essentially nationalistic, that the normative overtones of "aggression" disappeared amidst the cigar smoke of practical politics.

It is just at this point that the Left develops apoplexy. "Aggression" is absolutely correct when talking about Vietnam, so long as it is applied to American action there. Consequently, to speak differently, to be politic, to compromise and trade-off is to betray an indelibly stained conscious. Worse, it is proof positive that the liberal so indicted is prepared to try and make the best of this country, world, life; when the only moral thing to do is reject all three. This is accomplished by attending Bruce's lectures, and by planning for Armageddon.

There is a long tradition of people who have been frightened of life and its inherent uncertainties. Throughout they have found comfort in the company of the like-minded. During these occasions they have sometimes set down their thoughts, along with their desire for an end to it all, for finality, for closure. Their contributions have been described as *ersatz* religions, or more generally as Gnosticism. Its central tenet is the destruction of the old and alien, then passage to the new. The instrument by which this earthly salvation comes about is gnosis itself—knowledge.[40] The major herald of self-salvation through knowledge in today's world is Marxism.

No major mass movement began that way. Instead it derives, inevitably, from intellectuals and small groups. [41]

In his *Critique of Hegel's Philosophy of Right** Marx already had said that the class with which he identified "does not claim particular redress, because the wrong which is done to it is not a *particular wrong* but *wrong in general.*"[42] Even earlier than this, while putting together notes for his doctoral dissertation of 1841, he had made much the same italicized point as he spoke of *"a merciless criticism of everything existing."*[43]

The point is not to conduct an exegesis of Marx.

A quote from an American qualified to do that, Professor Robert Tucker:

> The radical is not simply a rebel but a visionary . . . His negation of what exists proceeds from an underlying affirmation, an idealized image of the world as it ought to be. Indeed, it is the very perfection of his alternative universe that explains the depth and totality, i.e., the *radicalness,* of his act of world-repudiation.[44]

The point, again, is not to do Marx, but rather to illustrate the contention that if one hurls a comprehensive No! against one's own moral inadequacy the stage is set for acceptance of an inviting, simplistic solution to all moral difficulties.[45] No human experience is more filled with moral ambiguity than war, no form of warfare more subtle than revolutionary war, and no conflict less acceptable to us than limited war.

Additionally, those within our societies whose vision and affirmation—the truly ideologized—have as their primary intellectual and spiritual source the Marxist tradition. Most members of the Left admit as much, some more forcefully than others.

The notion of a universal and interlocking conspiracy in which the Left intentionally does the bidding of communists is nonsense.

*From his *Economic and Philosophical Manuscripts of 1844.* Italics in the original.

It is unfortunate, too, for if such were the case control would be facilitated. And they need to be controlled, for their ideas and language are as seductive in a time of chronic instability, when everyone is seeking "the answer," as they are dangerous. With a good number of the ideologized being in the communications industry (which includes teaching) they have built-in outlets for their product. And something, one is convinced, ought to be done to counter this.

Debate is the first thing that comes to mind. It has to be dismissed, though, or at least seen for what it is in today's world. An ideology, such as the ideas promoted by the articulate Left, is founded upon a peculiar set of ideas concerning reality, man, and society.[46] In a debate, therefore, we do not read from the same sheet of music or, more correctly, "The universe of rational discourse collapses . . . when the common ground of existence in reality has disappeared."[47]

To return to earth, and to the issue of America at limited war, the thrust of this discussion of ideology and the ideologized can be seen if the remarks made in the Introduction concerning the corruption of the term "war" are recalled. The word was not corrupted by the Vietnam War, nor by any other single event. Instead, it and our entire language, and the thoughts and attitudes these words represent, have begun to succumb to the advance of ideology. The placard mentality of today is in large measure attributable to our simultaneous plea for symmetry in life (and in war), and to the pigeonhole answers advanced by the evangelical Left.

Again referring to the Introduction, mention was made of ethical disputes and of the "atom of irrationality" which would likely persist at argument's end. The opponent in the debate (Goliath, Son of Bruce) exemplifies in miniature a totally ideologized opponent. So the reason for the total opposition to rationality should be clear, if frightening.*

CF$_{sum}$

What has here been dubbed the Cartwheel Factor—the emerging from our unconscious of the need for something to fill the spiritual void which is the dominate, most dismal feature of the twentieth

---

*Frightening not just because there are Goliaths among us who have no more respect for the individual than for the language they use, but because of the ominous forebodings. It is obvious the Left does not disavow violence in general, nor war in particular. They just want to see us fight "the right" war. Our history of escalation should be borne in mind when the demands for economic and political reprisals against other governments are made. In a word, our Left is in favor of making the world over in its image. Once that road is started down the end can only be perpetual warfare.

century—developed in almost direct proportion to the likelihood of limited war. Initially, during George F. Kennan's tour at the National War College (1946–47) our people were too engaged in satisfying needs which had been arbitrarily deprived during the war years. This condition continued until the start of the Korean War, during which time there was zero preparation—in terms of theory, military ability, or public acceptance—for limited war. Instead, the foolish, flattering rhetoric of World War II came through. And we basked in the warmth of the nuclear fires everyone hoped never would be lighted.

Creation of still another department within the Executive Branch, Defense, one whose function still is to be determined, complicated matters still more as it began to compete with the Department of State.

Korea was a cataclysm. Total surprise, unilateral commitment by the U.S. under the pretense of a UN mandate, three distinct political goals. Overarching yet exemplifying the political nature of this war was the relief of General MacArthur. Despite the ridicule received by his "No substitute for victory" speeches,[48] he, not Harry S. Truman, understood America's heartbeat.

The nature of our politics precluded honesty in 1952, as it does today. President Eisenhower's lack of candor (to put the best face on it) provided only momentary satisfaction to our need for solidified time.

After Korea the economic dislocation which all wars bring on as they end, along with the promise of more defense for less money, led inexorably to an overreliance on nuclear weapons. Secretary Dulles' indiscreet use of language (especially as regards Eastern Europe) only compounded matters, since it made a "big war, holy war" mentality inevitable. His just hatred for communism, laudable though it was, provided standby fuel for the then-emerging Left, because of the Dulles reliance upon moral absolutes in wartime.

The possibility of assessing Korea for what it had been was lost far in advance of John Kennedy's nomination. For one thing, Generals Taylor and Ridgway confused the issues—and perhaps the future— by arguing that limited war was likely and needed to be fought (which was true), and that Korea had shown we were capable of waging such conflicts (which was false).

Kennedy's romanticism, coupled with a sliding commitment to a strong-willed South Vietnamese President, produced the first cracks in the liberal wall. The rise of a unified, ideologized bloc—herein called the Left—can be dated from that time. For while both liberal and Left see the world as their backyard, and each has his vision of the way matters ought to be, the former possesses a bubbly, uncontrollable compassion which, to the latter, is a sign of weakness. In order to advance his cause, the liberal will obey the dictates of politics. The Left would prefer character assassinations and, if that fails to work, the real thing.

In addition to the rapid ideologizing of American intellectual life since the end of World War II, there are four problems which stud the issue of limited war, just as the lust of ideology also strangles it. These are (1) the unstoppable flow of power to the President; (2) our instinctive adoption of the strategic value theory, a theory presupposed by the would-be wit who says Vietnam is of no importance since the VC have no navy and thus can't invade San Francisco. It is also presupposed by those who argue "we have to stop them somewhere." Limited war is future currency, tied to prestige, which Acheson described as "the long shadow cast by power." Displays of strength and will—ranging from the commitment to Greece in 1946 up through President Nixon's refusal to capitulate to the Senate's "Never-Again" club—are the essence of limited war;[49] (3) a cold or hot war's political goals, which are themselves part of the struggle, inseparable from the fighting, are not statable in advance. Our failure to appreciate the Korean negotiations and the communists' superb interlacing of battlefield violence with talk around the table was a principal cause of the current despair; finally, (4) our American character.

On the whole, we probably did better in Korea and Vietnam than smart odds-makers would have predicted.

As for the future, we have it on the word of a U.S. Senator: "No more Vietnams."

VIII THE NEXT ASSAULT ON NO-NAME RIDGE

Never Again!

—Anonymous

FACTORS TO CONSIDER BEFORE RESUMING THE ASSAULT

POWER TO THE PRESIDENT

Alternating with the war whoops and promises of no more Vietnams is a second wing of the Left's current offensive. The code words are "populism," "reform," "power to the people." These words support a vision of everlasting peace. With the decentralizing of government, with the return of power to its repository within the people, unnecessary and immoral military adventures will be ruled out on principle.

To insure and speed this return of power to the people, the Left asks only that it be given unparalleled power, the better to hasten the return of power to the people, and so forth.

Two sets of attitudes defined the American during the late 1930s: desire for release from the cruelties of the Depression, and no involvement in a war then already underway. This second class of opinions was highlighted in Chapter 1.

Simultaneous with the pleas for continued isolation from war's horror, our people wanted the following: a Federal limitation placed upon the number of hours of permissible labor for each business and industry (60 percent); a Federal Old Age Pension (90 percent); Federal aid to states for local schools (70 percent); free medical aid for the poor (80 percent); the assumption by the Federal government of the responsibility to see that all desiring a job have one (75 percent); the Federal Government to pay all living expenses for those out of work (70 percent).[1]

What they did not want—war—was beyond their individual control, as were the polling questions.

All sides in the upcoming fury were making preparations. Following the extremely unfavorable reaction to his "quarantine" speech of October 1937, President Roosevelt had to retrench publicly and lie low for two years. Nevertheless, he could quietly approve a mission to London on Christmas 1937, whose job it was to make plans for an Anglo-American command.

Thirteen months before Pearl Harbor a joint plan, code name DOG, was agreed upon. It called for a strong offensive in the Atlantic and a defensive posture in the Pacific. As the President had consistently ignored Secretary of State Cordell Hull, the Secretary refused even to look at the finalized British-American plan of March 1943.[2] It is difficult to blame Secretary Hull, as it is difficult to blame a Congress which was equally dumb to these goings-on.

"We probably do not need additional Congressional authority, even if we decide on a very strong action. A session of this rump Congress might well be the scene of a messy Republican effort."[3] The words came two wars later, after Bien Hoa came under attack, after the foundation for the Great Society was set.

All the Left is asking for is more of the same.

At the same time, one of the agonies of an era of limited war is the genuine need for Presidential discretion. The emerging array—or disarray—of friendships and rivalries, overlapping and issue-specific coalitions after Vietnam will require more not less leeway in foreign affairs. Heretofore there has been within the Executive a domestic symbiosis, each feeding upon the other. This more than any other problem demands resolution, yet it cannot be resolved so long as we demand more social legislation. And far from diminishing, the latter progresses geometrically. It is the best of political tender. We are yet to learn that this power can be used to lead us into war. The justified requests for Presidential discretion in matters foreign always should be viewed in this light.

During World War II, Korea, and Vietnam there was a progressive increase in the number of yes answers to the question, "Was it a mistake?"[4] At war's end we have been more than happy to give extra latitude to those who, it turns out, have been more than happy to accept it, the better to reorder priorities. An ironic consequence is the apparent identity of alarm voiced by some members of Left and Right.[5]

It is apparent only, for in their anguish the Left spokesmen promise only more of the same. They do this because they are incapable of engaging in truly radical thought.

WARS LITTLE AND PERSISTENT

The cloistered debate within the ranks of military intellectuals and Government officials toward the end of the Eisenhower Administration over our ability to wage limited war was fought over vacuous points.[6] At issue then, now, and ten years from now is not tactics or military procurement or any other fiber of military muscle. What is and forever will be at issue is political will, that is, the psychological and moral make-up of a nation. Failure to recognize this has in large measure produced today's melancholy.

This failure was due in part to the confusion surrounding the magic of political signals. A case in point is Korea, late 1950, when the patter of little feet meant not a blessed event but the introduction of wave upon wave of battle-tested ChiCom forces. Mao Tse-tung was cautious. Initially he probed. During this "unofficial" entry he built up his ground forces and began a massive infiltration into our rear. No heavy response issuing from Washington, Mao correctly concluded that he could intervene with impunity—save for perhaps a million human lives.

At President Truman's press conference of November 30, the specter of nuclear explosions was raised. The immediate consequence was a race across the Atlantic by Prime Minister Attlee. Four days later, on December 4, 1950, Mr. Attlee gained the twin assurances that no nuclear bombs would be dropped in Korea, and that we would seek a cease-fire.

Six months later, after the CCF offensive had failed and the allied forces stood poised to rip a hole and drive through the Communists, the order came down to again temporize. General Ridgway wanted to undertake limited but powerful offensive action—fight while talking—but was overruled. The general understood a U.S.-Communist limited war better than did his civilian leaders.

One side benefit of our conduct in Korea was the lifting of the last

224

veil of altruism. Our overcaution revealed to those allied with us not only indecisiveness but a gross selfishness crouching below.

There was a flurry of research and study into the problem of modulated force following the publication in 1957 of Osgood's excellent *Limited War,* a work already cited. Nothing that followed Osgood's effort is to comparable quality, being products of an era and mentality dominated by what Dean Acheson called the world's most boring subject: decision-making. One such work in 1962 mentioned constraint of public attitudes[7] but went no further, offered no help. A year later a warning was issued about our entering Vietnam, then a mumble about "somewhat contradictory pressures to end the war as quickly as possible'"[8] which might develop. No help was offered. Nor was there still another year along:

> Even though the Kennedy Administration recognized the limited-war problem and took steps, continued since,* to cope with it, we do not know if Congress and the public fully support these steps. And critical issues of armed force structure remain to be solved.

He concludes, preposterously, with the following: "But we have at last come to grips with these problems."[9]

And then we lost the war.

ON PUBLIC EDUCATION

"We must see that our public is educated to realities of Russian situation."[10] The style is clipped telegraphy, the words important and supplied by George Kennan. Both are extracts from his "long telegram" of February 1946. As much as any other man Kennan is identified with our acceptance of the limited war challenge (though "acceptance" is hardly the proper choice of words). As much as any other American he had an intuitive grasp of the single issue which would course through the next quarter century. From the outset he called for an enlightened public and, though he failed, his words from that bleak winter of '45–'46 need repeating:

> I cannot overemphasize importance of this. Press cannot do this alone. It must be done mainly by government, which is necessarily more experienced and better informed on practical problems involved . . . Our only stake lies in what we hope rather than what we have; and I am convinced we have better chances of realizing those hopes if our public is enlightened and if our dealings with Russians are placed entirely on realistic matter of fact basis.

*That is, during President Johnson's Administration.

He went on to describe world communism as a malignant cancer, and concluded with the observation that the period into which we were entering—the Cold War—would be essentially a matter of self-confidence, discipline, morale and community spirit of our own people. This, he said, "is a diplomatic victory over Moscow worth a thousand diplomatic notes and joint communiqués."

Secretary of the Navy James Forrestal agreed with our chargé d'affaires, and must have seen the implications for the creation of the Department of Defense and a modern defense community, which would come about one year hence, with Forrestal as the first Secretary of Defense.[11]

Something was lost between the drawing board and the work site for, as the editor of Forrestal's diary makes clear to us, "caution still ruled; there was no great campaign of education or basic realignment of policy, and it was not until a year later that President Truman was to raise the first . . . alarm with his message asking aid for Greece and Turkey in their battles against Communist infiltration."

Thus, the people were ignored, just as Congress would be at the outbreak of Korea.

An attempt to articulate something workable was made in early 1951 with the creation of the Psychological Strategy Board. It was composed of an Under Secretary of Defense and the director of the CIA. Its purpose was to plan and supervise the Cold War,[12] which is to say, develop and then practice political warfare. A few years and an administration later it was done away with.

A decade and a half ago the against-the-grain feeling was grasped, even as another plea for education was issued:

Perhaps the prevailing popular assumptions and predispositions concerning military power and policy are so antithetical to the requirements of a strategy of limited war as to be beyond the power of public explanation and persuasion to alter.[13]

That's the nub of the issue: persuading, becoming convincing. Even if there were the appropriate people and agencies in and out of government, the requirement would only be met in principle. The distance from there to the grass roots is considerable. For there would not be involved a mere transfer of statistical information or the names of foreign cities. Were this the case there would be no problem, since a member of the audience could add up the column of figures and check the spelling of the town's name for himself.

Not so with a problem as thorny as limited war.

A general statement of a way out has been suggested,[14] a way which simultaneously shows the need and difficulties involved. The procedure amounts to reaching into a community's consensus, anchoring an argument there by associating the controversial with the accepted.

Unhappily, as Goliath has shown, that's easier said than done.

And until Senators become saints, or saints Senators, it would be the worst sort of folly to centralize still more power in Washington. The distance between now and World War I and the people's willingness to tolerate "adroit salutes to peace instead of war,"[15] then lie quietly as the proper serum was administered, is infinite.

Who, then, will teach and persuade?

Our inbred assumption that progress is inevitable is not without disadvantages.

REASONS FOR FIGHTING: TO HOLD KEY TERRAIN OR TO KEEP A GOOD NAME?

The first view is virtually second-nature to us. It develops at quite an early age as a form of possessiveness, that is, keeping what we have. In wartime this idea, introduced earlier as the strategic value theory, is an argument about the enemy's greedy designs, his quest for territorial acquisition in general, warmaking potential in particular.[16] It is an argument tailored to the defensive justification for war, which is in turn consistent with our tradition of property rights. Before Hiroshima the strategic value theory—the seizing and holding of key terrain view—might have been convincing. It is utterly misplaced in an atomic age. The latter is characterized not by nuclear wars but by conventional ordnance, not a general conflagration but carefully scaled violence.

As we have seen to our sorrow, limited wars are won or lost (or whatever one does in a limited war) not because of a depletion of our armed population but because one side possesses greater determination. One reason the Joint Chiefs of Staff did not object too strenuously to Secretary Acheson's "defensive perimeter" speech of early 1950 (which excluded Korea) was because of the lack of the peninsula's military value* (not to mention the fact that Korea was an economic liability after that country was denuded by the Japanese). At the same time there was no inconsistency when, only five months later, the Secretary of State urged his President to commit American combat forces in order to save the Republic of Korea. For in truth

---

*Owing to the pinchpenny budget Congress had allocated them the JCS didn't have much choice in the matter.

we did not send our troops to save the ROKs. Instead they were dispatched as yet another act in the ongoing drama whose moral is the degree to which other nations perceive us as a determined, reputable people.

It was for the same reason we went into Vietnam—and Lebanon, Berlin, the Congo, and the Dominican Republic. Therefore, since we went in, in effect, to establish future credit and to keep our good name, repudiation of Vietnam by national leaders is as stupid as it is immoral. To project an image abroad of a powerful country apologizing for fighting a most difficult and limited engagement and, by implication, promising in advance it never will happen again, is to write the final scenario for the United States as a major power.

In recent years the Soviet Union has displayed an effective if cumbersome limited-war capability. A clear example is the crushing of Prague in 1968.* Six years earlier the Communist Chinese demonstrated much the same strength, as a full CCF division was infiltrated through the Himalayas into the Indian rear. Once in place, others blitzed in frontal assault.

If the other side knows we will fight as well as talk, there is a chance they will choose to talk.

If the United States loses her limited war capability, then she will cease to be a first-rate power. And there is no such thing as a "second-rate power."

ACCELERATING CARTWHEELS

Within the foreseeable future there will be a steady increase both in the number of cartwheel-turning players and in the savagery of their frolic. Sources of information will not be excluded. In fact, schools of journalism already have within their ranks the politicized, a euphemism for intellectual flab and moral pretense.

Specialized, paying markets are developing. A graduate who joins the advocacy press will enjoy the benefits of peer-prestige, perhaps a good income. The former will be quite limited, for mass media in America, TV news in particular, are gaining their just reward: disbelief by the general public. This will likely grow as society continues to unravel.

For those writers (and, within the next few years, TV people) who desire nothing more than the total liberation of all the people such that each can enjoy the freedom to develop to the fullest his unique-

*The Soviets had some logistical troubles during the Czech operation, but did the job through the use of trash and dump trucks for troop movement.

ness, positions already are available. If one is properly sensitive he might write an editorial eulogizing total freedom, such as follows:

> We will have workers' control, students' control, women's control, lovers' control and children control. We need to found a Left which speaks to each corner of our existence, A MARXISM OF EVERYDAY LIFE, an understanding and self-perception of every wheeze of existential desperation . . . We need a Left which can speak to our dream-fantasies and MAKE THEM COME TRUE, a Left which can energize our visions into social ANTI-BLUEPRINTS, for the release of people's spontaneous good will . . . It is not enough to Overcome and Repress: we must show all the world why the dictators must be controlled for their own protection and for the protection of all the people.[17]

It's more frightening than amusing.

The attack by way of Marx's "wrong in general" will continue and gain ever-widening acceptance by that segment of society which demands more of everything without effort, and which couches its demands in the language of the irrational: "Con III sees not merely a set of political and public wrongs, such as a liberal New Dealer might have seen, but also the deeper ills . . ."[18] Mani resurrected, speaking gibberish: "Unreality is the true source of powerlessness. We do not understand, we cannot control."[19] This latest Mystery is "a radical subjectivity designed to find genuine values in a world whose official values are false and distorted."[20] Therefore, III resolutely refuses "to evaluate people by general standards, it refuses to classify people, or analyze them."[21] It also refuses to make a damn bit of sense, wherein lies its appeal.

Looking down from the top rung of the ladder are the fully ideologized, among them an expert in the theory of revolutionary war. At this level of discourse the ether is compacted, and only the palest of words can survive. They survive because they have been dumped of all content. Ideology ceases being its murderous self and becomes instead only the harmless "value commitment of a people."[22]

In the Ba Tu region of Cambodia's Parrot Beak, there was for many years a VC political indoctrination center for recruits and backsliders. As the young person was being led from his village by the political cadre his family would form for a farewell.

The mother of the peasant would be informed that if her daughter rides the government school bus her recruited son would be shot.

Once inside Cambodia, the recruit would be told that if he holds the wrong thoughts while in the service of the people's revolution, his mother would be burned alive.

Our Left calls it a "no-nonsense social policy."

YOUR MODERN VOLUNTEER ARMY

Under circumstances more perverse than ironic, the Army has once again been ordered to reorganize, and to go all-volunteer. It was told to do so immediately, cheaply, and at the same time was told to solve its drug and race problems, immediately and cheaply. Then, with a "by-the-way" gesture, the Army was told to be prepared to fight at any time, under any conditions, immediately and cheaply. The transition is still underway, our soldiers are stranded somewhere between *From Here to Eternity* and *The Greening of America,* and will get along just fine so long as they are not asked to fight a war anytime soon.

A bitterness courses through much of today's Army, brought on in part by its own indiscretions and extravagances, its occasional insanities, in Vietnam. Consequently, every effort is being made to extinguish that awful memory in its entirety, to get back on the better graces of whomever it is that hates them so, and so forth. In ways reminiscent of the post-Korea period there is a yearning to return to the plains of Western Europe and thus to the stable, predictable, and noncontroversial environment which that sort of war offers. American defense efforts always have been directed primarily toward Europe; those priorites did not change even when the great Vietnam drawdown skeletonized our European forces. So that Army mission—the defense of Europe—is one of long standing.

But the matter runs deeper. Today there is above all a near-desperate need to apologize and then forget and, in time, be forgiven.

As the career soldier looks about him and sees empty spaces that were filled just a few years ago, he thinks of the unending stream of caskets he saw being air-mailed to the Mainland. That accounts for very few of the career slots. Then he thinks of a disappointed Congress that decreed in its most regal fashion, i.e., by way of the budget, that the Army should be cut, that "excess" should be removed by, say, half a million or so. That accounts for most of the rest of the empty spaces. Thankful to have job and income, more thankful still that the Reduction In Force is about over, he is so anxious to be forgiven for whatever he has done.

Vietnam should not be forgiven, nor the mistakes forgotten. The ungodly luxuries our soldiers provided themselves began as morale boosters. They ended as a debauchery and principal source of the black market. Worst, there quickly developed two classes within ranks: the haves and the have-nots, with the former much larger than the latter. Those who lived the gluttony of the rear area tended to feel guilty because of the effort to air-condition the Indochinese.

Awards and decorations became something of a joke in some units. In places it was standard policy to size-up the individual soldier's career potential, then decide which medals would look best on his record. Some senior officers awarded themselves valor medals for the same reasons. In a few ill-disciplined units towards the end of the war medals were handed out as rewards for complying with basic military directives. The list could be extended, but without purpose.

Body counts were akin to awards and decorations. In a war fought in the world's most rotten environment, where there simply were no ends, or goals, or purposes intelligible either to the senior commander or to the grunt on the ground, medals, promotions, and row upon row of rotting corpses soon stood in their stead.

GI humor in Vietnam reflects the utter vacuum the men fought in. Some soldiers stenciled the name of another on the plastic bag into which friendly corpes go ("body bags"). Others called mock formations and ordered the uninitiated to practice getting into the plastic affairs.

Unit mottoes never concerned life or love. A motto employed by a helicopter gunship company in the Delta is representative: "Death on Call."

The list could be extended, but without purpose.

Scapegoats have been in order following every military loss. Vietnam is no exception. Rather than selecting individuals who are culpable (which is arbitrary in an era of corporate nonresponsibility), a different tact might be considered.

When the President committed our forces to Vietnam he did so with the reputation for being the most savvy ex-member of the U.S. Senate. When he was told a short time later of the tremendous surge in popular enthusiasm for the war, he displayed that understanding of his people well with his famous remark, "Overwhelming support for an underwhelming period of time." He probably did not consider the degree to which his remark applied to the soldiers splashing through fecal streams, though he should have, as should all Presidents who send their soldiers out to fight.

Part of the answer to the disaffection that followed, and it would appear to be a sizeable part, is found in a pair of statements made by the President in the much-read booklet, "Why Vietnam?" The statements collided and fought each other to a standstill: "For behind our American pledge lies the determination and resources, I believe, of all the American Nation," but "We are ready now, as we have always been, to move from the battlefield to the conference table."[23] By mentioning fighting while talking, the President distinguished between them. Processes natural to Americans would quickly translate this surface distinction into the conviction that these are mutually exclusive activites. Thus, the promise of open-ended combat was made to superimpose itself upon our either/or character.

One of the practical consequences in Vietnam was the fixation on tactical operations. Another was that killing became an end in itself. After the withdrawal of civilian support it became the sole end.

This suggests that we took the wrong tactic initially, an easy statement for someone light years removed from the President's swivel chair. Nevertheless.

American soldiers are as much dominated by the sense of time as are the rest of our citizens. To an even greater degree is this true of need for finality. Finality in Vietnam could have been purchased only at the price of changing the rules of revolutionary warfare (which, as Sir Robert Thompson points out, we did half-heartedly, anyway).

American forces prevented the collapse of South Vietnam in 1965. This fact and our natural pugnacity combined to generate great support at home, where everyone knew the war would be won or lost. We should have capitalized upon the surge of enthusiasm. For example, had there been general mobilization of our Reserves at the time of the President's July 28 press conference, a political signal understandable to all concerned would have flashed. Had there been no favorable response from Hanoi, and with our forces having stemmed the tide in the South, stiffer measures could have been applied. No insurgency in the century has been completely successful without an outside logistics base. Consequently, after issuing appropriate instructions to other nations to remain calm, we should have struck the North a massive blow. Whether this blow was in the form of an invasion or crossing the nuclear threshold is immaterial.

Such a move would have cut off the insurgents' strength. Just as important, such a move would have satisfied citizen and soldier alike. It also would have led to Lyndon Johnson's coronation.

Instead of satisfaction there is disappointment. It runs through military and civilian alike, permeates every segment of the land. It finds expression in the U.S. Supreme Court's ruling on the Pentagon Papers case:

> The power to wage war is "the power to wage war successfully" [Mr. Justice Douglas]; "And paramount among the responsibilities of a free press is the duty to prevent any part of the Government from deceiving the people and sending them off to distant lands to die of foreign fevers and foreign shot and shell" [Mr. Justice Black].[24]

Those who sided with the newspapers stated—though quite without supporting argument—that disclosure would not "surely result in direct, immediate and irreparable damage to our nation or its people."(Mr. Justice Stewart).[25] The strategic value theory was held to be self-evident by a majority of our most-learned judges.

It appears to be held by a majority of our top military men.

The Army is today reorienting on Europe, wargaming mechanized and armored battles against Warsaw Pact nations. On the face of it the odds of an opponent taking us on in conventional warfare seem pretty long. The communists have stayed in power for a long time, and intend to stay there a while longer. Principal reasons for their longevity are prudence and caution; and there has since Korea been a fear of American irrationality during wartime. Nonetheless, the Army is planning on such an eventuality, such being a stated mission, such being safer than looking toward more limited affairs.

There is a problem. Even after deflating figures and converting to our size and type of units, the communists hold an overwhelming advantage in soldiers, tanks, and in artillery. To try and get along with what is close at hand and with what is likely to be forthcoming as the defense tide continues to ebb, there is underway a study on the feasibility of something called "force-oriented defense." It is designed for Western Europe, and amounts to selecting long avenues of approach through which an enemy would likely travel (called "attrition areas"). Here he would be engaged by numerically inferior forces armed with sophisticated antitank weapons. After the enemy's combat power ratio had been sufficiently reduced a counterattack would occur by our side.

To an outsider it looks for all the world like gigantic VC tactics adapted to a mech-armor environment.[26] It's called making do.

An outsider also would have to guess that ahead lies limited war challenges of greater frequency and likelihood than a ground attack in Europe. That was the opinion of our leaders ten years ago as the military structure was altered to meet the new demands. President Kennedy ordered the creation of the Strike Command, and had it headquartered at MacDill Air Force Base, Florida. It was especially made up as a "fire brigade" (for putting out "brush-fire wars"). It appeared ideally suited for limited war, given its blitzkrieg capability—integrated troops, troop carriers, prepositioned supplies and all.[27] Unfortunately, it wasn't all it was purported to be. During the 1967 Israeli-Arab war the Florida command got confused and transmitted this confusion to pilots of the aircraft which had been dispatched to get our civilians out of the area. One result was a blue-ribbon defense panel. It handed its report to Defense Secretary Laird in July 1970.[28] A year later STRIKE was done away with, its already restricted functions passing to an austere Readiness Command. This is in line with our general retrenchment.

The Soviet Union and Communist China are not pulling in, though. Within a few months of President Nixon's trip to Peking a new POL line was completed between the Chinese border and Hanoi. For their part, the Soviets look forward to the day the Middle East can be cut up into desert retirement parcels.[29]

Activities by both sides reflect, perhaps flow from, our spiritual retrenchment. One of the most influential actors and directors of the Vietnam drama, General Taylor, admits the misuse of our military probably marks the beginning of our decline.[30] The feeling is widespread, both in the Army and out. To our discredit the question of direction is being chanted rather than debated.

An exception is another principal in the Vietnam War, retired Marine General Victor H. Krulak, who stated the matter succinctly:

> It is a good idea to remind the American people that they must keep dynamic pressure on those charged with their defense to insure that they are preparing to fight the next war rather than the last.[31]

Who, then, will apply the pressure, or at least remind others to apply it? Will Eric the Vain assume the task?*

---

*Eric's sins are two in number. One is of omission, the second of commission. After a decade of monopoly on war coverage it is clear that one could watch network news until he was being swept away on the wings of an angel without gaining a flicker of understanding of modern war. This is because TV news is rated by its entertainment value, and is designed to allay fears.

The sin of commission proceeds from the former. A seventy-second analysis—which is not an analysis but only an exercise in moral puffery—tends to end on a comforting note. It therefore tends to reinforce the endemic belief that the complex issues of our time lend themselves to a simplistic if witty shuffling of ethical cliches, smugness rather than truth being the goal.

Our future is anything but bright. Limitations of wealth and resources are exceeded only by limitations of will. What ought one conjecture concerning the conflicts which might involve, or threaten to involve, the United States over the next decade or so? One would have to guess the next war to be similar to wars of the past only in one sense, namely, they will likely possess those characteristics which we, as Americans, are least capable of coping with. Such a conclusion is not inspired by knowledge of strategic goals but by common sense.An enemy would have to possess an overpowering death wish to take us on in World War II-style. For that would mean several of our divisions getting chewed up in a delaying action, the popular response to which would be the demand that we escalate to nuclear warfare.

A reasonable guess is that war will stay in the crowd, burrowing deeper with each advance in intelligence and police technology. An Australian specialist predicts a widening incidence of low-level urban violence.[32] War already has taken on its most hideous form to date in the guise of urban guerrillas; more is to come. Such is the judgment of Robert Moss, author of the work just cited. Moss makes two further points, putting them back-to-back. The effect is unnerving: although outside involvement (for example, by a communist power) has been minimal, "the incitement of civil violence is an obvious means of weakening an enemy or achieving a limited political goal." Secondly, he reminds us that domestic dissent in America already has imposed constraints on our foreign policy. Were such ever to get out of hand, "a full-scale minority revolt would cripple the nation's capacity for military intervention in other countries."

Which is what the marches on the Pentagon were all about.[33]

The condition the British now find themselves in in Northern Ireland is what might be for us, in Army jargon, the "worst case."* Were there a country whose survival is of interest to us to be in the process of being devoured from within and, even assuming the political will to use military force to correct the condition, at this time our military is incapable of responding. Yet just such an eventuality might come about, perhaps within the context of an externally supported revlutionary war. Assume that this occurs within one of the nations now receiving military assistance or one for other reasons considered important to us? What ought to be our response?

First, such a condition ought never be permitted to so degenerate. Our soldiers working in military assistance should be two cuts above

*The truly worst case would be an insurgency within the borders of the United States, where our soldiers would be used for internal security. An external enemy could wish for nothing better. Fortunately, such seems unlikely at present.

those serving in the infantry. A program with good potential already is underway.* To many, though, it smacks of early, early Vietnam. Thus far it has not received the priority treatment it must if the basics, that is, a good system of police and intelligence work internal to the recipient nation, are to be developed and worked to our full advantage.

If Walt W. Rostow's "crunch" reappears, then we ought to see if the minimal political will exists. At present, a majority of our people would not commit our troops to defend a neighbor as close as Mexico.[34]

Given a few atoms of will, we should profit from the sorry experience in Vietnam. A top commander is essential. He must be an American. It would be his task to make decisions both military and political, something akin to General MacArthur during the postwar days in Japan. All indigenous forces would be under the operational control of the American commander (who would, with this hat on, be the equivalent of a theater commander). All logistics would be strictly under American control.

Naval and Air Force limitations have been demonstrated both in Korea and in Vietnam. Consequently, infantry will have to be committed sooner or later.

Fiscal restraints and public attitudes being what they are, our regular forces will be small and, hopefully, of very high quality. Should our leaders commit us to war in the constabulary fashion here pictured,[35] the regulars would go in first and, while they are holding the line as best they can, reserves would be called up and given training along with the promise of early combat.[36]

If all else fails, then, to use an expression which the Joint Chiefs of Staff found useful if futile during Vietnam, we ought to give the enemy a "fast, full squeeze." Tactics or weaponry which would give us an early and popular goal ought not to be precluded *a priori*. Our national character demands force to be applied massively and abruptly. Under these conditions our Constitution can become an asset rather than the liability it has often been.

We are not a subtle people, and should not pretend we are.

Our soldiers should be trained accordingly.

General Dean was quoted at the conclusion of our discussion of the Korean War. He mentioned educating American soldiers for future wars of the Korean variety, that is, wars in which we would

*Military Assistance Officers Program offered at Fort Bragg, North Carolina.

take x-number of casualties and then go home to an indifferent public. That was in 1954.

Eight years before the general's statement, a similar promise was made by a bright, young colonel as he flew back to the Mainland to accept a desk assignment. If ever he should be in another war, the colonel said, he would make sure every man in his command knew what he was fighting for. To do this the "concrete objectives" would be made clear to every man who fought beside Colonel William C. Westmoreland.[37]

It is very late in the day, but not too late to work along the sensible lines suggested but never implemented by these two Army leaders. The task will be considerably more difficult than the future ground commander, Vietnam, imagined. A program of deceit and lies akin to some of those used on our men during World War II[38] is unthinkable. Not only have conditions changed, but such gross manipulation never would be tolerated. Nor should it be.

The problems faced by those who would acclimate our men to a limited war environment in advance of the event, that is, during peacetime, are but intensified versions of the issues faced by the President as he addresses his citizenry. The matter becomes highly personal to the man carrying a rifle. Otherwise, the overarching difficulties are the same.

One of history's lessons is clear: the goals pursued, and the goals one ends up with, cannot be specified in advance. Rather, if they *are* specified, then the leader must be prepared to go after his political objective regardless of cost. The spiritual disintegration which began churning after President Truman's admission that we could not, or at least would not, return to the Yalu after the CCF intervened —even though the latter was the national expectation—is one rather numbing example of this truth.

A more recent and more deadening example presented itself to us after President Johnson's "We will stand in Vietnam" gave way to a pleading for a coalition government in Saigon.

Limited-war objectives emerge from the flames of physical violence and the azure of diplomacy. They must change as a function of military power ratios, our relations with other countries and, most important of all, seething domestic pressures. The latter illustrates our people's attempt to reject rather than adjust to the post-unconditional surrender realities.

The connection between the preceding generalities and the often bloody specifics of the Army ought to be clear: How does one prepare today's soldiers for the eventuality of fighting a war which, should it last more than a few weeks, is almost certain to have its objectives change—this after some of our people in uniform already have been killed by the enemy? Or, how does one justify a war in which the physical survival of the United States is not obviously at stake, a war in which Evil is not going to be extirpated, a war whose outcome is unlikely to insure peace and fraternity eternal?

The second question is logically prior to the first. It is more easily disposed of as well.

American soldiers are servants of the people. As such, they fight wars on orders of the people's representatives. Thus, justification for fighting consists precisely in the soldier's receipt of the order. Any other justifying neither is necessary, desirable, nor consistent with our tradition of civilian rule. Otherwise, the soldier must be allowed to deny the justification of the war. And that runs counter to the notion of soldiers taking orders from civilians.

As for the specific issue of preparing our soldiers for the possibility of a limited war, the best approach is total honesty. Tell them that limited political goals are happenstance and flux, just because they are limited. Remind them of the uniqueness of our world wars (and of the soaring desertion rates, attempts at psychological conditioning notwithstanding); of the three mutually-exclusive goals President Truman both strove to obtain and was forced into accepting; of the laundry list of objectives five administrations sought in Vietnam; of the melancholia and disappointment any future war is bound to produce.

Chances are slim that any one will take on such a program anytime soon. It would be thankless and politically dangerous, for the vortex of Vietnam still exists. It is yet to swallow its final victim.

Should one attempt it, though, here are some suggestions: make the thrust at the bottom, not at the top. It is the man on the ground being shot at who most wants to know why he is on the ground being shot at. Brigade commanders may ask the question, but it will have a philosophical dimension which holds little appeal for someone on the ground being shot at.

Secondly, use the military facilities and personnel already in being for any program of instruction on the nature of limited war; integrate such teaching with the usual map and field exercises, and so forth.

Thirdly, keep the instruction, discussion, and practical work totally open, totally *apolitical.* There are members of the advocacy press who would like nothing better than to put another heel in the Army's ribs.

Limited war is at bottom a moral and psychological affair. Once into a conflict we make technical adjustments quickly. Our soldiers were deployed as divisions. Before long they had adapted and were working in three-man hunter-killer teams. Their target acquisition was superb, their ambushes as good as those of the VC. They ended up with all these accomplishments. And a high desertion rate.

"War" is being redefined. It is a joint undertaking. The Soviets are contributing, as are the Chinese Communists and the Americans. We are in the never-never land of war/peace/war, whose topography is shrouded in an eternal mist. We have been in the mist for some time, though the length of the heel marks would indicate some resistance to making the trip.

An Admiral writes correctly if mysteriously, "the nonwar strategies and tactics needed to counter the Soviet nonwar world conquest have yet to be perfected."[39]

If the tactics are perfected, and if "war" is defined, perhaps the same good fortune will befall "victory." Until then, a recommended definition: Victory shall, at any given time, mean an arbitrarily selected point along the consensus pH scale. (Note to self—consider something along the same lines for "just war.")

EPILOGUE

Richard Nixon took the very bad situation he inherited and turned it, if not to our advantage, then in such a way that no single country would be sole beneficiary of the outcome in Southeast Asia. For all the criticism his "peace with honor" received, it is a fact that he was the first President to set forth before the people a realizable goal, and then to pursue it with the few available resources he held at his disposal. His settlement satisfied neither supporter nor critic, for some wanted total victory, others wanted Saigon on its knees. That is the price paid for seeking a solution which avoids unacceptable friendly costs and, at the same time, stops short of the complete destruction of an opponent.

President Nixon inherited much more than a ground war in Asia. At home he was presented with a legacy of presidential warmaking which antedates by at least a year the Japanese attack on Pearl Harbor. It is fashionable to depict the current administration as grasping, satanic, and *sui generis.* Some legislators and not a few newsmen have succumbed to such foppery, proving that either they are ignorant or without principles. As has been argued throughout this study, the leap into extra-legality by a U.S. President began with Franklin D. Roosevelt, when wars were simple. That practice continues to this day, when wars are complex. A recent work devoted exclusively to this problem should be serialized in every newspaper, on every network news show.[1] At least Mr. Nixon used the power to shut down a war.

Current American policy is to so enmesh the world powers through interlocking economic and political arrangements that major war could work to the advantage of no one. At long last it is recognized that we cannot, through the use of military force alone, fashion an adversary's conduct so that it will advance the U.S. national interest.

Recognition of the world as basically amoral is evident in Dr. Henry Kissinger's series of essays on foreign policy.[2] But it is questionable whether Americans can adjust to a view of international relations as no more than a system of the shifting flow of power. Ideological foes serve an important psychological and spiritual function for a people. Since by definition the Cold War is over, and no longer are there any official enemies of the United States, one has to wonder what will be the result of the use of force should the U.S. find that necessary, again, in the near future.

In many ways the present is reminiscent of the opening days of the Cold War. At that time Kennan urged that the people be educated to the realities of the time. He called on the government to conduct the instruction on the assumption that it is better qualified to do the job than is a free press.

The lesson plan still was being deliberated when Korea exploded. After that the project was given up as impossible. It would have been political suicide for a national leader to promise the people periodic, low-level warfare for an indefinite future. Our press ignored the issue, and not without reason.

There is no single conception of the proper role of the press in American society. The usual argument in support of this state of affairs is that a pluralistic society is the best possible, and is best protected by a host of divergent press views. This position is more comforting than illuminating. It takes full advantage of a privileged First Amendment position without specifying what educational functions should be undertaken. But proper execution of the latter is the sole justification for privilege. The ordinary response by a member of the press is, more of the same! That would suggest that America has been well served by her press, that the evidence already is in. It is not unequivocal.

Publication of the *Pentagon Papers* was the greatest journalistic coup since the Spanish-American War. District Judge Murray L. Gurfein's denial of the government's plea was based, at least in part, upon the right of the American people to know what the government is doing. The individuals who published the papers were defending the same right. America is better off both for the judge's decision and for the conduct of the newspapers.

That is one argument, to be sure. It is not immune from doubt.

A different view is, first, that the newspapers involved disapproved of U.S. action in Southeast Asia to such a degree that they decided to punish and humiliate the country. The *New York Times* got a windfall thanks to Daniel Ellsberg. They carefully picked through the *Pentagon Papers* until defamatory materials were found. Others followed the *Times'* lead. The editorial positions of the *New York Times,* the *Washington Post,* and the *St. Louis Post-Dispatch* on the war have for years been paroxysms.*

Second, the influence of headlines upon the way one interprets a story has been demonstrated repeatedly. And few read the entire articles anyway.

Third, most Americans derive the bulk of their news from network television, a medium which issues headlines and little more to the viewing audience.

Fourth, these publishers could count upon support from a broad and growing assault upon authority. The mode of attack rather than its purpose is all-important today.

Finally, few people read both the pseudo-history, which was complied as Robert McNamara was stepping down, and the documents; very few compared what the papers had exerpted with the oceans of material from which they could draw; and only the tiniest hardcore has tried to put into scholarly perspective popular conceptions and available material.[3] And when counterevidence was brought forth it simply was ignored, as is the prerogative of a free press.

In support of this alternative argument is the tape recording of the editorial decisions leading up to publication by the *New York Times* of the *Papers.*[4] When asked by Mr. Catledge if it had been his and the other reporters' intention to "write a headline," Mr. Gold said it had not, and "We were just going to present an explanation. After all, the essentials—the large headlines about the Vietnam War—were known to everyone." The first example is cited: "We knew we bombed, uh, North Vietnam." The idea was to present "an explanation—not a dramatic one—but a very interesting, fascinating, and I think necessary one of how we got, how we arrived at these places." An expose "was the one thing that was not only the last thing on our mind but we rejected."

Mr. Catledge then asked Mr. Seigel if, perhaps, he pulled "out the headline-grabbing facts" and built articles around these. Mr. Seigel said no, but admitted to having taken notes, "as all reporters do."

---

*And never dissuaded by facts: "Over and over again, Nixon has tried to bomb Hanoi into submission. It has not worked before and it will not work today" (*St. Louis Post-Dispatch,* December 19, 1972).
It worked the next day.

Mr. Seigel: "I think the way we operated, ultimately, in deciding what to use and what not to use, was to say, 'This is what happened; how did we get to that point?' And then we looked for the material that was pertinent to that and it gave it a dramatic cohesion, outside of anything else."

He continues: "We could have included journalistic shorthand, we could have used the word 'secret' in the headline, and we could have embellished it. And people would have taken much more notice. That's not what we were doing! That's not what we were up to. Again, we were up to a calm explanation of what had happened."*

No better support of the retributive justice thesis here being adanced could be provided than that just given by the *New York Times* employees. Let anyone select "what happened," let him decide "how did we get to that point?" and throw in a dash of "dramatic cohesion," and Gandhi can be made to look like Attila the Hun.

The Ellsberg-Russo trial will be remembered for several reasons. The defense borrowed a tactic found useful, if dishonest, by some of the lesser civil rights people. This amounts to announcing one's act as the latest series in man's moral development, in which one breaks an unjust law, admits it, then pays the price in the hope society's conscience will be moved to replace the bad law. The twist is that, having squeezed the lemon dry, and having cornered all possible moral support, one goes into court denying he has broken any law, thus putting the monkey on Sam's back.

Second, the witnesses for the defense were basically a rerun of the New Frontier's "Who's Who," people whose motto it was, "make words not wars." Going beyond the simple notion of deterrence, the nation was protected during the sixties by a defense that was active, passive, offensive, defensive, direct, indirect, total, relative, absolute, finite, positive, negative, supreme, and of types 1, 2, and 3.[5]

From Arthur Schlesinger, Jr., to Morton Halperin one gained the impression during the trial that our national interest stops at California's shoreline, that the Vietnam War had been a big game, and that now that it's over we can all forgive and forget and return to the classroom.

This pushing of "war as defense of real estate" overlapped with the return of American prisoners. While the idea that trust and

*The subtitle of the book version of the *New York Times* edition of the *Pentagon Papers* is "The Secret History of the Vietnam War."

steadfastness are in any way related to the national defense was debunked by the Ellsberg boosters, returned POWs told of being beaten and having their limbs nearly torn off for refusing to weaken public support by making anti-war statements. So while the defense was fantasizing, the prisoners told what the target of the enemy had in fact been. The target had been the people at home; the weapon had been the erosion of faith, first in the war, then in the government. And there no longer seems to be any doubt that those persons who journeyed into the heartland of the enemy, against the desire of the government—whether to convey enemy statistics or to sing them lullabies—can take credit for much of the pain the prisoners endured.*

Ellsberg defense witnesses, therefore, were able to go beyond saying that Dan really was a nice guy who happened to have a thing for Xerox machines. Many took the opportunity to further dissociate themselves from a war that had gone sour. They knew only too well what happened to Walt Whitman Rostow, who is not yet used to grits.

A final item of interest from the trial concerns the general public. At one time they would have cast Danny's shoes in bronze—while he was standing in them. But postwar boredom set in and they just wanted to forget everything.

Assault on authority typified the sixties. With the coming of a new decade things mellowed some and the impulses receded a bit. Before they did, though a toll was taken which pushes well into the seventies.

An example is the case of two soldiers named Amick and Stolte. The Army court-martialed them for disloyalty following the soldiers' anti-war activity. A district judge overturned the decision because "disloyalty" is vague and therefore unconstitutional. The court said different people view patriotism differently, which is true but trivial. Judge Aubrey Robinson, Jr., finished writing the decison, then did a little soft-shoe routine: "A soldier certainly does not have the right to dispute the war aims of the United States when ordered to take a certain hill in the midst of combat."

*Prisoners who refused to meet with those who sought the defeat of the South Vietnamese received especially harsh torture by their captors.

As for the figures, Harrison Salisbury's 1966–67 trip to Hanoi stands out. He said "the overall disparity between the two [DRV and U.S. tabulations concerning lost aircraft] narrowed" only when Hanson Baldwin's respected estimate came out and contradicted government estimates.[6] But Baldwin was speaking of *all* aircraft downed both in and out of combat, and over North Vietnam, South Vietnam, and Laos to boot. DRV figures were claims about planes shot down by the agrarian reformers north of the Seventeenth Parallel only.

Does any one have any questions?

Assuming Southeast Asia can be held together, we are safe from futile military adventure at least until 1976. This is not to say there will not be forceful measures taken by the United States. Chances are that limited force will have to be applied. But it will be frugal and specific.

The next challenge will likely come around Presidential election time. Visionaries among us are following the traditional path in the backwash of Vietnam, constructing their utopias inwardly.[7] But there remain two major reasons for concern. First, to call upon Tocqueville a final time, we democrats "care but little for what has been, but are haunted by visions of what will be . . ."[8]

Second, if Republicans are successful when in office, they tend to produce a sated, bored America. Liberals know this. There are, today, opponents of American efforts in Vietnam who would wage war now if only they could find a repressive dictatorship . . . somewhere . . . anywhere.

It should be everyone's prayer that no such country can be found as 1976 comes into view.

NOTES

Introduction

1. The most prominent of those who criticize non-US contributions in Southeast Asia, and speak in glowing terms of such support during the Korean affair, are former Senator Eugene McCarthy and Congressman Robert E. McCloskey. Non-U.S. personnel in Korea (minus ROK forces) totaled 36,000; in Vietnam, 62,000. In response to charges that those who sent troops to Vietnam are U.S. "client states," it can be pointed out that the major contributor in Korea, after the United States, was Great Britain; she had been saved from certain bankruptcy by a $4 billion loan in 1946. In any case, the UN was irrelevant in Korea. See Chapter 3.

2. Roger Hilsman, Jr., *To Move a Nation* (New York, 1967), p. 129.

3. The expression is to be found in George Kelly, *Lost Soldiers—The French Army and Empire in Chaos, 1947–62* (Cambridge, Mass., 1965) Chap. 7.

4. Richard Wasserstrom, "Three Arguments Concerning the Morality of War," *Journal of Philosophy* 65 (1968): 578–589. The standard work on the American view of war is Robert W. Tucker, *The Just War* (Baltimore, 1960).

5. Examples are taken from E.P. Hollander and R.G. Hunt, ed.,

Current Perspectives in Social Psychology (New York, 1963), pp. 437–8.

6. Hans Speier, *Social Order and the Risk of War* (Cambridge, Mass., 1964), p. 333.

7. Napoleon's first major rallying speech, and his soldiers' promise to keep the tricolors "ever on the road to Victory," is found in David G. Chandler, *The Campaigns of Napoleon* (New York, 1966), p. 323. R. Palmer's *The Age of the Democratic Revolution —The Struggle* (New York, 1964) is a meticulous treatment of the evangelizing of the French Revolution. Baron De Jomini, *The Art of War,* tr. by Capt. G. H. Mendell and Lt. W.P.Craig Hill, U.S. Army (Westport, 1962), pp. 22–6.

Chapter 1

1. Hans Speier, *Social Order and the Risk of War* (Cambridge, Mass., 1964), p. 333.

2. Ibid., p. 403.

3. *Public Papers and Addresses of Franklin D. Roosevelt,* compiled by Samuel I. Rosenman (New York, 1950) 13: 116–7. Hereafter cited as PP-FDR.

4. Ibid., 13: pp. xiii; 104.

5. Quoted in John Hohenberg, *Between Two Worlds: Policy, Press and Public Opinion in Asian-American Relations* (New York, 1967), p. 7.

6. Quoted in William E. Leuchtenburg, *Franklin D. Roosevelt and the New Deal, 1932–1940* (New York, 1963), p. 197.

7. Lloyd A. Free and Hadley Cantril, *The Political Beliefs of Americans: A Study of Public Opinion* (New York, 1968), pp. 62–63.

8. Leuchtenburg, op. cit., pp. 219ff.

9. *Public Opinion Quarterly,* v. 5, no. 1, p. 159. Hereafter cited as POQ.

10. POQ, v. 5, no. 1, p. 158.

11. POQ, v. 5, no. 1, p. 158.

12. POQ, v. 5, no. 1, p. 334.

13. Hadley Cantril, *The Human Dimension* (New York, 1967), p. 44.

14. Sumner Welles, *Seven Decisions That Shaped History* (New York, 1951), p. 68.

15. PP-FDR, v. 10, pp. 29–31.

16. Cantril, op. cit., p. 37.

17. PP-FDR, v. 10, p. 63.

18. POQ, v. 5, no. 1, p. 486.

19. *London Observer,* reprinted in *Los Angeles Times,* January 1, 1972.

20. POQ, v. 6, p. 163; also PP-FDR, v. 10, p. 390.

21. POQ, v. 6, p. 149.

22. PP-FDR, v. 10, p. 515; 523–530.

23. Walter Millis, *American Military Thought* (New York, 1966), p. 400.

24. General George C. Marshall's First Biennial Report, in *Victory on the March,* Reports on the Progress of the War by President F.D. Roosevelt, Prime Minister Sir Winston Churchill, General George C. Marshall, and the U.S. Navy (National Educational Alliance, New York, 1944), p. 44.

25. Marshall, p. 48.

26. Marshall, p. 48.

27. Marshall, p. 50.

28. Marshall, p. 50.

29. Marshall, p. 52.

30. POQ, v. 6, p. 486.

31. V. O. Key, Jr., *Public Opinion and American Democracy* (New York, 1964), p. 11.

32. Cantril, op. cit., p. 73.

33. POQ, v. 6, p. 484; 654; 661.

34. POQ, v. 7, p. 173.

35. POQ, v. 9, p. 533.

36. POQ, v. 8, p. 587; v. 9, p. 389; 249.

37. POQ, v. 7, p. 100ff, "OWI and Motion Pictures," by Walter Wanger.

38. Elmer Davis, *Final Report to the President,* Journalism Monographs, no. 7, August 1968, Bruce H. Westley, ed., Association for Education in Journalism, Austin, Texas, p. 51.

39. POQ, v. 5, pp. 548ff.

40. POQ, v. 5, pp. 558–559.

41. Elmer Davis and Byron Price, *War Information and Censorship,* American Council on Public Affairs (Washington, 1943), part 1.

42. Ibid.

43. Ibid.

44. Davis, *Final Report to the President,* p. 28.

45. Ibid., p. 38.

46. FM 30–26, daed 21Jan42.

47. Sidney Kobre, *Development of American Journalism* (Dubuque, Iowa, 1969), pp. 689–90.

Chapter 2

1. Harry S. Truman, *Memoirs* (New York, 1955) 1: 516ff.

2. Ibid., 2: 105.

3. Ibid., 2: 104.

4. A standard rendering is Arthur M. Schlesinger, Jr., "Origins of the Cold War," *Foreign Affairs,* 46 (1967): 22–52. This thesis was questioned in Walter Lippmann, *The Cold War—A Study in US Foreign Policy* (New York, 1947). It is totally disregarded in Gar Alperovitz, *Cold War Essays* (New York, 1970). An even more animated version of what is herein referred to as "Left revisionism" is Gabriel Kolko, *The Politics of War* (New York, 1969).

5. George F. Kennan, *Memoirs 1925–1950* (New York, 1967), p. 271ff.

6. George F. Kennan, *American Diplomacy 1900–1950* (Chicago, 1951), pp. 95, 102, "National interest is all we can know and understand."

7. See Cabell Phillips, *The Truman Presidency* (New York, 1966).

8. Dean G. Acheson, *Present at the Creation: My Years in the State Department* (New York, 1969), p. 195.

9. Kennan, *Memoirs,* p. 359.

10. Truman, op. cit., 2: 96.

11. Ibid.

12. James V. Forrestal, *The Forrestal Diaries,* ed. by Walter Millis (New York, 1951).

13. Truman, op. cit., 2: 97.

14. Ibid., 2: 102.

15. Ibid., 2: 107.

16. A. H. Vandenberg, ed., *The Private Papers of Senator Vandenberg* (New York, 1952), pp. 341–47.

17. Robert A. Taft, *A Foreign Policy for Americans* (New York, 1951), p. 16.

18. Kennan, *Memoirs,* p. 320.

19. Acheson, op. cit., p. 225.

20. Kennan, op. cit., p. 321.

21. Ibid., p. 317.

22. Ibid., p. 322.

23. Truman, op. cit., 2:109.

24. Russell F. Weigley, *History of the United States Army* (New York, 1967), p. 496.

25. *The Public Papers of Harry S. Truman, 1945* (Washington, 1956), pp. 431–8; Truman, op. cit., 1:507–9.

26. Weigley, op. cit., p. 486.

27. Ibid., p. 497.

28. Ibid., p. 498ff.

29. Robert A. Falk, *The National Security Structure* (Washington, 1967), pp. 33–34; Weigley, op. cit., pp. 491–94.

30. Weigley, op. cit.

31. Harold Stein, ed., *American Civil-Military Decisions* (Birmingham, Ala., 1963), p. 467ff.

32. Truman, *Memoirs,* 2:48.

33. Forrestal, op. cit., pp. 512–3.

34. Ibid., pp. 46–7.

35. Acheson, op. cit., pp. 127, 160–3.

36. Stein, op. cit., p. 6.

37. Weigley, op. cit., p. 494.

38. Falk, op. cit., p. 36.

39. Truman, op. cit., 2:59–60.

40. Weigley, op. cit., pp. 489–93.

41. Stein, op. cit., 467ff; Forrestal, op. cit., pp. 430–1.

42. Truman, op. cit., 2:52.

43. Stein, op. cit., p. 483.

44. Forrestal, op. cit., p. 373.

45. Ibid., pp. 369–80.

46. Ibid., pp. 459–60.

47. Stein, op. cit., pp. 474–5; Truman, op. cit., 2:52.

48. Weigley, op. cit., p. 502.

49. Stein, op. cit., p. 485.

50. Taft, op. cit., pp. 21–2.

51. Dean G. Acheson, *A Citizen Looks at Congress* (New York, 1956), p. 55.

52. Truman, *Memoirs,* 1: 486.

53. Cecil V. Crabb, Jr., *Bipartisan Foreign Policy: Myth or Reality?* (White Plains, N.Y., 1957), p. 5.

54. Acheson, *Present at the Creation,* p. 95.

55. Vandenberg, op. cit., p. 548.

56. Ibid., p. 551.

57. Ibid., p. 339.

58. Ibid., p. 343.

59. Acheson, op. cit., p. 220ff.

60. George F. Kennan, *On Dealing with the Communist World* (New York, 1964), p. 34.

61. Acheson, *Present at the Creation,* p. 100.

62. Taft, op. cit., p. 13 (regarding UN membership): "I think we must recognize that this involves the theory of a preventive war."

63. Robert E. Summers, *Federal Information Controls in Peacetime* (New York, 1949).

64. Truman, *Memoirs,* 1:516.

65. Forrestal, op. cit., p. 93.

66. Acheson, op. cit., p. 197ff; Truman, op. cit., 2:95.

67. Acheson, op. cit., p. 133ff.

68. Truman, op. cit., 2:91.

69. Kennan, *Memoirs,* p. 495ff.

70. Acheson, *Present at the Creation,* p. 189.

71. Kennan, *Memoirs,* p. 500.

72. Ibid., p. 304.

73. Ibid., p. 309.

74. Ibid., p. 310.

75. Matthew B. Ridgway, *The Korean War* (New York, 1967), p. 245.

76. Dean G. Acheson, *An American Vista* (London, 1956), p. 72.

77. "Survival in the Air Age," *A Report by the President's Air Policy Commission,* Washington, D.C., January 1, 1948, p. 23.

Chapter 3

1. Matthew B. Ridgway, *The Korean War* (New York, 1967), pp. 264–5.

2. Roy E. Appleman, *South to the Naktong, North to the Yalu,* U.S. Army in Korea, Office of the Chief of Military History, Department of the Army (Washington, 1961), 1:21ff. The most imaginative view of the conflict is set forth in I.F. Stone, *The Hidden History of the Korean War* (New York, 1952). See p. xiff for the Great Soybean Mystery.

3. Glenn D. Paige, *The Korean Decision, June 24–30, 1950* (New York, 1968), p. 82. All times and dates falling within the first week of the war are taken from this work.

4. Ibid., p. 83.

5. Truman, *Memoirs* (New York, 1955), 2:336.

6. Appleman, op. cit., p. 44.

7. Truman, op. cit., 2:343.

8. Appleman, op. cit., p. 60ff.

9. Russell F. Weigley, *History of the United States Army* (New York, 1967), pp. 508–9.

10. *U.S. Marine Corps Operations in Korea 1950–53,* G-3, Historical Branch, U.S. Marine Corps (Washington, 1954), 1: chap. 9, "The Battle of the Naktong." Hereinafter cited as *USMC Ops.*

11. Ibid.

12. Douglas A. MacArthur, *Reminiscenses* (New York, 1964), p. 346ff.

13. Dean G. Acheson, *Present at the Creation: My Years in the State Department* (New York, 1969), p. 438ff.

14. Truman, op. cit., 2:332.

15. Ibid.

16. J. Lawton Collins, *War in Peacetime* (Boston, 1969), p. 14.

17. Acheson, op. cit., p. 405.

18. Ibid., p. 408.

19. *The Public Papers of Harry S. Truman* (Washington, 1958), year 1950, p. 491. Hereinafter cited as PP–HST.

20. Acheson, op. cit., p. 408.

21. Ibid., pp. 402–13, describes, in his own words, ambivalence toward the United Nations.

22. Margaret Truman, *Souvenir* (New York, 1956), p. 275.

23. Paige, op. cit., p. 178.

24. PP–HST 1950, p. 492.

25. Appleman, op. cit., p. 44.

26. Paige, op. cit., p. 245.

27. Ibid., p. 248.

28. Ibid., p. 254.

29. PP–HST 1950, p. 513.

30. Paige, op. cit., p. 268.

31. Acheson, op. cit., p. 412.

32. PP–HST 1950, p. 537ff. In his response General MacArthur said his Far East Command had "not the slightest responsibility for the defense of the Free Republic of Korea. With the President's decision it assumed a completely new and added mission." Ibid.

33. Truman, op. cit., 2:333.

34. Robert D. Heinl, Jr., *Victory at High Tide* (New York, 1968), 67ff.

35. Acheson, op. cit., p. 448.

36. MacArthur, op. cit. (New York, 1964), p. 358.

37. George F. Kennan, *Memoirs, 1925–50* (New York, 1967), p. 48ff.

38. Collins, op. cit., p. 143ff.

39. *New York Times,* August 9, 1950.

40. Kennan, op. cit., pp. 490–2.

41. Acheson, op. cit., pp. 445–6.

42. Truman, *Memoirs,* 2:359.

43. Ibid.

44. See Carl Berger, *The Korea Knot* (Philadelphia, 1964), for a brief exploration of the politico-military aspects of the conflict.

45. MacArthur, op. cit., p. 360.

46. Appleman, op. cit., p. 658.

47. Collins, op. cit., pp. 211–13.

48. *USMC Ops.,* 3:91ff. Communist China's decision to enter the war receives definitive treatment in Allen S. Whiting, *China Crosses the Yalu* (New York, 1960).

49. *USMC Ops.,* 3:355.

50. Truman, op. cit., 2:397.

51. PP–HST 1950, p. 724.

52. Collins, op. cit., pp. 232–3.

53. Truman, *Memoirs,* 2: 423.

54. Ridgway, op. cit., p. 101ff.

55. Ibid., p. 141ff.

56. PP–HST 1951, p. 222.

57. Truman, *Memoirs,* 2: 445–50.

58. Ridgway, op. cit., p. 165.

59. *Hearings,* p. 1782. Also, Acheson, op. cit., p. 531.

60. Letter to author, Department of the Army (DAIO–PI), dated February 24, 1972.

61. Ridgway, op. cit., p. 190ff.

62. Mark W. Clark, *From the Danube to the Yalu* (New York, 1954), p. 233.

63. *New York Times,* April 26, 1951.

64. *New York Times,* August 1, 1950.

65. Paige, op. cit., p. 227.

66. Acheson, op. cit., p. 652.

67. The most enthusiastic supporter of the decision to limit the Korean affair is the Britisher David Rees. See his *Korea—The Limited War,* (London, 1964). For one of the few worthwhile probes into the psychological damage the war did to the U.S., see Robert E. Osgood, *Limited War* (Chicago, 1957), p. 189ff.

68. Paige, op. cit., p. 189.

69. Truman, *Memoirs,* 2: 414.

70. Walter G. Hermes, *Truce Tent and Fighting Front,* U.S. Army in the Korean War, Office of the Chief of Military History, Department of the Army (Washington, 1966), 3: 509. For the type of fighting which characterized the final twenty-four months of the war, and the great political and psychological restrictions operative during that time, see Russell A. Gugeler, *Combat Actions in Korea* (Washington, 1970), chap. 19, "Combat Patrol."

71. Ronald J. Caridi, *The Korean War and American Politics: The Republican Party as a Case Study* (Philadelphia, 1968). The information on the GOP and the Korean War discussed in this section is taken from Caridi.

72. Ibid., p. 153ff.

73. William F. Dean, *General Dean's Story* (New York, 1954), p. 294.

Chapter 4

1. Robert E. Osgood, *Limited War* (Chicago, 1957), p. 189ff.

2. Marshall, p. 311.

3. Harry S. Truman, *Memoirs* (New York, 1955), 2:501.

4. Letter to author, Department of the Army, PIO, dated February 24, 1972.

5. Hans Morgenthau, "Perspectives: Industrial College of the Armed Forces," January 1971, p. 16.

6. See testimony given by General Mark W. Clark, *The Korean War and Related Matters* (Washington, 1955), p. 7.

7. Dwight D. Eisenhower, *Mandate for Change* (Garden City, 1963), p. 171.

8. For example, Cabell Phillips, *The Truman Presidency* (New York, 1966), pp. 305–6.

9. Speech, given June 28, 1950, in *Congressional Record*, 81st Congress, 2nd session, pp. 9320–22.

10. Truman, *Memoirs*, 2: 369.

11. Dean G. Acheson, *Present at the Creation: My Years at the State Department* (New York, 1969), pp. 451–3; 465.

12. Quoted Harold Stein, ed., *American Civil-Military Decisions* (Birmingham, Ala., 1963), p. 22.

13. Paul Peters, *Massive Retaliation—The Policy and Its Critics* (Chicago, 1959), p. 101.

14. David Ogilvy, *Confessions of an Advertising Man* (New York, 1963), p. 141.

15. Eisenhower, op. cit., p. 435.

16. Peters, op. cit., p. 36.

17. Eisenhower, op. cit., p. 131.

18. Nathaniel R. Howard, ed., *The Basic Papers of George M. Humphrey* (Cleveland, 1965), pp. 50–51.

19. *Humphrey*, p. 490.

20. Sherman Adams, *Firsthand Report* (New York, 1961), p. 161.

21. Howard, ed., op. cit., pp. 180–81.

22. Adams, op. cit., pp. 172–3.

23. Eisenhower, op. cit., p. 548.

24. See Heinz Eulau, *Class and Party in the Eisenhower Years* (New York, 1962), p. 143ff.

25. David B. Capitanchik, *The Eisenhower Presidency and American Foreign Policy* (London and New York, 1969), p. 55. For an early and emotional criticism of containment, see William Henry Chamberlain, *Beyond Containment* (Chicago, 1954).

26. Peters, op. cit., pp. 104–5.

27. Andrew H. Berding, *Dulles on Diplomacy* (New York, 1965), p. 24ff.

28. Ibid., p. 144.

29. Ibid., p. 139.

30. Peters, op. cit., p. 105.

31. Capitanchik, op. cit., p. 73.

32. Robert G. Nelson, *Freedom of the Press from Jefferson to the Warren Court* (New York, 1967), pp. 385–6.

33. Peters, op. cit., p. 284.

34. Ibid., p. 284.

35. Dwight D. Eisenhower, *Waging Peace* (Garden City, 1965), p. 363.

36. Eisenhower, *Mandate for Change,* p. 340.

37. Thomas K. Finletter, *Power and Policy* (New York, 1954), pp. 155–6.

38. Eisenhower, op. cit., p. 421ff.

39. Eisenhower, *Waging Peace,* p. 278.

40. Ibid., pp. 274–80.

41. Norman A. Graebner, *Cold War Diplomacy: American Foreign Policy 1945–1960* (Princeton, N.J., 1962), pp. 99–100.

42. Ibid., p. 100. The President later denied he ever intended to use force in liberating East Europe.

43. Eisenhower, *Mandate for Change,* p. 122.

44. Finletter, op. cit., p. 374.

45. John Foster Dulles, *War or Peace* (New York, 1950).

46. See Eisenhower's speech before the American Society of Newspaper Editors on April 6, 1954, in Graebner, op. cit., p. 129.

47. Emmet John Hughes, *The Ordeal of Power* (New York, 1963), pp. 205–6.

48. Graebner, op. cit., p. 144. Also, see Robert E. Osgood, et al., *America and the World* (Baltimore, 1970), p. 29.

49. Ibid.

50. Stein, ed., op. cit., p. 22.

51. Capitanchik, p. 41.

52. Ibid., p. 41.

53. Acheson, op. cit., p. 375.

54. Eisenhower, op. cit., p. 133.

55. Dean G. Acheson, *An American Vista* (London, 1956), pp. 86–87.

56. Eisenhower, op. cit., p. 449.

57. Russell F. Weigley, *History of the United States Army* (New York, 1967), p. 496. (All infantry and airborn divisions were affected.)

58. Acheson, op. cit., p. 373.

59. Peters, op. cit., p. 35.

60. John L. Galvin, *Air Assault: The History of Airmobile Warfair* (New York, 1969), p. 274.

61. *U.S. Naval Institute Proceedings,* November, 1965, p. 67.

62. Eisenhower, *Mandate for Change,* pp. 453–4.

63. Graebner, op. cit., p. 125.

64. Ibid., pp. 164–5; Eisenhower, op. cit., p. 353.

65. *Pentagon Papers, New York Times* edition (New York, 1970), document 10, p. 44.

66. Eisenhower, op. cit., p. 364.

67. Osgood, op. cit., p. 215.

68. Finletter, op. cit., p. 148.

69. Capitanchik, p. 62.

70. Adams, op. cit., p. 361.

71. Pentagon Papers, document 15, p. 54.

72. Ibid., pp. 76–7.

73. Eisenhower, op. cit., p. 453.

74. In Peters, op. cit., p. 110. For a denial that unanimity reigned among the JCS, see Matthew B. Ridgway, *Soldier: Memoirs of Matthew B. Ridgway* (New York, 1958), pp. 288–89.

75. Ridgway, op. cit., p. 327.

76. In addition to General Ridgway's book, the two most prominent were John Gavin, *War and Peace in the Space Age* (New York, 1958); and Maxwell D. Taylor, *The Uncertain Trumpet* (New York, 1959).

77. Weigley, op. cit., pp. 553–4.

78. In James N. Rosenau, *National Leadership and Foreign Policy* (Princeton, 1963), p. 51ff.

79. *Goals for Americans,* prepared by the President's Commission on National Goals (Princeton, 1960).

80. *Prospect for America,* The Rockefeller Panel Reports (Gar-City, 1961), pp. 111–13; for a statement on required forces, see. p. 151.

81. The sense of calm which President Eisenhower's years represent, and the basic rationality of the man's approach to social issues, are neatly summarized in Herbert Drucks, *From Truman through Johnson: A Documentary History* (New York, 1971), 1: 187–335.

Chapter 5

1. *Veritas,* Ft. Bragg, N.C., March 1971, p. 12. (Reprint of *Green Beret,* December 1970.)

2. *Veritas,* October 1970, p. 7ff.

3. *Veritas,* October 1970, p. 8. After the Tenth Special Forces Group was deployed to Bad Tolz, Germany, several hundred men were left behind to form the Seventy-seventh Group. In the summer of 1957 the First Special Forces Group was activated on Okinawa. In June 1960 the Seventy-seventh Group was consolidated, thus creating the Seventh Group. On September 21, 1961, the Fifth Special Forces Group was activated at Fort Bragg. Later the Eighth, Third, and Sixth operational Groups were formed. In 1966 the Forty-sixth Special Forces Company was organized, and deployed to Thailand.

4. *Public Papers of John F. Kennedy,* 1963, p. 889. Hereafter cited as PP–JFK.

5. PP–JFK, 1962, p. 28.

6. PP–JFK, 1963, p. 855.

7. *Montagnard Tribal Groups of the Republic of Vietnam,* Ft. Bragg, 1965, p. vii.

8. Roger Hilsman, Jr., *To Move a Nation* (New York, 1967), p. 450.

9. Russell C. Weigley, *History of the United States Army* (New York, 1968), p. 543.

10. John Kennedy, *Strategy of Peace* (New York, 1960), pp. 8–9.

11. Theodore Sorensen, *Kennedy* (New York, 1967), chapter 8.

12. Jay David, ed., *The Kennedy Reader* (New York, 1967), p. 124.

13. Hilsman, op. cit., p. 415; PP–JFK, 1961, p. 416.

14. PP–JFK, 1961, p. 658.

15. PP–JFK, 1962, p. 185.

16. PP–JFK, 1962, p. 322.

17. PP–JFK, 1963, p. 19.

18. Sorensen, op. cit.

19. PP–JFK, 1962, p. 121, and most press conferences from mid-1962 forward.

20. PP–JFK, 1962, p. 714.

21. Harwood L. Childs, *Public Opinion: Nature, Formation, and Role* (Princeton, 1964), p. 314: "The case of Cuba well illustrates the point . . . The Cuban crisis revealed a public policy being gradually, but decisively, molded by public opinion."

22. Sorensen, op. cit., p. 334ff.

23. PP–JFK, 1963, p. 893.

24. David, ed., op. cit., pp. 122–3.

25. Kennedy, *Strategy of Peace*, pp. 3–11.

26. David, op. cit., pp. 11, 15–6.

27. Ibid., pp. 4, 63.

28. Ibid., p. 124.

29. PP–JFK, 1963, p. 149.

30. PP–JFK, 1961, p. 400.

31. PP–JFK, 1963, pp. 295, 345, 442, 861.

32. PP–JFK, 1962, p. 453.

33. PP–JFK, 1962, pp. 232, 401, 535.

34. George Kelly, *Lost Soldiers—The French Army and Empire in Chaos, 1947–62* (Cambridge, Mass., 1965), p. 111ff.

35. Hilsman, op. cit., p. 427, Also, "International War: The New Communist Tactic," *Marine Corps Gazette*, January 1962, reprinted in *Guerrilla, How to Fight Him* (New York, 1962), pp. 22–36.

36. Kennedy, *Strategy of Peace*, p. 59.

37. PP–JFK, 1962, p. 12.

38. PP–JFK, 1962, p. 517.

39. Weigley, op. cit., pp. 527, 542. By 1963 the U.S. had moved from eleven to sixteen Army divisions.

40. Douglas Pike, *Viet Cong* (Cambridge, 1966).

41. Document no. 2, *Pentagon Papers, New York Times* edition (New York, 1970), pp. 121–4; document no. 5, pp. 131–8. No use is made of the study's interpretation of events.

42. Document number 107, *The Senator Gravel Edition of the Pentagon Papers* (Boston, 1972), 11: 660–61. No use is made of the study's interpretation. The first line of the mission of the Special Group (CounterInsurgency) reads. "a. To insure proper recognition throughout the U.S. Government that subversive insurgency ('wars of liberation') is a major form of political-military conflict equal in importance to conventional warfare." Such recognition did not and does not exist.

43. Headquarters, Department of the Army, Special Operations Research Office, *Casebook of Insurgency and Revolutionary Warfare* (Washington, 1962), p. iii.

44. Hilsman, op. cit., pp. 425–6.

45. *Loc cit.*

46. Hilsman, op. cit., p. 422

47. Document no. 3, *Pentagon Papers,* p. 125.

48. Ibid., doc. no. 6, p. 140; Doc. no. 7, pp. 141–3.

49. Ibid., doc. no. 8, p. 147.

50. Ibid., doc. no. 4, p. 128.

51. Ibid., doc. no. 9, pp. 149–50.

52. Ibid., doc. no. 10, p. 154.

53. Ibid., p. 441. Gravel edition, doc. no. 102, v. 11, p. 651, memo General Lemnitzer to General Taylor dated October 12, 1961: "The question of police or military organization for combatting VC insurgency should be laid to rest in that play . . ." It never was. Also, see Gravel, *op. cit.,* doc. no. 110, pp. 666–7.

54. Hilsman, op. cit., p. 429.

55. Hilsman, op. cit., p. 440.

56. Gravel, doc. no. 115, pp. 673–81.

57. PP–JFK, 1963, p. 137.

Chapter 6

1. Admiral U.S.G. Sharp, USN, CINCPAC, and General W.C. Westmoreland, USA, COMUSMACV, *Report on the War in Vietnam* (as of June 30, 1968), Washington, 1969, p. 99. Hereinafter cited as *S/W.*

2. John Galvin, *Air Assault: The Development of Airmobile Warfare* (New York, 1969), p. 292.

3. Gravel, *Edition of Pentagon Papers* (Boston, 1972), 4: 304.

4. Ward Just, *Military Men* (New York, 1970), p. 27. Just ridicules Jomini as "the former Swiss bank clerk," though there is no evidence he ever heard of Jomini before accepting the magazine assignment. In addition to numerous articles, Sir Robert Thompson's trilogy is a systematic development of his views. They include *Defeating Communist Insurgency* (New York, 1965); *No Exit from Vietnam* (New York, 1969); and *Revolutionary War in World Strategy 1945–1969* (New York, 1970).

5. *S/W,* pp. 79–80.

6. *S/W,* pp. 85, 92–3.

7. *S/W,* pp. 84, 95. The NVA units were the 95th, 32nd, and 101st Regiments.

8. *S/W,* p. 14.

9. *S/W,* p. 98.

10. Gravel, v. 111, pp. 463–7.

11. Gravel, v. 111, pp. 438, 440.

12. *S/W,* pp. 275–8.

13. *S/W,* pp. 99–100.

14. These were the 1st Marine Divisions, the 4th, 9th, and 25th Infantry Divisions, plus the 199th Light Infantry Brigade. Deployment dates are found at *S/W,* p. 275ff.

15. Major operations are found at *S/W,* p. 281ff.

16. *S/W,* p. 162.

17. The Marines enter Thanh Phong Peninsula (Gravel, v. IV, p. 389). The Units were the 23d Infantry Division (American), the remainder of the 101st Airborne Division, and the 27th Marine Regiment.

18. *S/W,* pp. 120–21. Also, Stephen T. Hosmer, *Viet Cong Repression and its Implications for the Future* (Lexington, Mass., 1970).

19. Gravel, v. IV, pp. 434, 447.

20. Gravel, v. IV, pp. 561–4. The Pentagon study group is not identified.

21. *S/W,* p. 133.

22. *XT,* p. 10ff.

23. William W. Kaufman, *The McNamara Strategy* (New York, 1964), pp. 271–2.

24. *Department of Defense Annual Report* (1962/63), p. 11; (1967), p. 140.

25. Walter G. Hermes, *Truce Tent and Fighting Front, The U.S. Army in the Korean War* (Washington, 1966) 3:512.

26. George Grivas, *General Grivas on Guerrilla Warfare* (New York, 1965), p. 3.

27. Department of the Army Pamphlet 550–106, *The Communist Insurgent Infrastructure in South Vietnam: A Study of Organization and Strategy,* Headquarters, Department of the Army, March 1967, p. xviii. Hereinafter cited as *550–106.*

28. Department of the Army Pamphlet 525–2, *Vietnam Primer,* Headquarters, Department of the Army, March 1967, p. 3. Hereinafter cited as *525–2.*

29. Gravel, v. 111, p. 43, memo dated March 14, 1964.

30. Gravel, v. 111, doc. 158, p. 505.

31. Gravel, v. 111, doc. 157, pp. 496–99, memo dated January 22, 1964.

32. Thompson, *No Exit for Vietnam, p. 138.*

33. *Headquarters, Department of the Army, Special Operations Research Office, Insurgency and Revolutionary Warfare: 23 Summary Accounts* (Washington, 1962), p. 42.

34. George F. Tanham, *Communist Revolutionary Warfare* (New York, 1961, rev. ed., 1967), p. 117.

35. F.L. Singer, *Pao Chia: Social Control in China and Vietnam, U.S. Naval Institute Proceedings,* November 1965, pp. 36–45. He is quoting Han Fei Tzu.

36. Tanham, op. cit., rev. ed., 132ff. Also *550–106,* pp. 97–99.

37. The major theorists are Douglas Pike and Sir Robert Thompson. Brigadier General Edward G. Landsdale (USAF, Ret.) presents his position in "Vietnam—Still the Search for Goals," *Foreign Affairs,* 47, pp. 92–98. There he argues for an instant application of traditional American goals in Vietnam, with

these gaining strength first at the bottom—in the villages—then floating to the top.

38. See Tanham, rev. ed., 132ff. Also *550–106,* pp. 97–99.

39. In Douglas Pike, *The Viet Cong* (Cambridge, Mass., 1967), p. 120ff.

40. *Defeating Communist Insurgency,* p. 168. For a very early and sketchy picture, see Country Study, *Republic of Vietnam,* The Military Assistance Institute, Department of Defense, Washington, January 1959, revised May 1965.

41. Department of the Army Field Manual 30–31, *Stability Operations—Intelligence,* Headquarters, Department of the Army, Washington, January, 1970, p. B-8. Hereinafter cited as *30–31.*

42. The primary political history is Joseph Buttinger, *The Smaller Dragon* (New York, 1958), 2 vols. Volume 3 is *A Dragon Embattled,* New York, 1967. This superb work was rarely read until the late 1960s. Pike's *Viet Cong* suffered a similar fate, though it is basic to an understanding of the infrastructure.

43. Gravel, v. 111, doc. 171, pp. 526–28.

44. Gravel, v. IV, pp. 291–4. Mr. John McNaughton tasked General Goodpaster.

45. Gravel, v. IV, p. 328. Message dated August 10, 1966, Ambassador Lodge to President Johnson.

46. Herman Kahn, "Toward a Program for Victory," Frank E. Armbuster, et al., *Can We Win in Vietnam?* (New York, 1968), pp. 304–46. Kahn called for a variation on the "oil spot" theory, with a four-phase frontierizing.

47. Letter from Director, Special Operations Research Office, American University, in Irving I. Horowitz, *The Rise and Fall of Project Camelot* (Cambridge and London, 1967), pp. 47–8.

48. *Pentagon Papers, New York Times* ed., doc. 82, p. 360. NSC memo dated September 10, 1964.

49. *S/W,* p. 230.

50. *S/W,* p. 90, pp. 148–9.

51. Directive 515–1, *Psychological Operations-Political Warfare,* Headquarters, U.S. Military Assistance Command Vietnam, dated March 2, 1968.

52. Adrian H. Jones and Andrew R. Molnar, *Internal Defense*

Against Insurgency: Six Cases, CRESS, American University (Washington, 1966), p. 8.

53. *S/W,* p. 91; Thompson, *No Exit from Vietnam,* p. 124; also Ernest B. Ferguson, *Westmoreland, The Inevitable General* (Boston, 1968).

54. Ferguson, op. cit., p. 307.

55. Thompson, op. cit., p. 167.

56. Ferguson, op. cit., p. 316.

57. For a description of the Quang Nam Pacification Project/People's Action Teams, see *U.S. Marine Corps Civil Action Effort in Vietnam,* March 1965–March 1966, Historical Branch, G-3 Division, Headquarters, USMC, Washington, 1968, pp. 54–60. Due to the ineptness of the South Vietnamese the VC were able to break the back of the project.

58. *S/W,* p. 17.

59. *S/W,* p. 18. The point is made throughout the work cited.

60. *Pentagon Papers, New York Times* ed., doc. 122, pp. 557–58, Cable Westmoreland to CINCPAC, dated March 18, 1967.

61. *Pentagon Papers,* Gravel ed., 3: 150–3.

62. Ibid., 3: 158–9.

63. New York *Papers,* doc. 80, p. 358, Draft Presidential memo, (DPM) dated September 8, 1964.

64. New York *Papers,* doc. 85, pp. 365–66, paper, "Action for SVN," dated November 6, 1964.

65. Gravel, vol. 3, doc. 224, pp. 604–6, DPM dated November 7, 1964.

66. New York *Papers,* doc. 91, p. 419, letter to Secretary of Defense (SecDef), "Military Disposition and Political Signals."

67. New York *Papers,* doc. 92, pp. 423–5, memo to President Johnson, dated February 7, 1965.

68. Gravel, vol. 3: 171–3.

69. Gravel, v. 3, doc. 179, p. 542, message CINCPAC to JCS dated August 17, 1964.

70. Gravel, v. 3, doc, 183, p. 550, JCS memo to SecDef dated August 26, 1964.

71. Gravel, v. 3, doc. 230, pp. 628–30, JCS message 955–64, no addres-

see, dated November 14, 1964; same volume, doc. 193, p. 564, JCS memo to SecDef dated September 9, 1964.

72. New York Times *Pentagon Papers,* doc. 86, pp. 368–70, memo JCS to Assistant Secretary Bundy, "Additional Material for Project on Courses of Action in Southeast Asia, dated November 19, 1964. Ambassador Taylor wanted the announcement made public.

73. Gravel, 4: 3ff, JCS memoranda of January 18, April 14, April 26, May 10, and May 22, 1964.

74. Ibid., 4: 58–114.

75. Ibid., p. 310ff.

76. Ibid., 1: p. 611.

77. Peter Paret and John W. Shy, "Guerrilla Warfare and U.S. Military Policy: A Study," in *The Guerrilla—How To Fight Him,* (New York, 1962), p. 52.

78. Gravel, vol. 3, doc. 177, p. 540, message MACV to CINCPAC dated August 16, 1964.

79. For example, see *S/W,* p. 104.

80. Gravel, vol. 2., p. 601, cable to Ambassador Lodge dated October 18, 1966.

81. Ibid., vol. 2, pp. 601–25.

82. Ibid., vol. 3., p. 45, CJCS memo to SecDef dated February 18, 1964.

83. *Pentagon Papers, New York Times* ed., doc. 99, pp. 444–5, cable dated April 17, 1965.

84. *S/W,* p. 174.

85. Gravel, vol. 3, pp. 468–71; vol. 4, doc. 257, pp. 606–9, message MACV to CINCPAC dated June 13, 1965.

86. *S/W,* p. 98.

87. Ferguson, op. cit., p. 319.

Chapter 7

1. John Hohenberg, *Between Two Worlds: Policy, Press and Public opinion in Asian-American Relations* (New York, 1967), p. 320. The reporter was Seymour Topping.

2. AR 360–60, dated December 7, 1951.

3. AR 360–65, dated August 15, 1952. The 1966 revision of this AR

was not substantive. There were related FMs published in 1954 and 1967, plus a classified document.

4.   Robert C. Miller, "News Censorship in Korea," *Nieman Reports,* v. 6, no. 3, 1952, pp. 5–6.

5.   Christopher Rand, "Reporting the Far East," in Louis M. Lyons, ed., *Reporting the News: Selections from Nieman Reports* (Jan.–Apr. 54) (Cambridge, 1965), pp. 307–312.

6.   James Aronson, *The Press and the Cold War* (Indianapolis and New York, 1970), p. 103ff.

7.   Ibid., pp. 240–41.

8.   Hohenberg's treatment (chap. 6, "The War in Vietnam") is a good, objective treatment.

9.   Hohenberg, op. cit., p. 310.

10.   Ibid., pp. 315–16.

11.   Letter to Author, Headquarters, USMC (G-3, Historical Branch), dated March 9, 1972.

12.   CBS broadcast of Dec. 19, 1971, reprinted in *Soldiers,* Headquarters, Department of the Army, March 1972, pp. 7–8.

13.   *Los Angeles Times,* January 2, 1972.

14.   "Absentee and Desertion Rates," DOD, OASD (Mand RA) MPP, Sept. 16, 1971.

15.   Committee on Freedom of the Press, *A Free and Responsible Press* (Chicago, 1947), Harold L. Nelson, ed., *Feeedom of the Press from Hamilton to the Warren Court* (New York, 1967), p. 387.

16.   Robert P. Wolff, *Philosophy: A Modern Ecounter,* (Englewood Cliffs, N.J., 1971), pp. 410–11.

17.   Ibid., p. 413.

18.   Ibid., p. 408.

19.   Ibid., p. 408.

20.   Ibid., p. 414.

21.   Hugo A. Bedau, "Military Service and Moral Obligation," Virginia Held, Kai Nielsen, and Charles Parsons, ed. (New York, 1972), pp. 136, 143. *Philosophy and Political Action.*

22.   Bedeau, op. cit., 143.

23.   Ibid., pp. 145–50.

24. Michael Walzer, "World War Two: Why Was This War Different," *Philosophy and Public Affairs,* Fall 1971, p. 19.

25. J. M. Spaight, *Bombing Vindicated* (London, 1944), p. 74.

26. See David Irving, *The Destruction of Dresden* (New York, 1965).

27. Harold Riegelman, Col. (USA), *The Caves of Biak* (New York, 1955).

28. Carl Cohen, "Conscientious Objection," in A. K. Bierman and J. A. Gould, ed. *Philosophy for a New Generation* (New York, 1970), p. 245.

29. Cohen, op. cit., p. 239.

30. Jan Narveson, "Pacifism: A Philosophical Analysis," *Ethics,* July 1965. For a carefully contrived argument against Narveson's position, see Ronald B. Miller, "Violence, Force and Coercion," in Jerome A. Shaffer, ed., *Violence: Award Winning Essays in the Council for Philosophical Studies Competition* (New York, 1971), pp. 9–44. Ernest van den Haag's *Political Violence and Civil Disobedience* (New York, 1972) employs Miller's distinctions and still agrees with Narveson.

31. J. Glenn Gray, *On Understanding Violence Philosophically* (New York, 1970), pp. 18–19. Being, as he says, a "crypto-pacifist," Professor Gray would not agree with the argument of this book.

32. Lewis W. Walt, General, USMC, *Strange War, Strange Strategy* (New York, 1970), pp. 31–32.

33. Jonathan Daniels, *The Time Between the Wars* (New York, 1966), p. 345.

34. American Civil Liberties Union, "Freedom in Wartime," *Annual Report* (New York, 1943), pp. 3–11, in Nelson, ed., op. cit., pp. 266–67.

35. W. W. Rostow, *The View From the Seventh Floor* (New York, 1964), p. 115.

36. *Pentagon Papers,* Gravel ed., v. 3, doc, 238, p. 647.

37. *RW,* p. 3.

38. Gray, op. cit., pp. 22–24.

39. Walter Goldstein, "The American Political System and the Next Vietnam," David S. Sullivan and Martin J. Sattler, eds.,

Revolutionary War: Western Response (New York and London, 1971), p. 97.

40. Eric Voegelin, *Science, Politics, and Gnosticism* (Chicago, 1968), p. 11. Apologies to Dr. Voegelin. In addition to Voegelin, *The New Science of Politics* (Chicago, 1952), works of immediate interest include Hans Jonis, *The Gnostic Religion* (2d ed.; Boston, 1963); Norman Cohn, *Pursuit of the Millennium* (2d ed.; New York, 1961); E. L. Tuveson, *Millennium and Utopia* (Berkeley, 1949); Gerhart Niemeyer, *Between Being and Nothingness* (Baton Rouge, 1970); Willmoore Kendall and George W. Carey, *The Basic Symbols of the American Political Tradition* (Baton Rouge, 1970).

41. Voegelin, *Science, Politics, and Gnosticism,* p. 83ff.

42. T. B. Bottomore, tr. and ed., *Karl Marx, Early Writings,* (New York, 1963), p. 58.

43. In Robert C. Tucker, *The Marxian Revolutionary Idea* (New York, 1967), p. 182.

44. Ibid., pp. 182–32. See p. 218ff for a discussion of Marx's aesthetic utopia.

45. Niemeyer, op. cit., p. 97.

46. Ibid., p. 139.

47. Eric Voegelin, "On Debate and Existence," *The Intercollegiate Review,* 3 (1967): 143.

48. A recent example is Robert McClintock, *The Meaning of Limited War* (Boston, 1967), Chap. 7, "The Lessons of Limited War."

49. See James L. Payne, *The American Threat: The Fear of War as an Instrument of Foreign Policy* (Chicago, 1970).

Chapter 8

1. Cantril, 1968. Polling dates were between July, 1937 and April 1939.

2. Harold Stein, ed., *American Civil—Military Decisions* (Birmingham, Ala., 1963), p. 18.

3. *Pentagon Papers,* Gravel ed., v. Vol. 3, doc. 219, p. 593. DPM W.P. Bundy dated November 5, 1964.

4. Robert B. Smith, "Disaffection, Delegitimization, and Consequences, Aggregate Trends for World War II, Korea, and Vietnam," in Charles C. Moskes, Jr., *Public Opinion and the Military Establishment,* v. 1, Sage Research Progress Series on

War, Revolution, and Peacekeeping (Beverly Hills, 1971), p. 226. For legitimization, see p. 237ff.

5. See, e.g., David S. Sullivan and Martin J. Satler, eds., *Revolutionary War: Western Response* (New York and London, 1971), p. 116ff. He predicts more Vietnams, but blames our "national security managers."

6. This argument is found at Alvin J. Cottrell and James E. Dougherty, "The Lessons of Korea: War and the Power of Man," in Allen Guttman, ed., *Korea and the Theory of Limited War* (Boston, 1967), pp. 79–92.

7. Klaus Knorr and Thornton Read, ed., *Limited Strategic War* (New York, 1962), chap. 8. They here discuss seelective nuclear responses.

8. Morton H. Halperin, *Limited War in the Nuclear Age* (New York, 1963), p. 25.

9. Seymour Dietchman, *Limited War and American Defense Policy* (Cambridge, 1964), p. 254.

10. George F. Kennan, *Memoirs, 1925–50* (Boston, 1967), pp. 558–59.

11. James V. Forrestal, *The Forrestal Dairies,* ed. by Walter Millis (New York, 1951), p. 135ff.

12. Robert A. Falk, *The National Security Structure* (Washington, 1967), p. 41

13. Robert Osgood, *Limited War* (Chicago, 1957), p. 280.

14. C. H. Perelman, *Justice* (New York, 1967).

15. Kent Cooper, *The Right to Know* (New York, 1956), p. 84.

16. See James L. Payne, *The American Threat: The Fear of War as an Instrument of Foreign Policy* (Chicago, 1970), chap. 5, "The Demonstration of Will," for an elaboration of this argument.

17. Undated editorial in Milwaukee's "Kaleidoscope," in Robert J. Glessing, *The Underground Press in America* (Bloomington, 1970), pp. 158–9.

18. Charles A. Reich, *The Greening of America* (New York, 1970), p. 246.

19. Ibid., p. 13.

20. Ibid., p. 242.

21. Ibid., p. 243.

22. Eqbal Ahmad, "Revolutionary War and Counter-Insurgency," in Sullivan and Sattler eds., op. cit., p. 38.

23. Reproduced in *Public Papers of Lyndon B. Johnson, 1965* (Washington, 1965), 2: 774–6.

24. *Pentagon Papers, New York Times* ed., pp. 654, 663.

25. Ibid., p. 658.

26. See Major Joseph Keyes, "Tactics for Force-Oriented Defense —When You're Outnumbered and Outgunned," *Infantry,* July–August 1972 (Ft. Benning, Ga., 1972), pp. 23–31.

27. See the argument by Colonel Wesley W. Yale, et al., *Alternative to Armageddon* (New York, 1970). The argument presupposed STRIKE, which is no more.

28. See *Report to the President and the Secretary of Defense on the Department of Defense,* by the Blue Ribbon Panel, July 1, 1970 (Washington, 1970). Also, *Statement of Secretary of Defense Melvin R. Laird Before the House Armed Services Committee on the FY 1972–1976 Defense Program and the 1972 Defense Budget,* March 9, 1971 (Washington, D.C., 1971).

29. For a picture of the likely outcome of sloth reinforcing retrenchment in the West alongside Soviet expansion, see General Sir Walter Walker, "A Glance at the Future," *Military Review,* September 1972, pp. 21–31.

30. Maxwell D. Taylor, General (USA, ret.), *Swords and Plowshares* (New York, 1972), chap. 35, "Adjustments to Declining Powers."

31. *Seminar,* no. 13, December 1971, La Jolla, Calif. p. 26.

32. Robert Moss, *The War for the Cities* (New York, 1972), p. 247.

33. For a chilling but realistic picture of future contexts in which we will have to fight see Richard F. Rosser (Colonel, USAF), "Civil-Military Relations: 1980s," *Military Review,* March 1972, pp. 18–31.

34. Albert H. Cantril and Charles W. Roll. Jr., *Hopes and Fears of the American People* (New York, 1971), p. 47.

35. See Morris Janowitz, *The Professional Soldier* (rev. ed., New York, 1971), "Epilogue—Towards the Constabulary Concept," for a similar but clearer idea. In Secretary Laird's *Annual Defense Department Report FY 1973* there are but two pages (50–52) devoted to limited, e.e., "subtheatre/localized," wars. For those given to studying conceptual models, see Lincoln P.

Bloomfield and Amelia C. Leiss, *Controlling Small Wars: A Strategy for the 1970s* (New York, 1969). A more readable blueprint for the future is Frank Kitson, *Low Intensity Operations: Subversion, Insurgency, and Peacekeeping* (Harrisburg, 1971).

36. A joyfully optimistic picture of the Reserves in the early Kennedy years is George F. Eliot, *Reserve Forces and the Kennedy Strategy* (Harrisburg, 1962). When they were partially mobilized the Reserves were disappointing to all concerned.

37. Ernest B. Ferguson, *Westmoreland: The Inevitable General* (Boston, 1968), p. 317.

38. The record of one such program for the massaging of our soldiers' minds during the World War II is found at Carl R. Hovland et al., *Studies in Social Psychology in World War II,* vol. 3, "Experiments on Mass Communications," Princeton, 1949. Chap. 8, "The Effects of Presenting 'one side' versus 'both sides' in changing opinions on a controversial subject," is most illuminating. (The soldiers were promised anonymity, then matched up with their responses by handwriting analysis and biographical information.)

39. Rear Admiral George H. Miller, USN, "Needed—A New Strategy for the Preservation of the Republic," *Sea Power,* December 1971, pp. 5–11.

Epilogue

1. Merlo J. Pusey, *The Way We Go To War* (Boston, 1971).

2. Published in book form as *American Foreign Policy* (New York, 1969). Dr. Kissinger likewise explains his role as adviser to the President in this book.

3. For example, Robert F. Turner, "Myths of the Vietnam War," *Southeast Asian Perspectives,* September 1972.

4. *Times Tapes,* "The Pentagon Papers," side 2, copyright *New York Times* 1972. The reporters' syntax is their own.

5. Andre Beaufre, *Deterrence and Strategy* (New York, 1966), p. 25.

6. Harrison E. Salisbury, *Behind the Lines: Hanoi Dec. 23, 1966– Jan. 7, 1967* (New York, 1967), pp. 139–40. Salisbury's current euphoria is due to the "new Chinese man." See his *To Peking —And Beyond* (New York, 1972).

7.   This American postwar phenomenon is explored in Harold V. Rhodes, *Utopia in American Political Thought* (Tucson, Ariz., 1967), pp. 23–24.

8.   Alexis de Tocqueville, *Democracy in America* (New York, 1841), 2:78.